THE CRITIQUE
OF HUMANISM

THE CRITIQUE
OF HUMANISM

A SYMPOSIUM

Edited by
C. HARTLEY GRATTAN

KENNIKAT PRESS, INC./PORT WASHINGTON, N. Y.

CRITIQUE OF HUMANISM

First published in 1930
Reissued in 1968 by Kennikat Press

Library of Congress Catalog Card No: 68- 26241
Manufactured in the United States of America

ESSAY AND GENERAL LITERATURE INDEX REPRINT SERIES

EDITOR'S NOTE

THE occasion that called forth this symposium was the return to a more central position in American criticism of the New Humanists, the disciples of Irving Babbitt and Paul Elmer More. Broadly speaking, the book was conceived as an experiment in pamphleteering in the modern manner: its aim was to bring together within the covers of a single book a variety of essays which would in times past, and under similar circumstances, have been published separately. Since the editor had this idea in mind, he did not presume to dictate the opinions of those he asked to contribute or to influence them either directly by laying down dogmas to which his associates must subscribe, or by implication of invitation; for indeed he was only too happy to gather together in one place so diverse a collection of writers. The remarkable thing is that working absolutely independently the writers contributing did not repeat specific attacks, cite similar passages from the writings of the New Humanists, or, in general, tread on one another's toes more frequently than they did. Coming to the problems raised from their special fields of interest, they saw the weaknesses of the New Humanism from, I may say, thirteen different angles; and, in looking at this blackbird from so many different points of vantage, saw him every time differently.

Editor's Note

When the subject of the New Humanism was raised once more, it was recognized that, to parody one of Mr. Babbitt's famous remarks, the New Humanists had asked many of the right questions, but that they had given the wrong answers. It was admitted that the forceful restatement of the questions was a direct challenge to those critics dissenting from the Humanist answers to criticize the answers and offer alternative ones. The book resulting from the acceptance of the challenge has two sides. It has a destructive side: it is critical of the New Humanism, in fashions ranging from disappointment with certain inadequacies of the New Humanism to a total rejection of its ideological basis. It has another side also; and the reader will be making a grave mistake if he overlooks the important fact that most of the writers contributing give him, either directly or by implication, a constructive statement. Indeed it is next to impossible to reject the Humanist answers without implying one's own answers. Some of the writers here represented have not been content with implication; they have gone on to state directly and unequivocally their social, moral and esthetic beliefs.

While there is a considerable negative unity, there is very little unity at all constructively. This is not a group statement, but a real symposium: a sort of round-table discussion at which the guests, in their different voices, offer their different opinions on the same subject. The reader will discover that the book does not represent a school of writers; nor does it give evidence of any unified trend in American literary and social criticism. There are signs, however, of a new interest in social problems on the part of writers who were formerly preoccupied with esthetics. There is a certain general search for the ideals of a true humanism which is not that of More and Babbitt. All the contributors come together at certain points and some few agree on an appreciable number of points; but no one of the writers is in agreement with any one of his fellow writers on all points. This is as it should be, for the arts will probably be the last refuge of individualism and it is entirely logical that the critics of the arts should be individualists also. The broader implication of this symposium is, perhaps, that the non-academic critics of this country will not march under any single banner, no matter how pretty the device it displays.

C. H. G.

CONTENTS

THE NEW HUMANISM AND THE
SCIENTIFIC ATTITUDE—Grattan

The New Humanism and the Scientific Attitude

> I conjure you, my brethren, *remain true to the earth*, and believe not those who speak unto you of superearthly hopes! Prisoners are they, whether they know it or not.
>
> Despisers of life are they, decaying ones and poisoned ones themselves, of whom the earth is weary: so away with them!
>
> They have something whereof they are proud. What do they call it, that which maketh them proud? Culture, they call it; it distinguisheth them from the goatherds.—FRIEDRICH NIETZSCHE.

WORDS are the common property of all men. There has been a complete and elementary communism in words from time immemorial, and with the spread of popular education, they have become even more communized than ever. It is a peculiar quality of words that they respond with ease to the flux and flow of life, taking on new meanings and discarding old ones with remarkable nonchalance. In the case of most words this chameleon-like quality is of small importance, but others have, in the course of the years, acquired a high emotive quality and their use calls into being, more or less automatically, certain states of mind. A word of the latter type is "humanism." For several centuries now it has been the badge and banner of an

3

appreciable group of writers and thinkers. It has been used to signify an interest in the concerns of the mundane world, an interest which has found expression in the desire to accomplish the good life here and now. It has, as I say, been an emotive word, suggesting not a doctrine but an attitude; it has not been a sectarian battle cry, but a word connoting a concern for man and his earthly welfare. Naturally a word of such respectable meaning has been, from time to time, appropriated to describe a wide diversity of personalities and points of view, but it has never, so far as I know, been appropriated by a doctrinaire group until our own day.

The very fact that humanism has such emotive power and such a broad meaning makes it peculiarly distasteful for one whose allegiance to humanism has never wavered to attack a doctrine which is known as the New Humanism. For something like thirty years now, Professor Irving Babbitt has been advocating this doctrine which is sectarian in essence and humanistic only in name. Throughout his works there is a noticeable inability to appreciate the emotive power of words or, to forego charity, a disposition to use words with a heavy emotive connotation to defend his doctrine and disparage his enemies. Together with this peculiarity there exists another which would seem to provide the means of escaping from this disastrous technique of advocacy and controversy: the desire for precision of definition. The close reader of Mr. Babbitt's works, however, soon discovers that Babbitt defines by studying words and never by studying things. He has never realized, apparently, that words are not things or even parts of things and that by studying words in their historical usages we may be drifting farther and farther away from the thing rather than getting closer to it. How peculiarly disastrous this sort of business is, is clearly expressed in a passage from *The Meaning of Meaning* by Ogden and Richards:

. . . words may come between us and our objects in countless subtle ways, if we do not realize the nature of their power. In logic . . . they lead to the creation of bogus entities, the universals, properties and so forth. . . . By concentrating attention on themselves, words encourage the futile study of forms which has done so much to discredit Grammar; by the excitement which they provoke through their emotive force, discussion is for the most part rendered sterile; by the various types of Verbomania and Graphomania, the satisfaction of naming is realized, and the sense of personal power factitiously enhanced.

These observations are particularly pertinent to any discussion of Mr. Babbitt's work. He has carried word-mongering and definition-making to the point of madness, until one of his ardent disciples is forced

5

to observe of Babbitt's most recent writing: "Professor Babbitt has had perforce to limit himself so closely to 'conclusions' and to use so many words in special senses which he has elsewhere expounded at length, that new readers will be puzzled rather than illuminated or attracted." It is hardly surprising, then, that Mr. Babbitt cannot see that he has committed an error of major proportions in appropriating the word humanism to designate his particular doctrine. He is more apt to congratulate himself on his brilliant strategy in forcing his opponents to attack a doctrine masquerading under a term which all sensible men regard as representing a most respectable and desirable attitude.

In attacking the New Humanism, then, I am not casting aspersions upon the attitude which more than any other will lead to the good life. Furthermore, I am speaking for myself and not for the other contributors to this symposium. I am attacking, as an individual, a peculiarly doctrinaire frame of mind which is hostile to the good life. Perhaps as acutely as any one of the subscribers to the New Humanism I am aware of the forces in modern society which would seem to defeat the good life. Indeed a close perusal of *Democracy and Leadership* convinces me that I have a clearer and more humanistic (in the proper sense) perception of the difficulties than Mr. Babbitt. Nor am I, as are the New Humanists, suf-

ficiently egotistic to believe that I alone have perceived the subversive forces at large in modern
society.

In any logical effort to achieve the good life one
must begin by a perception of one's own difficulties
and dilemmas. It is just because the majority of men
do not understand that the difficulties and dilemmas
by which they are plagued can be resolved that most
of our discontent with present-day conditions is
loosely described as a passing unhappiness. It is for
the thinker to bring the matter to the consciousness
of men and point out to them that a way out must
be discovered. Professor Babbitt would have it that
the solution is a purely individual problem. The
"root of the whole matter is in the psychology of the
individual," he writes. Others have located it there
also, but they differ from Mr. Babbitt in not letting
it remain there. For he goes on to say that the war
of the cave (i.e., the moral struggle within the individual) is an irreducible fact which cannot be resolved by any other method than the repression of
such trends in the human personality as he calls undesirable. Instead of attempting to achieve a balance
between the individual and the environment which,
after all, is the true nature of the problem, he ignores
the environment entirely and concentrates on the individual. His diagnosis is therefore partial and his
prescription inadequate; it resembles the diagnosis and

prescription of the Christian preachers; and his remedy really differs from that of the Christian preachers only in the fact that he does not promise a final resolution of all troubles in Heaven.

In maintaining this position he has erected some very dubious dogmas which I shall examine in detail later. For the moment, it is enough to emphasize the fact that the problem has two aspects, the individual and the environmental. One of the most acute thinkers in this field in recent time, Walther Rathenau, realized perfectly the nature of the problem. Rathenau could discover no merit in the lives of what he called the "purpose-ridden" men. They seemed to him to be past masters of the art of endlessly duplicating and extending the barrenly external forms of industrialism. They did so in the face of the facts that their activities meant the proletarization of the masses of mankind and the emptying of their own lives of cultural significance. He therefore first attempted to prescribe a remedy for his own difficulty: how to free himself from being "purpose-ridden." He did so by evolving a new concept of the "soul." (It is necessary to protest against the introduction into modern discussions of words which carry heavy emotive connotations derived from their use by religionists.) Rathenau did not mean the soul in any conventional sense. He meant the organization of the interior life in such a fashion that man can bring

8

his personal life to perfection. He saw, however, that it is only after we have ordered the environment that we can have orderly interior lives, and consequently he was led to a form of economic radicalism far more revolutionary than any propounded by the Marxists. This perception marks Walther Rathenau off from the other critics of modern society, even those who offer essentially the same prescription for regeneration. The latter do not see that the "soul" is not something uninfluenced by external environment. The burden of all sensible critiques of modern society must be against its economic structure. The only difficulty is that we must recognize the possibility, emphasized by Oswald Spengler, of our being unable to change the direction of societal evolution. It may just be that we are in a "civilization period" or even that we are victims of a culture (assuming that Spengler's distinction lacks validity) which enforces externalization, increasingly made obvious by the indefinite extension of its outstanding feature, mechanized industry.

Rathenau saw, furthermore, that there can be no retreat from mechanization. It must be accepted as an irreducible fact. We must proceed to turn it to the service of man. Man must master things, a not impossible task logically viewed. Rathenau offered a program for the mastering of industry as organized at present which involved the utilization of forces imperfectly realized under private competitive control. In doing so he changed the nature of the state (also in harmony with forces any clear-sighted observer can see at work) from a primarily political to a primarily economic instrument. In essence he proposed an economic system which would recognize that—as a friend of mine has pointed out is true of America increasingly—we are governed by trade associations, and which made the state the arbiter between them and regulator of them. He saw that the dominance of the political motif in the minds of the governing classes made the realization of his program difficult even in one state, let alone on an international scale as the system ideally should operate.

But the important point is not that Rathenau's system for rearranging the economic system of Western society may be unrealizable because of the interference of the passions which have survived from more primitive times; that it is impossible because of cultural lag, to use the terminology of William F. Ogburn. The important point is that he asked the question, "Why?" and fortified himself against what Nietzsche calls nihilism ("Nihilism: no aim, no answer to the question: Why?") by developing his concept of the soul, and then made the next step, which is to attempt to order the environment so that the soul may be a possibility instead of an anachronism.

Professor Babbitt's hostility to the external forces governing man's conduct can be explained on two grounds. In the first place he is traditionally Christian in his dislike for this world; he would perpetuate the anachronistic distinction between the things which are Cæsar's and the things which are God's. After all, all things are man's. Before God created man, man created God, G. Stanley Hall used to tell us; and it is not doing violence to anything in particular if man reclaims what he, in a misguided moment, assigned to God. Nor can there be any objection, even from Mr. Babbitt, if man reclaims the right to deal with what has been Cæsar's, for man, even at the height of the Christian dispensation, has always had the privilege of erecting his own Cæsar. Reclaiming the traditional provinces of human endeavor, man can then proceed to create a truly humanistic world, denying no part of reality and affirming all that is good. Instead of leaving Cæsar to run amuck, he will curb Cæsar, making him a servant instead of a master, and he will attempt to achieve the good life on earth rather than in some chimerical Heaven.

Mr. Babbitt himself worships Cæsar in his present incarnation. In effect he has said to him: "You can rule man's environment, but I'll see to it that the individual sticks to his mutton, which I conceive to be his personal psychic life." And to himself Bab-

11

bitt muttered a Machiavellianism: "I'll trick Cæsar by gaining control of education and making him a Humanist and all will be as it should be." This business of giving Cæsar a *carte blanche* and hoping to control him by making him subscribe to Humanism and by forcing his slaves to subscribe to some catchwords, the nature of which is to be dictated by Mr. Babbitt, leaves Babbitt himself in a position to be a complete conservative. It is his conservatism which makes him unwilling to formulate any scheme for modifying the environment. Not even the Transcendentalists of early nineteenth-century New England made such a grotesque error. Mr. Babbitt lives in a most unholy awe of State Street. He will never be able to write of Humanism as Emerson wrote of Transcendentalism: "The view of Transcendentalism in State Street is that it threatens to invalidate contracts." The Transcendentalists at least escaped the life-hating Christian tradition sufficiently to attempt to achieve a new environment, misguided and essentially childish as those attempts now seem. For when it comes to social matters what do we find Babbitt doing? We find him criticizing imperialists not because of the damage they do to the people they subject to their rule; not for their wasteful exploitive methods; not because they endanger the peace of the world; but because they do not exercise the will to refrain, the inner check which is to keep man firmly at

12

his own business, the business of being saved! And, similarly, he condemns labor leaders, not for the unintelligence of their social program primarily, not for their failure to serve their own interests intelligently, but for their failure to be decorous. Social reform, Babbitt would have it, is a humanitarian business, and "humanitarian" is one of the words which he has for his own purposes infused with a denigrative emotive content. That is the mask he puts on when he wishes to asperse the activity of social reformers, but I suspect that he is rationalizing a prejudice. I suspect that he is horrified, in his rôle of conservative, at their menace to the institution of property narrowly conceived. Babbitt writes of "the institution of property that genuine justice and genuine civilization both require." And implicit in all his writings on social matters is the conviction that the desirable economic arrangement which will give us genuine justice and genuine civilization is the exploitive capitalism of late nineteenth-century America. It will be regulated only by the will to refrain; its leaders will be restrained by the inner check. Babbitt seems to forget that some of the most arrant pirates of that capitalism, like Carnegie and Rockefeller, were pious Christians. That did not prevent them from engaging in the most consummately devilish cut-throat competition and exploitation; nor will the inner check prevent the most unrestrained exploitation of

13

the masses of mankind. The world is not so simple as Babbitt's philosophy implies. The individual and the environment react constantly. They are not separate entities. And most individuals unconsciously derive their dynamic motives from the environment. Even the most profoundly Humanistic individual could hardly do otherwise than bow to the non-humanistic environment in which he found himself immersed.

Dr. Babbitt's colleague, Paul Elmer More (with whom I have chosen not to deal), has clearly perceived the nature of Babbitt's dilemma, which is the dilemma of Humanism. He sees that Humanism, in spite of all protestations to the contrary, is not of this world. It is a technique for preparing man for the next—a sort of substitute Christianity. But, curiously enough, it tends to deny the next world. Mr. More believes this to be a fallacy, a weak link in the Humanist chain of logic: ". . . the humanist who thinks to stand without religion is desperately beset by forces that would sink him to the level of naturalism. He may cling stubbornly to values that are the creation of his own fancy [sic!]—for a while; in the end he will be overcome by the brutality of facts." Consequently Mr. More believes that the Humanist must, in self-defense, subscribe to the good old religion which is good enough for him and which he defines thus:

. . . it must come into the heart of man, not without austerity of command, yet with salutary hope, assuring us that our practical sense of right and wrong, of beauty and ugliness, is justified by the eternal canons of truth, and that the consequences of our deeds in this little segment of space may follow the soul in its flight into regions beyond our utmost guessing. It must fortify the purpose of the individual by inspiring him with a conviction that the world in which he plays his part is not a product of chance or determinism, but the work of a foreseeing intelligence, and is itself fulfilled with purpose. It must lend new meaning and larger values to visible phenomena by seeing in them shadows and symbols of invisible realities, and by exhibiting them as servants to a spiritual end. It will so knit the future with the present, so bind together the eternal and the temporal, that the torment of frustration will be assuaged, the sting of transience blunted, and the triumph of the grave overthrown.

Amen!

II

The Humanist argument runs as follows: By a free will which is at once selective (and not causally determined) and a mechanism of ethical control, man is enabled to select his mode of life. There is a profound dualism between man and nature. Man, to be human, must live by values which are higher than anything deducible from nature. Man has intuitive glimpses of a higher reality behind the flux and flow of nature. On the basis of these glimpses he is enabled to formulate a code of values which is opposed to nature and therefore human, to guide him in living. The man who denies this higher reality and derives his values from nature is a naturalist. The man who identifies higher reality with God is a religionist and accepts his code of values on the basis of divine revelation or from admitted authority exterior to himself, to which he submits himself for guidance. But there is a medial position which, while opposed to naturalism, is yet not prepared to accept divinely revealed or externally imposed values. The man in this position seeks to formulate his values from a close study of those glimpses of antecedent reality discernible in literature and from life scrutinized through literature. Such a man is a Humanist.

The Humanist asserts free will as a fact. It is necessary for him to do so because he believes that man can by his own choice live on any level he desires. Thus, if there is no free will he thinks that there can be no Humanists. For one becomes a Humanist by cultivating values which are not naturalistic; values indeed which are opposed to the naturalistic trends in human personality; and one can only do this by exercising choice.

The difficulty here is the fact that the Humanists

have failed to examine their concept of "free will" —they have left it hanging in mid-air so to speak. But having posited a dualism between man and nature (an idea which will be examined below) it follows that they consider the will to be located in the human aspects of the personality, not the natural. Their will, as has been remarked, is both selective and a mechanism of ethical control. Babbitt describes it as an "inner check" operating upon the expansive trends of the personality, and since it is ethical in quality it is alleged to be *indispensable to the practice of Humanism*. But, to quote C. J. Herrick, "The coinage of a high-brow name for an unknown factor is not an adequate solution of a scientific problem, though this subtle device has at times retarded scientific advance for generations."

The Humanist will, then, is a metaphysical concept not to be defined, measured, or described in terms that are acceptable to the scientific mind. It is an arbitrary intrusion into the personality from the outside, not integral with it. Its action is not causal but arbitrary. It is a figment of the imagination, without validity to any one with an elementary knowledge of modern scientific thought on the subject.

The joke of the matter is that it is quite unnecessary in the accomplishment of the Humanist desire to arrive at so-called freedom of choice. Modern scientific determinism assumes the reign of law everywhere. "The scientific method," writes Dr. Herrick, "admits of no appeal to mystical agencies which do not knit into a unitary system of natural processes and of no logical arguments whose premises are not verifiable experiences." Man being continuous with nature it follows inescapably that the mind is as much subject to the rule of causal sequence as the rest of the body. There are no discontinuities in nature. We admit cheerfully that part of our conduct is controlled in the same fashion. Admitting this does not lead to fatalism or to subjection to the law of chance. For, writes Herrick,[1]

Our common and trustworthy experience is that mental acts (thoughts, emotions, volitions, and the like) are causative factors in human conduct. . . . When therefore, we say that conscious experience is a causative factor in human behavior it must be understood that we regard this experience as one part only of a protoplasmic activity involving structural changes in the nervous system, whether we know what these latter are or not. Thinking is a part of living and all living involves structural alterations of the vital substance. . . . Some of our experiences we objectify as external things; another complex of experiences we objectify as our own animal bodies; still other experiences we do not objectify at all and

[1] See *Fatalism or Freedom*, by C. J. Herrick, the best modern scientific statement of this problem I have ever seen.

18

call them ideas, hopes, sentiments, aspirations, ideals, and so forth. These are just as truly functions of our body as is our breathing. They are natural events. Their causes are preceding natural events, some outside our bodies, some inside, some easily demonstrable physiologically, some known only introspectively. Their results are still other natural events, some mental, some physiological, some perhaps profound changes in external nature. . . . When . . . discrimination is made consciously in view of the probable future consequences of each of the possible ways of reacting to the situation we call the act a choice. . . . Whichever alternative I may choose it is clear that every step is causally determined in the same sense that my reflexes are said to be causally determined. . . . This power to choose, that is, to shape our conduct in view of one out of several possible future contingencies, is no supernatural or miraculous endowment which enables us to flout the laws of nature; it operates within the natural realm and in harmony with natural law.

These correlated passages make it abundantly clear that in dismissing the Humanist "free will" (in both its aspects) as a metaphysical concept of no validity or worth, we do not fall into a paralyzing worship of fatalism nor into a drifting world of chance. Quite the contrary. All that we dismiss is a metaphysical concept of no use whatsoever. Its utility as an illusion is another matter entirely.

19

Equally dubious is the Humanist assertion that there are three distinct levels of experience. These levels, they say, are in an ascending scale of excellence. Since any hierarchy of levels of living is quite arbitrary in origin and invidious in intent, overemphasis of what may perhaps be justified on the plea of expedience is dangerous. It is hardly necessary, when you have no ulterior motive, to assign a higher and lower position to modes of life. It is best to recognize that they are different approaches to the problem of living. Furthermore, such invidious distinctions soon lead to an attitude of patronage or glorification toward the mode not practiced. In this fashion any critical examination of the alternative modes is precluded and, indeed, the accepted mode becomes so self-contained as to make impossible coöperation for common ends.

The Humanist classification is revelatory of the distinctions they draw in discussing the modern world and modern literature. The lowest level is the naturalistic. On this level living proceeds on the basis of mere unregulated animality. It is in no way given significance by a discipline of values. It is expansive and materialistic. It is expansive because on the emotional side Rousseau is its prophet and Rousseau emphasized the free play of natural impulses at the expense of an imposed discipline, and materialistic because of its allegiance to the Baconian cult of science.

On the Humanistic level, on the other hand, the emphasis is on discipline—on control through the ethical will. Humanism is a doctrine and a discipline of aspiration without being a religion. According to Babbitt the great Humanistic virtue is "decorum, or a sense of proportion." In other words, Humanism enables man to discipline his natural impulses in the interests of finer living. It is, in Humanist eyes, an athletic discipline, not supine and drifting, but resistive and aspiring. While the Humanist recognizes that man is after all an animal and subject to natural laws—a product of evolution and an integral part of nature—he asserts that man has glimpses of a state higher than the natural to which he aspires. The formulation of his aspirations gives him knowledge of what is *human*. Human law is not in any way subject to the natural law of the universe. It is, indeed, opposed to the natural. Professor Norman Foerster writes: "Humanism assumes . . . that the essential elements of human experience are precisely those which appear to conflict with the reality explored by naturism." Humanism, then, is a scheme of values above man. To practice these values he must suppress his naturalistic self.

Assuming a medial position, the Humanist tacitly admits that the religious plane of living is either higher than or complementary to his own. Mr. Foerster characterizes religious experience as "the supreme

21

level of life." Mr. Babbitt writes: "The honest thinker, whatever his own preference, must begin by admitting that though religion can get along without Humanism, Humanism cannot get along without religion." It is this hospitality toward and deference to religion that is carrying so many young Humanists over into religious sects. Humanism is merely a point of rest on the threshold of the church. The Humanist is prevented, by his inability to accept any revealed truth, from progressing to the highest plane. But experience is proving that that inability soon breaks down amongst the disciples of Humanism. It is no wonder that Foerster did not meet the challenge of T. S. Eliot's remark: "There is no avoiding that dilemma: you must be either a naturalist or a supernaturalist." The Humanist prefers to rest in the position of an ally of dogmatic religion. As long as the "inner check" is in good working order he can resist the cries of T. S. Eliot and G. K. Chesterton, inviting them into their respective ponds with the plea that the water is fine! It is not unjust to say that Humanism is a refuge for those persons who want to be religious without assuming the responsibility of defending a dogmatic orthodoxy of the conventional kind. They want the moral elevation without the supernatural sustention.

But "the central assumption of Humanism," writes Foerster, echoing Babbitt, "is that of a dualism of man

22

and nature." Babbitt's famous work, *Rousseau and Romanticism*, is devoted in considerable part to the assertion of this dualism. One of his main indictments of the naturalists, whether Rousseauistic or Baconian (the writer of this paper is undoubtedly what Babbitt would call a Baconian), is that they deny the duality of man and nature. This duality is an idea developed before the experimental technic was applied to man. It is an idea held in common by the Greek philosophers and the Christian theologians. The difficulty is to determine in what particular the human mind (for the duality arises in the mind) is subject to a power outside of nature. To achieve duality one must introduce from the outside of nature and arbitrarily something that is not naturally there. "There is no separate 'mind,' " writes Doctor John Dewey, "gifted in and of itself with a faculty of thought; such a conception of thought ends in postulating the mystery of a power outside of nature and yet able to intervene within it. Thinking is objectively discoverable as that mode of serial responsive behavior to a problematic situation in which transition to the relatively settled and clear is effective." This position, which accords with the findings of science,[2] entirely eliminates the possibility

[2] See Herrick, *op. cit.*, page 40: "There is abundant scientific evidence . . . that thinking is a function of the body (and of the brain more particularly) just as truly as walking is a function of the body (and of the legs more particularly). Both of

of a discontinuity between the human and the natural, for the "human," it must be understood, resides in the mind—according to the Humanist. Such a discontinuity as Humanism demands can only be based on the idea that the mind is a "spectator"; or that it runs parallel to the body in some undefined way; or that there is an interaction with no causal relation between mind and body. None of these positions is tenable. For as a matter of fact organic acts are an integral part of all mental processes. "Man is continuous with nature."

The Humanist feels it necessary to posit this dualism because he relegates science to an inferior position and seeks to aggrandize Humanistic and religious values. By such aggrandizement he hopes to save his values from scientific (experimental) scrutiny. The Humanist critic of science denounces all scientific progress since Newton as largely false and so preserves from scientific scrutiny those aspects of life about which the Humanists presume unscientifically to dogmatize. He rejects all modern psychology, biology, and sociology. In these fields the Humanist would have us rely on what Veblen has called "lore"—the "wisdom of the ages." In fact he glories in the fact that his values are not naturalistic but "human" and these functions have well-known, definitely assignable organs, and the scientific evidence for relating the function with the organ is of the same sort and equally convincing in the two cases."

24

as such in opposition to the naturalistic. This opposition leads to what Joseph Wood Krutch has called the "paradox of Humanism," which is that most of the values which the Humanists glorify are values which are least human in the ordinary sense. Instead of realizing that values which are to gain general allegiance and have an important part in practice must grow naturally out of life as the mass of cultivated mankind lives it, the Humanist demands that values require, for their achievement, a deliberate effort of a hypothetical free will acting arbitrarily. He is thus demanding that the discontinuity between ideals and practice be perpetuated. The Humanist fails to see that life is not so ascetic an affair that men may brood on ethical "choices." They have not indeed, under modern conditions of living, time to engage in abstract spiritual exercises of any kind, and if the values which are to be regarded as valuable to man and society do not have a natural and inevitable continuity with action, they are bound to remain unobserved and consequently trivial and unimportant—noble and amusing anachronisms.

Humanist values, it will be recalled, are derived from intuitive glimpses of higher reality—of the antecedently real. In the eyes of the Humanist the apprehension of the antecedently real is what gives man knowledge. Dr. John Dewey's latest and most

25

important book, *The Quest for Certainty,* is in part devoted to a devastating critique of the doctrine. Dr. Dewey points out that the idea of an antecedent reality was first developed by the Greeks and was adapted to Christian epistemology by identifying the universal with God. It was the idea common to all variations upon the doctrine that behind the shifting appearances of this world there was a preexistent perfect scheme. Man progressed in knowledge insofar as, by the operation of his intellect, he apprehended this scheme. In seeking to provide a philosophical basis for modern science, Sir Isaac Newton borrowed this Greek idea and made it the purpose of science to reveal through the experimental method the preëxisting scheme. In this way he grafted an antique anachronism upon what was an entirely new and remarkable method for arriving at knowledge. He subverted his most original contribution to human thought to the most powerful and perverse idea that had survived from the era before experimental science became a possibility.

Though Newton thus provided philosophy with a method for reconciling scientific advances with the necessities of its pre-experimental position, he effectively cut off any chance for science immediately to contribute to philosophy a new theory of knowledge. For, while experimental science proceeded to advance knowledge by one method, the philosophers continued to say that it was advancing by another. The issue was the so-called Newtonian World-machine. The fault of evolving this monstrosity, if fault it was, must not be laid at the door of the scientists, but at the door of the philosophers, who by insisting that experimental science was revealing a preëxisting scheme of the universe, provided the basis of the whole idea.

Dr. Dewey discards this outmoded notion and evolves a theory of knowledge from the methods of experimental science. He states the experimental method of arriving at knowledge thus:

While the traits of experimental inquiry are familiar, so little use has been made of them in formulating a theory of knowledge and of mind in relation to nature that a somewhat explicit statement of well-known facts is excusable. They exhibit three outstanding characteristics. The first is the obvious one that all experimentation involves *overt* doing, the making of definite changes in the environment, or in our relation to it. The second is that experiment is not a random activity but is directed by ideas which have to meet the conditions set by the need of the problem inducing the active inquiry. The third and concluding feature, in which the other two receive their full measure of meaning, is that the outcome of the directed activity is the construction of a new empirical situation in which objects are differently related to one another, and such that the *consequences*

27

of directed operations form the objects that have the property of being *known*.

But while the Humanists profess to derive their values by the intuitive apprehension of the universal elements discernible behind the flux and flow of experience, they really derive them from the study of past literature; or confirm their intuitions by reference to the "wisdom of the ages." To be sure a Humanist of Babbitt's order is chiefly famous for the destructive moralistic criticism he has leveled against the writers and schools of writers who have subverted his values, notably Rousseau and his alleged derivatives and abettors. But Foerster, who is somewhat of a missionary, has told us frequently that the true Humanistic values are to be found in what is known as classic literature (not necessarily the literary classics, by the way) and above all in Greek literature. (It should be pointed out, however, that Dr. Babbitt derives his doctrine that the ethical will takes primacy over the intellect, from Oriental sources.) The point here is that Humanistic values are derived from past formulations, and particularly from formulations arrived at in a primitive society where the authors could not conceivably imagine many of the most vital and complex problems of modern living. Even if we accept, as the Humanists apparently do, the idea that literature is in a certain sense a criticism

28

of life, it is impossible to accept this method of deriving values for living. Dr. Dewey has a passage which clearly defines the quality of values to be derived from literature, since literature is a projection of experience, criticized, if at all, on a non-scientific basis:

"Experience" once meant the results accumulated in memory of a variety of past doings and undergoings that were had without control by insight, when the net accumulation was found to be practically available in dealing with present situations. Both the original perceptions and uses and the application of their outcome in present doings were accidental—that is, neither was determined by an understanding of the relations of cause and effect, of means and consequences, involved. In that sense they were non-rational, non-scientific.

But really it is a perversion of literature to make it a source and support for moral dogmas, just as it does violence to culture history to trace all modern ills back to Rousseau or Bacon. Humanism is based upon a fundamental misapprehension of the purpose of literature. Literature is not a source of moral precepts; nor a source of a pseudo-religious discipline; it is a phase of experience. It is not the whole of experience, but one aspect of it. For any complete life-experience it is indispensable, because in literature

29

we have a most satisfactory technic for clarifying and organizing the meanings of life. Literature (and all art) concentrates experience. Literature suggests, realizes and embodies meanings. It has this quality in common with the other arts—painting, sculpture, music. The right use of literature will assist us in "clarifying further perceptions and enjoyments." In this approach to art "appreciation is the intelligent apprehension of what is significant and meaningful in a picture or a poem in pictorial and poetical terms, what emotions are relevant to that esthetic impression, what light or meaning it throws over other experiences including those not popularly regarded as esthetic." [3] In this sense literature is knowledge —in a broad sense scientific knowledge. "Anything that may be called knowledge," says Dewey, "or a known object, marks a question answered, a difficulty disposed of, a confusion cleared up, an inconsistency reduced to coherence, a perplexity mastered." And "taste . . . is the outcome of experience brought cumulatively to bear on the intelligent appreciation of the real worth of likings and enjoyments." [4]

Our quarrel is not with values as such. It would be an indefensible position to maintain to deny that values are necessary to civilized living. None of us

[3] Irwin Edman, "A Philosophy of Experience as a Philosophy of Art," in *Essays in Honor of John Dewey.*

[4] I have elaborated a theory of literary criticism in *The Nation,* April 30, 1930.

has quite resigned the hope of some sort of good life. "The problem of restoring integration and coöperation between man's beliefs about the world in which he lives and his beliefs about the values and purposes that should direct his conduct is the deepest problem of modern life," writes Dr. Dewey. Our quarrel is with the method by which Humanist values are derived. Since this is our objection to them it would be pointless to engage in an extended debate over the particular values to which Humanists give allegiance. For it is impossible to accept them on the Humanist say-so, since they were arrived at by a method which is open to the condemnation of being unscientific. Humanistic values, indeed, cannot be regarded as ends in themselves. They are rather data to be used in arriving at valid values. ". . . the conclusions of prior knowledge are the *instruments* of new inquiries, not the norm which determines their validity."

Values, to present a definition, are "whatever is taken to have rightful authority in the direction of conduct." To be useful they cannot be prohibitions against certain ways of living, nor can they be idle hortatory injunctions in favor of certain modes of conduct. They, above all, cannot rely for their authority upon an alleged agreement with a hypothetical antecedent reality.

It is utterly idle to think, as the Humanists do, that one can transfer the values of one social congelation,

31

imperfectly apprehended through literature, to another social congelation and expect them to be absolutely relevant. We must reach a more fundamental basis for the construction of values than this. Agreeing with the Humanists that it is impossible to accept values imposed by external authority or divine revelation, we must go a step beyond the Humanists and demand that the values to which allegiance is finally to be given, be arrived at according to the scientific method in coöperation with true esthetic appreciation.

Admittedly we are here advocating the use of the scientific method in a field where it has been least active and consequently least successful. Furthermore, little has been done in the field of esthetics of conduct in relation to scientific findings, though Havelock Ellis has done notable pioneering. The disparity between the knowledge we possess about the physical world and that which we have about man and society is what gives the Humanists their chance. Since our scientists have been, by the nature of the society in which they have worked, more inclined to develop those phases of knowledge which can be used in their applied aspects for the pecuniary aggrandizement of individuals, the other phases have been neglected. At the present time, however, we are witnessing a progression from the physical to the social sciences. To be sure a great deal of what is called social science to-day seems grotesque and may eventually prove to be worthless, but since science is a progressive development, that is not reason to reject its findings altogether. Furthermore science in the social realm can never be so exact—the control can never be so perfect—as in the physical realm. The imponderables are more in number and less easy to control.

Nevertheless, if we are to have values which are to have any reasonable finality for living, they must be the product of the application of the scientific technic. In arriving at scientifically approvable values past formulations will serve as data. Not only will the scientists utilize the Humanist formulation as a tool, but they will also be prepared to use religiously supported values, those cultivated by sophisticates as well as rustics, and indeed any values, in the same fashion. What the final formulation will be no man can say. It is sufficient to observe that the values which science will approve will not be in contradiction to the natural constitution of man and allegiance to them will not be predicated upon any metaphysical free will nor upon any recognition of the unprovable allegation that there is one law for nature and another for man.

III

The remedy for the present situation is not less science but more science. The extension of the ex-

33

perimental technic into the human and social realms is bound to be the most fruitful adventure of modern times. But it must be clearly understood that we have as yet no way of measuring what will be the effect of a general adoption of a scientific attitude by those with influence upon society. It is not now a part of the equipment of any group except an infinitesimal and usually uninfluential minority. Even those men who have mastered the scientific attitude as applied to some special branch of knowledge—for example, physics—frequently betray in other fields the fact that they are not completely scientific. What we need is not more courses in science in the universities, but a greater effort to get the scientific *attitude* firmly planted in the minds of those who subject themselves to higher education. Though certain "philanderers upon the outskirts of knowledge" are now engaged in a revival of the old disparagement of science, they direct their criticism at courses about science—against scientific information, not the scientific attitude. We, let it be admitted at once, do not need more courses of this sort, but if in some way the essentials of the scientific attitude could be freely communicated it would be a marked advance. ". . . science," writes Dr. Dewey, "has been taught too much as an accumulation of ready-made material with which students are to be made familiar, not enough as a method of thinking, an attitude of mind,

34

after the pattern of which mental habits are to be transformed." And a similar position has been taken by other distinguished proponents of the scientific attitude.

Even if the courses in science as now conducted are continued there are several common errors that can be corrected. Mr. Foerster states that "in its true function, science is merely descriptive." Nothing could be more inadequate as a definition of the "true function" of science. Charles Singer, a leading authority on the history of science, has written: "Nor is the advance of science to be measured by the vast accumulation of observations but by the degree to which these observations are brought under general laws. The function of science, we must repeat, is to classify, which is simply and intimately to unify." Science is, in its essence, an art of control. If it was "merely descriptive" it could control nothing. When such misapprehensions of what science actually is and does prevail with a man who presumes to define the place of science in the intellectual scheme, it is no wonder that J. B. S. Haldane can exclaim in despair that "there has been a complete failure to integrate into its [society's] intellectual structure the scientific ideas which have furnished its material structure." The prevailing intellectual dilemmas can mostly be traced to the failure of this integration. When the integration is accomplished it will not mean the triumph of what old-fashioned sentimentalists call materialism. It will mean that mankind will in some sense gain possession of the intellectual heritage which is rightfully its own.

NOTES ON BABBITT
AND MORE—Wilson

Notes on Babbitt and More

THE following notes deal with the essays by Irving Babbitt and Paul Elmer More in the Humanist symposium, *Humanism and America.*

"HUMANISM: AN ESSAY AT DEFINITION,"
BY IRVING BABBITT

(1) *The law of measure on which it [Humanism] depends becomes meaningless unless it can be shown to be one of the "laws unwritten in the heavens" of which Antigone had the immediate perception, laws that are "not of to-day or yesterday," that transcend in short the temporal process.*

This seems to me a grotesque misapplication of the famous speech from Sophocles. Let me point out, in the first place, that what Antigone says is " ἄγραπτα κἀσφαλῆ θεῶν νόμιμα"—"unwritten and unfailing laws of the gods"—and that Professor Babbitt, in changing "gods" to "heaven" (which is particularly inappropriate in this case, as Antigone has just specified the gods of the underworld), is following the Victorian tradition of Jebb and Jowett, who, by substituting such Christian words as "God" and "heaven" for the pre-Christian conceptions of the Greeks, almost succeeded in giving Sophocles and Plato the aspect of pious English dons. But Babbitt has turned

Sophocles into something worse and even more alien to his true nature: he has turned him into a Harvard Humanist. In the scene in question, Antigone is not talking about the law of measure or anything remotely resembling it—she has disobeyed Creon's edict by performing funeral rites for her brother and she is justifying herself for her insubordinate conduct. There is no self-control about Antigone's behavior: she has committed an act of passionate personal loyalty, regarded as excessively rash and wrong-headed by everybody else in the play, including her own sister, whose "inner check" is more highly developed than Antigone's. When Creon demands how Antigone has dared to break the law, she replies fiercely that such a law as his edict is contrary to the laws of the gods.

The Romantic might, in fact, turn this scene against the Humanist with more appropriateness than the Humanist can use it against the Romantic. Antigone has the same hasty intemperate insolent nature as her father Œdipus—we are told so explicitly in the play—and she is asserting her individual will in defiance of law and expediency—she is making an impulsive and desperate gesture. Aristotle—"a true Humanist," according to Babbitt—says of this passage, in showing the distinction between conventional and natural law, that Antigone vindicates the latter in asserting "ὅτι δίκαιον, ἀπειρημένον,

40

θάψαι τὸν Πολυνείκη, ὡς φύσει ὂν τοῦτο δίκαιον,"—
that her act, though it violated the prohibition, had
the sanction of natural right, was "right according
to nature." Now Antigone, of course, is not a nineteenth-century Romantic, and Aristotle does not
mean by "nature" quite the same thing that Rousseau
does. But what Rousseau means does have something
in common with what Aristotle means that Antigone
means, whereas what Antigone means can't by any
possible stretch be associated with Babbitt's "law of
measure." Babbitt grossly misrepresents Sophocles
when he applies Antigone's speech in this way: "The
laws unwritten in the heavens" is one of Babbitt's
favorite quotations: he has used it again and again in
order to give us the impression that Sophocles has en-
dorsed the Humanist "will to refrain." Yet, as I say,
if it is a question of slinging classical texts, the old-
fashioned Romantic who is Babbitt's bugbear—if
there be any such still alive—might turn Antigone's
outburst against Babbitt—and might even add, as
Antigone does:

σοὶ δ' εἰ δοκῶ νῦν μῶρα δρῶσα τυγχάνειν,
σχεδόν τι μώρῳ μωρίαν ὀφλισκάνω.

Babbitt elsewhere in this essay says that Sophocles
"ranks high among occidental Humanists," though he
admits—making reservations in regard to the opinion
of Matthew Arnold—that "perfect poise is no doubt

41

impossible; not even Sophocles succeeded in seeing life steadily and seeing it whole." I don't know in precisely what respect Professor Babbitt considers Sophocles to have fallen short of perfect poise; but it is certainly true that Sophocles' characters are usually remarkable for anything but poise—they are as violent and as harsh as the people in the plays of Eugene O'Neill. Where the "law of measure" comes in is certainly not in the conduct of Sophocles' characters—the hot-headed over-confident Œdipus; the "fierce child of a fierce father," Antigone; the relentless and morbid Electra, etc.—but in Sophocles' handling of his material—the firmness of his intellectual grasp, the sureness of his sense of form, the range of psychological insight which enables him to show us spending themselves against each other the rages, the ambitions, the loyalties, of so many passionate persons, and all to die in the clear air, leaving only with the echo of their tirades the vibration of the taut verse. In a world dominated by the law of measure, however, there would be no Humanist masterpieces such as the tragedies of Sophocles—since Babbitt claims them, with reservations, as Humanist masterpieces—because there would be no violent passions to write about. This might be a good thing—perhaps we ought to be glad to do without the Sophocleses if we could get rid of the unruly passions. But, on the other hand, we ought perhaps to think twice before

letting ourselves in for a world where the sole masterpieces were Humanist symposia.

(2) *It would not be easy to argue with any plaus-
ibility that the typical modernist is greatly concerned
with the law of measure; his interest, as a glance at
our newspapers should suffice to show, is rather in the
doing of stunts and the breaking of records, in
"prodigies, feats of strength and crime," the very
topics that, according to the traditional report, Confucius banished from his conversation.*

In this respect, our age is no worse than any other.
What is done to-day for the people by the newspapers
was done formerly by the composers of ballads, and
ballad literature has always been occupied with prodigies, feats of strength and crime. The *Iliad* itself was
presumably made out of ballads—and, in any case,
there can be no question that it deals with prodigies,
feats of strength and crime. The Greek dramatists,
including Sophocles, got their themes from Homer or
similar sources. It is true that the genuine poet is
able to do with such stories something which the re-
porter is not usually able to do, but the material that
he deals with is the same. And the general run of the
ballads of any age has been as crude as newspaper
stories. The sages of our own time—Professor Babbitt, for example—are, I should say, as little preoccupied with the prodigies and crimes of the news-

papers as Confucius was with the common gossip.

(3) *In the case of such encroachments [of Naturalism upon the domains of Humanism or religion] there is not only a quarrel between the Naturalist and the Humanist, but a quarrel of first principles. When first principles are involved the law of measure is no longer applicable. One should not be moderate in dealing with error.*

It has apparently never occurred to Professor Babbitt that one should be moderate about being too sure that one is oneself absolutely right and that others are absolutely wrong—though Mr. More, in his companion essay, quotes from Whitehead against the dogmatists of Darwinism, Cromwell's, "My brethren, by the bowels of Christ I beseech you, bethink you that you may be mistaken!" We might have thought that if the law of measure were valuable anywhere, it was valuable in the domain of ideas, where the failure sufficiently to observe it has notoriously bred war and persecution from the beginning of the world. Babbitt surely did not learn from Plato, whom he invokes in the next paragraph, that we should be so sure of our own opinions that we need not be moderate with people who happen to have different ones. The hero of Plato's novel of ideas is Socrates, but Plato's dialogues are a novel, none the less, and the impression, I think, which most people get from them, though they may be persuaded by Socrates' opinions, is that the world has a good many aspects and that there is a good deal to be said on all sides. The people in Plato who follow Babbitt's precept that we "should not be moderate in dealing with error" are the judges of Socrates. I doubt whether even Aristotle was so sure that he was right as Babbitt. If Babbitt wants to find a tradition for his policy in dealing with error, he must look not to the Academy and the Lyceum, but to the councils of the Inquisition, the revolutionary tribunal of the Terror and—to come closer to Professor Babbitt's home—Dedham Courthouse and Boston State House.

(4) *Positively one may define it [the higher will] as the higher immediacy that is known in its relation to the lower immediacy—the merely temperamental man with his impressions and emotions and expansive desires—as a power of vital control* (frein vital).

So Paul Elmer More asserts (in *Aristocracy and Justice*) that if a man "retires into himself and examines his own motives and the sources of his self-approval and discontent . . . he will discover that there is a happiness of the soul which is not the same as the pleasure of fulfilled desires, whether these be for good or for ill, a happiness which is not dependent upon the results of this or that choice among our

45

desires, but upon the very act itself of choice and self-control."

Now why the deuce is virtue, with the Humanists, always made to reside exclusively in what Babbitt calls the "will to refrain"? "Humanism," says Professor Babbitt, in making a distinction between Humanism and religion, "is not primarily enthusiastic." So far as I can see, it is not enthusiastic at all. Professor Babbitt goes on to say that the Humanist, though he "cannot afford to be an enthusiast in Rousseau's sense, on the other hand should not neglect the truth of Rousseau's saying that 'cold reason has never done anything illustrious.'" But the writings of the Humanists strike us with a chill even more mortal than that of reason. And how can one take seriously a philosophy which enjoins nothing but negative behavior?—as if humanity were not, now as always, as much in need of being exhorted against coldness and indifference and routine as against irresponsible exuberance—especially Anglo-Saxon humanity. As if Boston and New York, Manchester and London, were not obviously suffering from a lack of normal human fellowship and normal human hope and joy rather than from the demoralizing effects of unbridled "humanitarian" sympathies, indiscriminate emotional "expansiveness" or universal orgiastic dissipation—as if our clerks, our factory workers and our respectable professional and business classes were all in danger of

46

falling victims to the rhapsodical enthusiasm and the lawless individualism of Romanticism! If it is a question of refraining, these people are all good Humanists: they have either been compelled by society to refrain from most of the enjoyments, from the exercise of most of the faculties, which make the amenity of human life at its best, or they refrain because their educations have been too limited to enable them to conceive their own esthetic and emotional possibilities, or because their natures are too poor to have any.

As a matter of fact, however, Professor Babbitt, as I have noted above, has managed to exempt his own professional activities from the law of measure, the obligation to refrain. He has made it plain that, in "dealing with error," we are no longer under the necessity of being moderate; and as Professor Babbitt, in his writings, is always engaged in "dealing with error," it is never necessary for him to be moderate. Professor Babbitt—and the other Humanists—are relieved of the obligation of being decorous as soon as they put pen to paper. It is not decorous to look for nothing but mistakes in the writings of your contemporaries, it is not decorous always to call attention to these mistakes with a sneer; it is not decorous to take a word like Humanism, which has always formerly been applied to the great scholars, philosophers, satirists and poets of the Renaissance, and to insist that it ought to be regarded as the exclusive property of a small sect of schoolmasters so fatuous that they do not hesitate to assign schoolmasters' A's, B's and C's in Humanism to "Homer, Phidias, Plato, Aristotle, Confucius, Buddha, Jesus, Paul, Virgil, Horace, Dante, Shakespeare, Milton, Goethe, Matthew Arnold, Emerson and Lowell"—it is not decorous to assume that you yourselves are the only persons who have taken seriously the vices and woes of your own time and that everybody else except yourselves is engaged either stupidly or perversely in aggravating them. But as all this comes under the head of dealing with error, and as, in dealing with error, one should not be moderate, the Humanists are unfortunately obliged to confine the pursuit of their ideal of decorum to the transactions of their private lives, where comparatively few of us are able to benefit by it.

(5) *This movement* [*the modernist movement*] *has, from the eighteenth century and in some respects from the Renaissance, been marked by a growing discredit of the will to refrain. The very word renunciation has been rarely pronounced by those who have entered into the movement. The chief exception that occurs to one is Goethe (echoed at times by Carlyle). Any one who thinks of the series of Goethe's love affairs, prolonged into the seventies, is scarcely likely to maintain that his* Entsagung *was of a very austere*

48

character even for a man of the world, not to speak of a saint.

It seems to me that assumptions are here being made in regard to sexual morality which require a good deal of proving on Babbitt's part. He goes on to say, a little further down the page, that "the real Humanist consents, like Aristotle, to limit his desires only in so far as this limitation can be shown to make for his own happiness." If one disapproves of Goethe's love affairs, but if the end to be achieved is happiness, one should first show that these love affairs did not make him happy. It seems to me that Professor Babbitt should shoulder the burden of proof and show that it did not do Goethe good at the same time that it did the ladies no harm for him to fall in love after he was seventy. But these are questions which Babbitt and More will never argue, as to which they will always simply make assumptions, just as they assume that virtue should consist mainly of the exercise of the will to refrain, because these opinions are not really conclusions from any sort of evidence, but merely the unexamined prejudices of a Puritan heritage which Babbitt and More have never outgrown, in spite of all their fascinated and tireless voyages among the varied countries of the mind, and which they mistake for universal and eternal moral laws because—they have themselves put this forward as their final and overwhelming justification—when they look into themselves, they find them there.

49

THE CRITIQUE OF HUMANISM

"THE HUMILITY OF COMMON SENSE," BY PAUL ELMER MORE

(1) *It is a nice question to ask whether belief in the absolute irresponsibility of the artistic temperament has engendered the modern ideal of absolute art, or the contrary. . . . The point I would make is the falseness and futility of the logical deduction that art can . . . dispense with the stuff of humanity or nature, or can weigh anchor and sail off into a shoreless sea of unreality.*

In the first part of Mr. More's essay, marked by his usual intellectual arrogance, which he incongruously entitles "The Humility of Common Sense," he is occupied with the old "art for art's sake" doctrine as it has been formulated by some of its most recent champions. Now I should agree with Mr. More that the artist should not be irresponsible and that he cannot dispense with humanity and nature—I should even agree that "art for art's sake" has given rise to a good deal of nonsense, as indeed what doctrine has not? But it seems to me that Mr. More has failed to understand how this point of view has been inevitably produced by a particular situation. Art is, of course, like market-gardening, road-building and banking, a means of supplying certain human needs—it is one of our devices for adjusting ourselves to the world, and, as the Humanists are so zealous to insist, raising

50

our condition above that of the animals; and it is preposterous for artists to talk as if they were able to work *in vacuo,* or as if it were possible for them to remain indifferent to the effects of their work on human life. But in the course of the nineteenth century, they began to be driven to talk in this way, to make a cult of art for its own sake, by the progress of the industrial revolution and the rise of the middle class. It was one of the fatal defects of the kind of society to which these events gave rise that it neglected or discouraged the esthetic appetites for which the artists had formerly provided. And as they found esthetic values depreciating, as they found themselves becoming almost outlaws, the artists grew desperate and embittered. They swore, if they had any spirit, that they were going on to practice their craft in spite of the fact that nobody wanted their wares, and they thus arrived at the slogan of "art for art's sake." The fact that they should have felt the necessity for asserting the value of what they were doing was a witness to their maladjustment, to the abnormality of the situation in which they found themselves—but, given this situation, the very assertion of one's faith in esthetic values, the dogged devotion to the practice of art, not infrequently called forth qualities of the highest heroism. It is true that the isolation of the artist, his consciousness of swimming against the current, had sometimes—especially toward the end of the century—the effect of deforming his work. But, none the less, what student of literature who is not content merely to praise or blame a work of art, referring it to ideal moral and esthetic standards, but who makes an effort to see it in its relation to the other forces of the society in which it was produced, will assert that even the *fin de siècle* poet could or should have done otherwise? In the generation of the middle century, even so great a man as Flaubert had found it possible to save his soul only through the cult of art. Yet the idea that, despite the cynicism of a Flaubert or the perversity of a Baudelaire, their novels and poems might show the application of an austere and triumphant discipline, the exercise, in dealing with the materials supplied them by their imaginations, of a rigorous will to refrain, and might thus fortify their readers as well as entertain them— this is something which Mr. More seems incapable of conceiving. He apparently believes that the only way in which it is possible for a writer to discipline himself in these bad days is to write literary criticism like his own and Babbitt's, which, though it is distinguished by thorough reading and sound writing, has obviously not required a discipline a fifth as exacting as that which has gone to produce some of the works of which it so superciliously complains.

Aside, however, from its special significance in this

special situation, the slogan of "art for art's sake" has a further validity which would continue to hold good even in an age which did not, like our own, freeze out the artists and make them defiant. From this point of view, Mr. More's attitude is open to the same sort of criticism as that of the imaginative but rather unintelligent socialist of the type of Upton Sinclair: Upton Sinclair disapproves of works of art which do not point explicitly a socialist moral, as Paul Elmer More disapproves of works of art which do not point explicitly the moral of self-control. Each insists upon denouncing as irresponsible and futile all the writers in whom it is impossible for him to find his own particular moral stated in his own particular terms. Now, aside from the fact that reality has many aspects and may be expected to suggest more than one kind of moral, and aside from the fact that fine workmanship itself must always convey an implicit moral, it is further true that in the arts as in the sciences a certain freedom for experimentation is necessary—one must allow a good deal of apparently gratuitous, and even empty or ridiculous work, if one wants eventually to get masterpieces. Gregor Mendel was dead eighteen years before any one had even suspected that his hobby of interbreeding green peas was anything other than a harmless monastic diversion—Gauss's non-Euclidean geometry, which he had been too timid during his lifetime to publish, and

Ricci and Levi-Civita's calculus had seemed the idlest of mathematical exercises till Einstein found them just the tools he needed ready to his hand. But, in general, the gratuitous experimentation of the scientific world is known only to its own laboratories and studies, whereas the corresponding work of the literary world is likely to be published and circulated more widely. When it happens to fall under the eye of an Upton Sinclair or a Paul Elmer More, he is infuriated by what seems to him its fatuity: he demands to know what these writers think they are good for. Well, they may not be good for anything, but, on the other hand, they may be valuable—one has to wait and see what comes of them, what other writers get out of them. Virgil, a poet held in high repute by Mr. More and the other Humanists, had laid under contribution not merely Homer but also the romantic rebel Apollonius, whose rebellion had failed at Alexandria, but from whom Virgil was to derive so much of his misty, subtle and tender feeling for humanity and nature— just as the other Alexandrians had nourished the other Latin poets, and hence the whole European tradition. The Alexandrians, like the modern poets, had been cut off by political events from participation in the life of a great society, and they had come to cultivate art for art's sake. But will Mr. More, taking into consideration their original contributions to poetry no less than the fact of their having kept alive the

54

poetic tradition of Greece, contend to-day that the Alexandrians were not justified?

(2) *They* [*"a few restless souls" among "the radical writers of to-day"*] *hold deliberation to be the foe of liberation. Hence the later theory, exemplified in English by James Joyce, that art shall not reproduce a picture of life as the Humanist sees it, or even from the point of view of the realist, but for its subject matter shall descend to what they call the pure "stream of consciousness." The hero of fiction shall have no will, no purpose, no inhibition, no power of choice whether for good or evil, but shall be merely a medium through which passes an endless, unchecked, meaningless flux of sensations and memories and emotions and impulses.*

But Joyce does not exemplify anything of the sort: his characters are all going about their business like the characters of any other novelist. Bloom, Dedalus, Mrs. Bloom and the others do have their wills, their purposes, their inhibitions, and they make their moral decisions—indeed, these moral decisions are the crucial events of *Ulysses*. What has probably misled Mr. More is Joyce's method of presenting the human mind directly, as it is aware of itself from hour to hour, from moment to moment. The minds of Joyce's characters are sometimes relaxed or confused, at other times lucid and intent: it depends on the character and the situation. The principal way in which *Ulysses* differs from the kind of novel to which Mr. More is accustomed is not in its depriving its characters of moral sense or will, but simply in its method of making us watch their consciousnesses as if they were beehives under glass, and of making us watch them through the whole of a day—it is a difference of technique, and of speed and scale. But I cannot suppose, as a matter of fact, from the inappropriateness of Mr. More's remarks about Joyce, that he has ever done anything more than look into him, and I will venture to say that the Humanists' high-handed habit of disposing jeeringly of contemporary writers whom they plainly haven't read is an even more serious scandal to their cause than their misrepresentation of the ancients, whom they have at least conscientiously studied. So Mr. More, in *The Demon of the Absolute*, has described Dos Passos's *Manhattan Transfer* as "an explosion in a cesspool" without apparently the faintest suspicion that Dos Passos intends his novel as an indictment of the same social conditions of which Mr. More himself has always taken such a gloomy view. But not only is Mr. More unable to recognize in *Manhattan Transfer* the work of a man who, like himself, has, as he once wrote of his own state of mind, been "deafened by the 'indistinguishable roar' of the streets" and can "make no sense of the noisy jargon of the market place" and who finally causes his hero to escape from the modern American city with as much relief as Mr. More ever did when he went into his celebrated retreat at Shelburne; he has not even succeeded in informing himself from any other sources as to Dos Passos's general point of view. If Dos Passos had been a second-rate eighteenth-century essayist, Mr. More would know everything about him, political opinions and all—if he had been the humblest New England poet (of the seventeenth century, that is) Mr. More would have read him through.

(3) *"The only way of mitigating mechanism," he [Whitehead] says, "is by discovery that it is not mechanism." And so, instead of admitting humbly that mechanism is mechanism while beside it there exists something of a totally different nature, and that the ultimate nexus between these two fields of experience surpasses our comprehension, he must demonstrate mechanism out of the world altogether.*

But why *should* Whitehead admit humbly that mechanism is mechanism and that humanity exists beside it as something of a totally different nature? Why *should* he assume that the ultimate nexus between these two fields of experience surpasses our comprehension? I do not feel with Mr. More that the effect of Whitehead's metaphysics is to "make a travesty of the inorganic world," that it threatens "to deprive humanity of what is distinctly human."

57

Why should Mr. More take for granted that to change our idea of humanity is necessarily to degrade it? There can be no advances in philosophy without the altering of old conceptions. And I cannot, for the life of me, see that Mr. More has any other real objection to Whitehead's ideas than that they would, as he believes—and I am not sure that he is right even here—tend to discredit the distinction between "man" and "thing" upon which his own Humanistic philosophy is based. He makes no attempt to show that Whitehead's speculations are not justified, that his arguments are not sound; he makes no effort whatever to discuss the scientific findings—the conception of the "event," for example, as the ultimate unit of both the organic and the inorganic worlds—upon which Whitehead has based his metaphysics and which he did not himself invent. He merely asserts that Whitehead should never have undertaken to account for the relations between the organic and the inorganic world. He says that he "admits" this "humbly," but one gathers from his tone that he would, if he could, get out an injunction against all wanton metaphysics directed to this end, just as he would, if he could, get out an injunction against all experimentation in the arts. Yet if the philosophers of the past had been willing to accept so humbly the apparent paradoxes of experience, we should have no philosophy at all, and Mr. More would have no Plato and no

58

Platonists to beguile his academic retirement. I cannot avoid coming to the conclusion that Mr. More's primary objection is to having any one, either in science or in art, find out anything new, and I cannot explain this state of mind except on the hypothesis that Mr. More is really an old-fashioned Puritan who has lost the Puritan theology without having lost the Puritan dogmatism. Mr. More is more certainly than Professor Babbitt a man of some imagination; he is able to follow the thought of the modern world, as appears from his very intelligent and often sensitive expositions of the ideas of other writers (if they are not absolutely contemporaries)—but some iron inhibition always comes into play in the long run to restrain Mr. More from agreeing with anything which he finds in modern philosophy or art. Everything he encounters there seems to terrify him, even when, as in the case of Whitehead, one would think he ought to find it reassuring. One law for man and another law for thing is the whole of philosophy for More, as the will to refrain is the whole of morals. Outside these—anywhere, that is, except among the brave little band of Humanists—he sees only the abyss. It is as if Mr. More, on one of his sides, were capable of meeting on his own ground the great modern philosopher or poet, but as if some other element in his nature—which he tries to foist upon us, too, as the universal and eternal moral law of the "inner check"

—had operated to make him afraid of philosophy and poetry, so that, in spite of his vigorous intellect and his esthetic sensibility, he is unable to allow himself to profit by any book not written sufficiently long ago to have acquired an academic sanction almost equivalent to a religious one.

A certain passage from Whitehead's *Science and the Modern World* is quoted by Mr. More as follows: "When Darwin or Einstein proclaim[s] theories which modify our ideas, it is a triumph for science." Mr. More is going on to criticize this passage, but in the meantime he has observed that Whitehead has been so indiscreet as to write "proclaim" as a plural verb after two subjects connected by "or," and where any ordinary critic would either have left Whitehead's sentence as he wrote it or have made him a present of the singular ending without calling the reader's attention to it, Mr. More has put it in brackets, as who should comment scornfully "[sic]!" Mr. More may not be able, or may not dare, to imagine, as Whitehead has done, a metaphysical explanation of the relations between the organic and the inorganic worlds, but he can, and, by Heaven, he will, correct Whitehead's grammar!

HUMANIZING SOCIETY—Cowley

HUMANIZING SOCIETY

THE opposition lately encountered by the disciples of More and Babbitt can be explained in part, though only in part, by a fundamental confusion in the minds of the American Humanists themselves, a confusion between humanism with a small "h" and their own sort of capitalized Humanism.

Humanism with a small "h" is a general attitude which is very difficult or impossible to define. Partly it is an emphasis on the qualities it considers to be essentially human. Partly it is a defense of human dignity, of human possibilities; partly it is an opposition to all the forces that threaten them, whether these forces be religious, social, governmental, economic, or those of an anti-human philosophy. This attitude received its name during the Renaissance, when it was revived by the study of Greek and Roman antiquity. The Chinese sages were humanists in their time, and so, it might be added, are vast numbers of thinking men to-day.

The Humanism we spell with a capital letter is a body of doctrine assembled by Professors Irving Babbitt, of Harvard, and Paul Elmer More, of Princeton. These two men are among the foremost American critics of their generation, and this in itself surrounds their philosophy with a certain prestige. Their system appeals, moreover, to the critics who wish to apply fixed standards to literature; and it is not uncongenial to the somewhat conservative temper of the younger generation. Thus, in the midst of enemies, this doctrinal Humanism has grown in power. To-day there are Humanist magazines, Humanist publishers, Humanist professors in all the larger universities; there are Humanist critics, scientists and political thinkers (if not Humanist artists); and the movement has even enlisted the editorial support of the New York *Times*, which doesn't quite know what it is all about, but which feels, somehow, that Humanism is safe and reactionary. Yet in spite of all these activities, American Humanism is only one school of thought among many: it is a movement that may be compared in scope with Ethical Culture, or at the most with Christian Science.

Now, the Humanists themselves have unconsciously confused their specific cult with the general attitude. When Babbitt, for example, speaks of founding a Humanist university or of banding his followers together into a Humanist "communion" from which most of us will be excluded for doctrinal reasons, he is evidently referring to the cult. When, on the other hand, he speaks of humanism as something comparable in importance with religion in general—when he says that "a more definite feeling of limitation . . . lies at the base of both humanism and religion," or

64

that "the question remains whether the more crying need just now is for positive and critical humanism or for positive and critical religion," or again that "the solution of this problem as to the relation between humanism and religion . . . lies in looking upon them both as only different stages in the same path"—in all these instances he is obviously referring to humanism as a general attitude, and one which is shared not only by Socrates and Confucius, but also by many contemporary writers whom Babbitt himself disowns. His followers profit vastly by this confusion. It enables them to claim all the humanist past for their modern doctrine; it enables them to speak of "Homer, Phidias, Plato, Aristotle, Confucius, Buddha, Jesus, Paul, Virgil, Horace, Dante, Shakespeare, Milton, Goethe . . . Matthew Arnold in England and Emerson and Lowell in America" as their own collaborators; and at the same time it subjects them to a great deal of justified ridicule which they might have avoided by a little Socratic thinking.

Their philosophy should be considered in itself. And so, in the present essay, I intend to deal chiefly with capitalized Humanism, though I shall sometimes contrast it with other forms of the general attitude which impress me as being more valid. I shall deal with the doctrines of More and Babbitt, first as theories, then as practiced in their own writings and those of their disciples; I shall point out the social implications of these doctrines; and lastly I shall try to criticize them from the standpoint of imaginative writers in general.

II

American Humanism begins with the assumption that life can be divided into three planes: the natural, the human and the religious. It holds that we should cultivate the second of these planes, not in opposition to religion, but rather to the natural plane, which is represented to-day by the scientific descendants of Francis Bacon and the romantic descendants of Jean-Jacques Rousseau. Thus, says Robert Shafer writing in *The Bookman:*

Against romanticism, humanitarian sympathy, mechanistic or vitalistic determinism, the doctrine of progress and the like, has been opposed a skeptical criticism of life and letters which rests ultimately on the proposition that man differs not alone in complexity of organization, but in kind, from the animal, and that his happiness depends upon his recognition and cultivation of that element in his being which is distinctive of him. This is held to be possible; man is held to be, within limits, capable of responsible choice. . . . To choose is to discriminate, and, for this, habituation to self-restraint is essential; it is, indeed, the foundation on which the whole structure of distinctively human life rests.

66

Everything is reduced, in the end, to the morality of the individual. By practicing self-restraint, by applying the *law of measure*, by the *imitation* of great models chosen from the antiquity of all nations, he can arrive at the Humanistic virtues of poise, *proportionateness, decorum,* and finally attain "the end of ends"—which, Babbitt says, is individual happiness.

These are the general doctrines of Humanism, and it seems to me that they can be accepted, so far as they go, by many opponents of More and Babbitt. They can also be criticized, but chiefly for what they omit. They can be criticized in theory, first, for their incompleteness as a system of ethics and, second, for their total disregard of social and economic realities.

The ethic of Humanism consists of a single precept: namely, that we should exercise self-restraint (or the will to refrain, or the Inner Check, Veto Power, *frein vital, Entsagung* or whatever else it may be called at the moment). We are offered no other guide. But why—we ask like children repeating a Shorter Catechism—why should we exercise self-restraint?

A. In order to achieve decorum.

Q. And why should we achieve decorum?

A. The end of ends is happiness. (Be good and you will be happy. If you can't be good, be careful. With all their paraded learning, all their analysis of texts, all their quotations from the French, German, Latin, Greek, Sanskrit and Chinese, can the Humanists tell us nothing more than this?)

In theory, they can tell us nothing more. In practice, we find them basing their moral judgments on a set of conventions which have nothing to do with their logic. In practice, at this critical point in their philosophy, they renounce a "positive and critical" humanism for tradition and theology. Yet this silent renunciation, which damages their own position without benefiting the church, was quite unnecessary. Without ceasing to be strictly humanist, they could have developed a complete system of ethics, but only by considering man in relation to society. This they have failed to do: in this increasingly corporate world of ours, they have confined their attention to the individual.

Economically, socially, their doctrine is based on nothing and answers no questions. Out of what society does Humanism spring, and toward what society does it lead? Has it any validity for the millhands of New Bedford and Gastonia, for the beet-toppers of Colorado, for the men who tighten a single screw in the automobiles that march along Mr. Ford's assembly belt? Should it be confined to the families who draw dividends from these cotton mills, beet fields, factories, and to the professors who teach in universities endowed by them? Can one be Humanist between chukkers of a polo match, or can the steel workers be Humanists, too—once every three weeks, on their Sunday off? Has Babbitt any social program?

In his "Democracy and Leadership," which gingerly touches on some of these problems, he rejects the whole conception of social justice as a dangerous fallacy. He asserts that the economic problem, including the relations between capital and labor, runs into the political problem, which runs into the philosophical problem, which in turn is almost indissolubly bound up with the religious problem. The root of the whole matter is in the psychology of the individual. For unemployment, low wages, long hours, intolerable working conditions, for all the realities of the present system, he has one solution, perhaps the most unreal that could be offered. "The remedy," he says, "for the evils of competition is found in the moderation and magnanimity of the strong and the successful, and not in any sickly sentimentalizing over the lot of the underdog."

Yet it would be incorrect to say that Babbitt offers no social program. For all his hatred of terms like humanitarianism and social justice, he does suggest a mild path toward a Humanist utopia. "The first stage," he says, "would . . . be that of Socratic definition; the second stage would be the coming together of a group of persons on the basis of this definition

. . . the third stage would almost inevitably be the attempt to make this convention effective through education." Babbitt seems to contemplate the salvation of society through a private school system culminating in a Humanist university. For one of his collaborators, Frank Jewett Mather, Jr., of Princeton, the salvation of the country seems even simpler. He says, in a recent group-statement of the Humanist faith:

We contributors to this symposium have actually seen a few humanists made, have helped a little to make them perhaps; and we are dealing with spiritual values which transcend ordinary statistics. A few thousand genuine humanists in America would make our society humanistic; a hundred humanist painters, sculptors, architects, musicians and men of letters would make our art solidly humanistic.

A few thousand Humanists in business and the professions, a hundred Humanists in the arts. . . . I submit that these rash professors, in their aversion for utopian visions, have produced the lamest utopia ever imagined. The vast economic machine that is America would continue to function aimlessly; great fortunes would continue to grow on the ruins of smaller fortunes; millions of factory workers would continue to perform operations so subdivided and standardized as to be purely automatic; two million former workers, the "normal" army of the unemployed, would seek vainly for the privilege of performing the same dehumanizing tasks; the Chicago beer barons would continue to seek their fortunes and slaughter their rivals, revealing once more a deplorable ignorance of the Inner Check; the students in the new Humanist university, after the two-o'clock lecture on Plato, would spend an hour at the talkies with the It Girl—and meanwhile, because of a few thousand Humanists, our society, our government, our arts, would be genuinely and ideally Humanistic.

III

When a philosophy like that of More and Babbitt presents itself as a way of life, it is dangerous for that philosophy to omit important aspects of life. These gaps in thought do not remain empty. They are filled unconsciously, irresistibly, by the conventions that prevail in the world surrounding the philosopher. If these conventions are blind and narrow, the philosophy will be blind and narrow in practice, however enlightened it may seem in theory.

Such has been the misfortune of American Humanism. At birth, the world that surrounded it was the American university of the 1890's, and from this world the Humanists have borrowed their underlying convictions. Economic problems at Harvard or Princeton before 1900 were less urgent than

71

they became after the War: the young instructor was sure of being fed and clothed; he was comfortably lodged; and his salary was fixed by an individual arrangement with the university. The moral problem, however—or at least the problem of self-restraint— was of primary importance. Any sort of enthusiasm was suspicious. Any failure to restrain one's impulses toward frankness of judgment, freedom of thought, sympathy with the dispossessed, and love most of all —love for one's neighbor or his wife—might lead to immediate dismissal. And what was Babbitt's reaction? "The wiser the man," he says, "the less likely he will be to indulge in a violent and theatrical rupture with his age. He will like Socrates remember the counsel of the Delphian oracle to follow 'the usage of the city.' " Even Socrates himself, as Babbitt adds in another passage, "was perhaps needlessly unconventional and also unduly inclined to paradox."

The American Humanists, less paradoxical than Socrates and more faithful to the usage of the city, have adopted the older conventions of the universities where most of them teach. One of these conventions is a snobbery both intellectual and social—a snobbery which does not seem out of place in a professor's drawing-room, but which becomes grotesque when applied to literature and art. Paul Elmer More, for example, damns a whole school of American fiction,

72

partly for literary reasons, but partly because its leading members are men of no social standing, men "almost without exception from small towns sprinkled along the Mid-Western states from Ohio to Kansas . . . self-made men with no inherited background of culture." One of More's disciples, Seward Collins, couples this accusation with another; namely that some prominent American writers are "the sons of recent arrivals in this country." It is as if Parnassus were a faculty club, at the doors of which More and Collins stood armed with blackballs. It is as if the world of letters were a university—one which applied the quota system to Irishmen and Jews, and which demanded a signed photograph with every request for admission.

Sometimes the snobbery of the Humanists is carried from the sphere of esthetics into that of government, and here it leads them into a dangerous alliance with the forces of reaction. Babbitt, for example, is not unwilling to have his Inner Check on conduct reinforced by the outer check of civil authority: he speaks with approval of the policeman who arrested Raymond Duncan for wearing a Greek costume in the streets. Paul Elmer More, in the same fashion, feels that the cause of Humanism was somehow strengthened by the Princeton officials who "rusticated" a student for his "aspiration towards free morals in literature." Seward Collins vehemently defends the Watch and Ward Society; his only regret is that there are not two such societies in Boston. And this alliance between Humanism and reaction was emphasized some years ago at the Scopes trial, when Bryan took a book on evolution by Louis Trenchard More—brother of Paul Elmer More and author of the leading essay in the Humanist symposium—along with him to Dayton, Tennessee, in order to confute the ungodly biologists and establish the Bible as the one American textbook of natural science.

And so these angry professors, in following the usage of the city, have come to defend the social and intellectual prejudices of the universities where they teach and the churches where some of them worship. To themselves, they seem to play a more distinguished rôle. Gorham B. Munson claims for his Humanist colleagues the virtue of swimming against the current; but so, apparently, do straws caught in an eddy. Norman Foerster absolves himself and his condisciples from "the professorial vices of pedantry, indolence, timidity and . . . sluggish tolerance"; he commends their boldness in attack. Boldness of a sort they have, but it is not the courage of lonely men treading their own paths: it is the boldness of reactionary professors in the classroom, lecturing to students most of whom agree with their ideas and none of whom will rise in rebuttal.

IV

Partly from the moral atmosphere of our Eastern universities in the 1890's, the Humanists imbibed another quality, one which their enemies describe as Puritanism. The word is dangerously vague: it connotes or denotes a number of characteristics, good or bad, sentimental or realistic. The single quality to which I refer is clear, definite, unmistakable: it consists in a profound belief in chastity, a belief which forms no part of their official theories, which is revealed only in their practice of criticism, and yet which is so fundamental that it distorts the moral, the social and especially the literary judgments of the American Humanists.

Babbitt, for example, in the course of his long attack on Rousseau, happens to discuss the question of wages. "If a working girl falls from chastity," he says, "do not blame her, blame her employer. She would have remained a model of purity if he had only added a dollar or two to her wage." He is speaking ironically, of course: he is implying that the girl would have fallen no matter what her wages were. Now, I expect this judgment to be utilized—perhaps it has already been utilized—by those of Babbitt's pupils who are now employing girls in the cotton mills of Fall River and New Bedford. If chastity is all-important, if chastity is unaffected by wages, why should they ever raise wages? . . . One might answer, from the standpoint of a humanism just as valid as Babbitt's, that a working girl may be chaste or unchaste and still remain human, but that it is almost impossible to be either human or Humanist on ten or twelve dollars a week.

Elsewhere in speaking of Goethe, he adopts the same tone as with the working girl. "Any one," Babbitt says, "who thinks of the series of Goethe's love affairs prolonged into the seventies, is scarcely likely to maintain that his *Entsagung* was of a very austere character even for a man of the world, not to speak of the saint." By what right does Babbitt summon him to the Dean's office?—a little jestingly, it is true, but still with profound disapproval, as if Goethe were a Harvard or Princeton sophomore with aspirations toward free morals in literature. And by what right does the professor deliver this lecture? Is he speaking in behalf of humanistic standards, to be deduced from the conduct of a hundred generations of sages, including Socrates, Dante and Goethe himself—or is he applying the religious standards of the Reformation? And is he willing to assure us that his opinion of Goethe's books, as books, is not affected by this smoking-room gossip about Goethe's life?

He believes, not without justification, that morality and esthetics cannot be separated, but he destroys the value of his esthetic judgments by confusing morality

76

in general with the one virtue of chastity. "Restoration Comedy," he says with a professorial smile, "is a world not of pure but of impure imagination." "A greater spiritual elevation . . . is found in Wordsworth's communings with nature than in those of Rousseau and Chateaubriand." The reason, he explains, is because in Wordsworth "the erotic element is absent." At other times he delivers lectures on the sex-life that could not be surpassed by the professor of Mental Hygiene in a fresh-water college. Yet Babbitt, after all, never quite reaches the heights of chaste absurdity that are attained by Paul Elmer More.

Consider More's "Note on Poe's Method," an essay that mingles some keen literary judgments (and others less keen) with an inexcusable ignorance of the poet's life. At the end, after deciding that "Poe remains chiefly the poet of unripe boys and unsound men," More goes on to say:

Yet it is to the honor of Poe that in all his works you will come upon no single spot where the abnormal sinks to the unclean, or where there is an effort to intensify the effect of what is morbid emotionally by an appeal to what is morbid morally. The soul of this man was never tainted. [That is, Poe lied, flattered, slandered, drank to excess, took opium; his characters indulged in strange forms of necrophilia; but neither they nor their author committed fornication.] . . . If you wish to understand the perils he escaped, read after "The Sleeper" one of the poems in which Baudelaire, Poe's avowed imitator and sponsor to Europe, gropes with filthy hands among the mysteries of death. [That is, in which he writes of physical unchastity.]

On the next page, after delivering this judgment which reeks of Rufus Wilmot Griswold, S. Parkes Cadman and all the psychological and literary ingenuousness that could very well be packed into a single paragraph, More turns to a new subject, "My Debt to Trollope." . . . As a "professed Trollopian," he praises the ethical atmosphere of Trollope's novels, regretting only that Trollope the moralist should yield so much to Trollope the entertainer; he exults over the fashion in which the good little Trollopes are rewarded and the bad Trollopes punished by the great Trollope their creator; and meanwhile he pauses to comment on the one class of modern writers who have followed Trollope's virtuous example:

The only form of literature to-day wherein you may be sure that the author will not play tricks with the Ten Commandments is the detective story; the astonishing growth of which brand of fiction can be traced in no small measure, I suspect, to the fact that there alone murder is still simply murder, adultery simply adultery, theft simply theft, and no more about it.

78

In other chapters of the same volume, More writes about Joyce, Dos Passos and the Superrealists, but he appears not to have read them very carefully. Like most contemporary writers, they seem to him unchaste. He reads detective stories.

V

Among the Humanists in general, there is a real antipathy toward contemporary literature. They do no "creative" writing themselves and they hold an undying grudge against those who do. Whether it was originally imbibed, like other prejudices, from the atmosphere of the classroom and Professors' Row— where contemporary literature is expounded only by lecturers bent on uplifting the professors' wives, and where it is written only by immature students— would be difficult to decide. We can safely say, however, that a dislike for modern imaginative writers is revealed in the works of almost all the American Humanists. It is shown once more in their recently published symposium, "Humanism and America."

Out of the fifteen contributors to that volume, there is only one who has written a mature poem— and T. S. Eliot, in point of doctrine, is far from being a strict Humanist. There is not one contributor who has written a serious novel, a drama, or even a passable sketch (though I am told that one of them, under an assumed name, turned out a detective story which

More probably enjoyed). At the end of the symposium, the editor has collected a sort of White List containing "most of the recent books that are humanistic in a strict sense." The list includes not one novel, one poem or one drama.

But perhaps I am laying too much stress on the importance of "creative" literature. Criticism, too, can be creative: it can express new values in a style that pleases the senses as well as the intellect; it can have form, vision, imaginative power. Perhaps their philosophy has endowed the Humanists with these qualities? . . . Turning back to the book, we find that with a very few exceptions—notably those of Eliot and More himself—the fifteen critical essayists write either colorless prose or prose that is conspicuous for its muddled metaphors, harsh rhythms, awkward vocabulary and lack of original ideas.

Six of them deal directly with modern American literature. Might it not seem that they would find at least one book to praise? They find many: they praise the collected works of More and Babbitt, but they praise not one poem, drama or novel. . . . No, I am doing them an injustice. I seem to remember that in one essay, "Pandora's Box in American Fiction," Harry Hayden Clark finds a novel to recommend. It is a dull and correct book by a dull, correct and estimable author; it is not the best of her novels, but merely the most didactic; it is, in a word, *The*

Brimming Cup, by Dorothy Canfield Fisher. Read it and see what our arts would become if controlled for their own good by the "hundred humanist painters, sculptors, architects, musicians and men of letters" who are needed to make them "solidly humanistic."

VI

Outside the room where I am writing, a flooded New England river bends over the dam of an abandoned paper mill, sometimes falling in one smooth sweep, sometimes rising in spray under the March wind. The sky is gray, with floating, clear blue islands; there are flurries of snow in the intermittent sunlight. And, in this place of winds and waters, it seems futile to attack the Humanists—just as futile as it would be to rage against the branches circling in an eddy beneath the dam.

The opinions they express—I think, looking out the window—the old attitudes to which they cling, have as much right to survival as these New England houses rising squarely from the ground. They remind us of the past; and this is, I feel, the special value in the controversy over Humanism. It distracts our attention as readers and critics from the masterpieces of the moment—from "the greatest poem since 'John Brown's Body,'" from "the last word in American fiction"—and directs it toward questions of permanence, toward a judgment based

81

on centuries. The Humanists, moreover, have performed another service to American letters: they have reaffirmed the connection between ethics and esthetics, thereby helping to rescue art from the sort of moral vacuum to which it had been condemned by another school of critics. But—I think as the first lights flash out in the village—they have made art the servant of morality. And what have these Humanists ever said about the humanizing functions which art in itself performs?

All good art—at least all good literary art—has a thesis. Its thesis is that life is larger than life—that life as portrayed by the creative imagination is more intense, more varied, more purposeful or purposeless, more tragic or comic, more crowded with moral decisions, than is the life we have been leading day by day. Sometimes we are discouraged by the contrast; sometimes we merely escape into the world of art. Sometimes, however, we try to reinterpret our lives in the light of the artist's vision. The new values we derive from his work, when projected into our own experience, make it seem more poetic, dramatic or novelistic, more significant, more sharply distinguished from the world of nature—in a word, more human.

But art has another humanizing function perhaps no less important: it is the humanization of nature itself. The world about us was alien in the beginning; vast portions of it are alien to us to-day. Before man can feel at ease in any milieu, whether that of forest, plain or city, he must transform the natural shapes about him by infusing them with myth. Perhaps I am choosing a too pretentious word; perhaps I should merely say that certain streets in New York are rendered habitable for me by snatches of old ragtime, that I never *saw* a telephone till I saw it in one of Charles Sheeler's drawings, that my memory of Hawthorne transforms and humanizes a New England village like this. I might say that this creation of myth, by whatever name we call it, has continued since the earliest times; that it is, indeed, a necessity of the human mind. It is a sort of digestive process, one that transforms the inanimate world about us into food without which the imagination would starve.

Now, this double humanizing function of literature, and to a lesser degree of the other arts—this creation of value and myths—cannot wholly be performed by the masterpieces of the past. The values of Sophocles still hold good to-day, but to interpret them in terms of our own life requires more knowledge of Greek civilization than most of us possess— more even than is possessed by Babbitt himself, whose picture of Sophocles is that of a rate-paying Victorian professor. The myths of Homer still people the shores of the Ionian Sea, but they are alien to the prairies, the sky-presuming city, and even to this

New England village of old men. Our own myths, our values, must be renewed from generation to generation. They will so be renewed as long as artists live; they will be renewed in spite of the critics who cling to exiled legends and values long since dead.

One of the real tasks for American critics to-day is to assess our contemporary literature on the basis of this double humanizing function. They will find that some values and myths have been created or renewed. They will find that E. E. Cummings, John Dos Passos, Hart Crane, Yvor Winters, Glenway Wescott, William Carlos Williams, Elizabeth Madox Roberts—to mention a few names at random—have each succeeded in humanizing some district, landscape, year or city. They will also find, I fear, that our mechanical civilization has outmarched its artists. Once more, as in Shelley's day, "We want the creative faculty to imagine that which we know; we want the generous impulse to act that which we imagine; we want the poetry of life: our calculations have outrun conception; we have eaten more than we can digest." . . . But what has this got to do with American Humanism? And what, in turn, has Humanism to do with the scene outside my window: with the jobless men who saunter in the dusk, or the dying village, or the paper mill abandoned across the river—this mill whose owners have gone South where labor is cheap?

HUMANISM AND VALUE—Hazlitt

HUMANISM AND VALUE

BEFORE we examine the logical credentials of the New Humanism, we may profitably ask ourselves what it is that has been impelling young writers recently to announce their conversion to the doctrine.

We find a number of motives, some of them more creditable than others. There is, to begin with, a reaction from the cult of unintelligibility and incoherence, and from the new barbarism and the tough-guy school of literature; and this reaction is to a large extent sound. Further, the younger generation is impressed by the fact that the Humanists seem to have a wider knowledge of the literature of the remote past than most of their opponents. And again, in so far as Humanism may be thought of as a form of classicism, it was bound to follow upon an era of romanticism. Just as a period of traditionalism is succeeded by one of revolt, so revolt in turn is succeeded by revolt from revolt, i.e., by another wave of traditionalism. Historic perspective should enable us to hazard the prediction that the wave of traditionalism just beginning will probably go farther; but it should also enable us to predict that it in turn will not be permanent.

Behind this endless see-saw are two main causes. Either traditionalism or revolt, when it reaches a high point, tends to discredit itself by its own excesses. And even if it does not, critics tire of the old theories and the old gods, and want new theories and new gods, if only for the sake of something fresh to talk about. Hence the present shouts of down with Mencken, down with Dreiser, down with Lewis, down with Cabell; hurrah for the youngsters under thirty and the critics over sixty! It is the same motive, at bottom, that periodically leads a bored and restless voting public to turn the Republicans out and put the Democrats in. This phenomenon is recurrent and immemorial, both in politics and literature. It deserves a special name. We might call it, after its most famous victim among the Greeks, the *aristidization* of old heroes.

Perhaps an even deeper appeal of Humanism is an appeal that authority has always made, and now makes with particular force. Amid the booming, buzzing confusion of new discoveries, doctrines, theories, isms, opinions, it is peaceful, it saves a great deal of anxiety and mental effort, to bow one's head to a traditional authority. Further, many of the conclusions of science, particularly when one does not understand them and imagines that they imply a purely mechanistic view of the world, seem depressing, and the "New Humanism," and, even better, the old-time religion, appeal as quiet and comforting sanctuaries. It is this that lies behind T. S. Eliot's adoption

88

of Anglo-Catholicism and the Humanist's dislike of
what he calls "naturalism." Of course, if you decide
to let an authority give you cut-and-dried answers to
your problems, there is still the problem, hardly less
difficult, of deciding *which* authority shall do it. In
practice, however, that problem has not troubled the
religious branch of the Humanists at all. There is
not the slightest possibility that any one of them will
emerge as a Buddhist or a Zoroastrian; they allow the
problem to be decided for them by geography and
social considerations: Mr. Eliot is an Anglo-Catholic
because he is a British citizen.

The Humanists, as I have already implied, are not
very well acquainted with science. And this, I think,
as well as the uncomfortable conclusions to which
they imagine science leads, accounts to a large extent
for the fact that they seldom refer to science except
to depreciate or to patronize it. In brief, they ration-
alize their scientific ignorance. They wish to con-
vince themselves that knowledge they do not possess
is not knowledge of the first importance. If one
knows Greek, but not physiology, then it is well to
dismiss physiological knowledge as merely "utilitarian," first being careful to imply subtly that utili-
tarianism is identical with philistinism. At all events,
a good Humanist knows how to emerge with the conclusion, or at least the innuendo, that literary studies,
particularly if they are of literature far enough in

89

the past, are the only kind with a genuine cultural, or as he would put it, a genuinely "human," value.

Not least among the causes for the present vogue of Humanism is the desire of the critic to have a theory, a "philosophy," a "point of view." If he does not give clear evidence of such a philosophy, or if it is merely implicit in his criticism, he is likely to be accused of being devoid of "ideas." It is convenient for him to have a philosophy that he can state explicitly, and that has already been neatly labeled. He yields to the temptation to take some one else's philosophy, ready made, and to take all of it, coat, vest, trousers, shoes, socks, without too curious a scrutiny. If, finally, we include those youngsters who are going in for Humanism for no better reason than to be on the band-wagon, we have listed virtually all the main motives behind the attempt to resuscitate this singular movement.

When we come to examine the meaning and validity of Humanism as a doctrine, we are confronted by the initial difficulty of deciding (as space limitations forbid dealing with all of them) just *whose* Humanism we are going to examine. There are apparently grave differences among the Humanists themselves. There is, first, the schism between the religious and the non-religious Humanists. Mr. Eliot, criticizing Mr. Babbitt, has maintained that the humanistic point of view is at bottom "auxiliary to and dependent upon the religious point of view." Further, the European humanists do not seem to have too much respect for their American brethren. Ramon Fernandez, translated by Mr. Eliot in the January *Criterion,* goes so far as to say that the American Humanists "do not seem to have tested their notions by a rigorous critique, and are easily entrapped in their own pretensions."

It is the doctrines of the American Humanist that now concern us, so we shall turn to their acknowledged leader, Irving Babbitt. We may begin with one of his latest encyclicals, which appears in the *Forum* of February, 1930. What first strikes the reader who has had any acquaintance with exact reasoning is the amazing looseness with which Mr. Babbitt, as well as all the other Humanists, employs crucial terms. Around each of these terms hangs a heavy fog. There is first the word "Humanism" itself, which Mr. Babbitt confesses he has not been able to make clear in a series of volumes. Then there is "standards." Then there is "humanitarianism." Finally there is "nature," with its derivatives "natural" and "naturalism"; and these terms are used more loosely than any of the others. John Stuart Mill once devoted a long essay entirely to the confusions and fallacies inherent in various uses of the word "nature," but he might just as well never have written so far as Mr. Babbitt is concerned. Mr. Babbitt falls

91

into the same fallacy as his arch-enemy and mighty bugaboo Rousseau; the only difference being that Rousseau was all for freeing and glorifying something that he thought of as "the natural man," and Mr. Babbitt is all for suppressing something that he calls "the natural man." At cue time the reader of Humanist propaganda will find the word "naturalism" applied to variations on Rousseau's doctrines, and at another time the word, after an invocation of the name of Sir Francis Bacon, will refer to the scientific investigation of natural processes; and the ill-repute that attaches to the term in its first sense will somehow be carried over to the second.

But Mr. Babbitt commits this sin of ambiguity and vague extension on a far greater scale when he comes to the word "Rousseauism." (His animus against Rousseau is far greater than it is against Bacon.) Now Rousseau was an extremist, and in many ways an ass, and it is very easy to discredit some of his more important views. But Mr. Babbitt takes advantage of this fact to attempt to discredit every view, no matter how well established, that is either superficially similar to one of Rousseau's, or may be made to seem so; and he attempts further to strengthen his case by pretending that the views he is attacking have their historic origin in Rousseau. The trick is an ancient one; indeed, it is accurately described in that ironic little masterpiece, "The Art

92

of Controversy," in which Schopenhauer lists, numbers, and names the various shady stratagems for getting the better of an opponent in a dispute. Mr. Babbitt's two main controversial devices fall under Stratagems I and XXXII. The first "consists in carrying your opponent's proposition beyond its natural limits . . . so as to exaggerate it." Stratagem XXXII consists in putting your opponent's assertion "into some odious category; even though the connection is only apparent, or else of a loose character. You can say, for instance, 'That is Manicheism, . . . or Spinozism, . . . or Naturalism,' . . . and so on. In making an objection of this kind, you take it for granted (1) that the assertion in question is identical with, or is at least contained in, the category cited— that is to say, you cry out, 'Oh, I have heard that before'; and (2) that the system referred to has been entirely refuted, and does not contain a word of truth."

Substitute the word "Rousseauism" above, and you have almost the entire *Forum* argument of Mr. Babbitt uncannily summed up.

Any one who cared to use Mr. Babbitt's method of argument against him could easily show, with far less stretching of terms, that the serpent's doctrine of "naturalism" made its appearance centuries before Rousseau. The following sentence from Montaigne is typical: "As I have said elsewhere, I have for my

93

part adopted, very simply and crudely, this ancient rule, 'that we cannot go wrong if we follow Nature,' and that the sovereign precept is 'to conform to her.' " Spinoza's naturalism was, of course, on its theoretical side even more thorough.

Yet it is probably unjust to Mr. Babbitt to imply that he has employed this dialectical device as a conscious trick. The man is too sincere for that, and he has been arguing this way for too many years. Rousseau and his doctrines have become an obsession with him—one might almost say a monomania—and they play for him the rôle that the devil and his temptations did for the medieval saint. That is why Mr. Babbitt can accuse any one who does not agree with him of "Rousseauistic emotionalism" with the same facility as the late Mayor Hylan could accuse all his critics of being tools of the traction trust. But all this means that it is impossible to take Mr. Babbitt seriously as a thinker. His antagonism to Rousseau distorts all his views, if it does not actually dictate most of them: it drives him to an opposite extreme; he is clearly a victim of "the subservience of contradiction."

No reader can go very far with him, moreover, unless he is willing to take over a shallow and jerry-built metaphysics and an antiquated psychology that insist first on a dualism between man and nature and then on another dualism between what Mr. Babbitt calls our "expansive desires" (the existence of which we are obviously meant to deplore) and what he calls "the higher will." Nearly all of his writing comes down to a mere shuffling of these terms, in pairs neatly set off against each other—"humanism" against "naturalism" or "Rousseauism," "emotionalism" against "reason" (the latter, of course, being identified with Humanist doctrine), "expansive desires" against "higher will," and so on, until the reader has had enough. Mr. Babbitt does not use these terms for simple reference, but emotively—that is, they are mere signals for certain attitudes on the part of the reader.

It is not necessary to spend much time over the "constructive" side of Mr. Babbitt's doctrine. "Decorum is supreme for the humanist." "The humanist exercises the will to refrain." The insistence, you will notice, is always on the purely *negative* virtues. Apply them to literary criticism. We are above all to judge a writer, not by his originality or force, not by his talent or genius, but by his decorum! That is, we are to praise him for a virtue within the reach of any learned blockhead. And we are presumably to denounce him if he lacks the virtue of decorum— i.e., we are to denounce Villon, Rabelais, Marlowe, Shakespeare, Carlyle, Nietzsche, Dostoevski, Melville, and Whitman. As for "the will to refrain," it is the outstanding merit of the cartoonist Webster's hero— the Timid Soul, Mr. Caspar Milquetoast.

To sum up, a small clique of the self-anointed have arrogated to themselves a name that stood, in the fifteenth century, for a genuinely liberating attitude, and degraded it to a synonym for a tight academicism. The whole doctrine has become little more than a rationalization of neophobia and a piece of special pleading for the genteel tradition. At its best, it is a mere revival of a singularly dogmatic and narrow classicism. There are, of course, sound criteria in the classic tradition, unduly neglected in the criticism of the last decade. But the critics who wish to apply these criteria will be well advised if they do not load themselves down with the millstone of dogma that the Humanists are so eager to hang round their necks.

II

The fact that the doctrines of the Humanists are narrow and even a bit ludicrous does not relieve us from the need of adopting positive attitudes of our own. This need is peculiarly great when we come to the question of value. Here the present writer feels that he must differ both from the religious Humanists, represented by T. S. Eliot, and from those critics of Humanism who, like Allen Tate, insist that "religion is the sole technique for the validating of values."

It would, of course, be futile to attempt a full account of value in the short space at my disposal.

It is hardly possible to do more here than to indicate a general position. And this position, I fear, will be dismissed both by the religious and non-religious humanists as hopelessly "naturalistic."

I may begin by remarking that the entire antithesis between Humanism and Naturalism, upon which the Humanists lay their greatest stress, seems to me artificial and false. It is perfectly consistent to believe both (a) that man is, and cannot cease to be, a part of the general order of Nature (which the Humanists are fatuous enough to deny), and (b) that man has certain distinctive and even unique qualities which set him off from the other animals. This second belief, as I understand it, is central to the Humanism of Paul Elmer More. I willingly concede its truth, and yet I cannot draw the corollaries from it that Mr. More does. For it does not seem to me, in the first place, that *every* difference between ourselves and the other members of the animal kingdom is necessarily in our favor, and, partly as a consequence of this, it does not seem to me that we should regard a given action, pursuit, or attitude as necessarily virtuous *simply* because it is peculiarly human. Dogs, for example, have so vastly superior a sense of smell that they must regard our own with contempt, and it is a mere truism that they exhibit gratitude and loyalty not only more uniformly but for the most part more intensely than ourselves. They are at

97

least as courageous as we are, and less frequently inclined to be bullies. The phenomenon of house-training, common to nearly all adult dogs, is in itself sufficient to discredit Mr. Babbitt's belief that only man can control his immediate desires. If the dog's "higher will," in this instance, has obvious natural causes, if it may be reduced to memories of punishments and rewards, in short, if it is merely a product of social approval and disapproval, so, for the most part, I fear, is the "higher will" in man. If we turn to even more humble creatures, we find that ants and bees have a more smooth-running social organization than our own, that the individual ant or bee subordinates himself to the general welfare with a completeness seldom approached even by the rarest human being. The animal mother, once more, will sacrifice her comfort or her life for her offspring with a complete lack of hesitation that would shame many human mothers. Finally, the lower animals, for the most part, are far less obsessed by sex than we are.[1] Our "moral" superiority to the animals, in brief, is by no means thoroughly established.

The Humanists, of course, usually fall back upon the assertion that at least in his possession of a reasoning faculty[2] man is unique. This contention like-

[1] For an expansion upon this comparison, consult Joseph Wood Krutch's *The Modern Temper*.

[2] It is hardly necessary to point out that most of the humanists still credit the old faculty psychology. Indeed, it is one of their

98

wise has still to be proved. Köhler's experiments on apes, and even recent studies of the higher insects, reveal that these beings are capable of responses which can hardly be described otherwise than as intelligent action. Waiving this point, however, and granting for the moment that man has a monopoly of reason, I do not see how this proves the necessary superiority of reflective over instinctive action in all circumstances. The ability to reason is not an unmixed blessing. Its defective exercise leads to conclusions of poor survival value, like those of chiropractic or Christian Science. And even a sound reasoner may unfortunately be sunk too deeply in reflection while crossing a street against the traffic.

In brief, it does not seem to me either that a complete scheme of ethics or a sound hierarchy of values can be based merely on the assumption that man's dignity consists in the exercise of his peculiarly human traits. Indeed, it would seem more plausible to set up exactly the opposite criterion, and to hold that the first need of man is "to be a good animal." Such a contention does not compel one to adopt the philosophy of the big-muscle school, represented by Mr. Bernarr MacFadden, nor does it mean that one

central dogmas, as, for example, in Mr. Babbitt's conception of the will as an entity divorced from the desires. If Mr. Babbitt's "higher will" is not a crude reflection of the older faculty psychology it is only because he sees that will as an uncaused or supernatural agency.

need overlook the frequent phenomena of the sickly genius. It means merely that we must recognize the purely animal quality of health (as Plato did), both as a value in itself and as a necessary condition for the existence of many other values. A man cannot be even a Humanist unless he has comparatively recently done something so distressingly bestial as to eat a meal.

A sound theory of values will be "naturalistic" in that it will be neither exclusively "human" (in the sense that it would ignore the great range of appetites and activities which we share with the lower animals—hunger, sex, sleep, exercise, etc.), nor will it be supernatural, like that of Mr. Eliot and Mr. Tate. It will be developed along the lines already laid down by numerous writers, among the more recent of whom are John Dewey, Bertrand Russell, I. A. Richards and a number of economists. While none of these writers has yet given us a completely satisfactory theory, they have separately indicated important aspects of such a theory, and they have been moving in a fruitful direction.

We may begin with Bertrand Russell, whose theory is stated in the simplest terms. It is set forth in his chapter on Ethics in his *Philosophy*, and we may paraphrase it somewhat, substituting the term "value" where Russell uses the term "good." Value is derivative from desire. This does not mean quite

100

simply that the objects and activities of value are the desired, because men's desires conflict, and "value" is mainly a social concept, designed to find an issue from this conflict. The conflict, however, is not only between the desires of different men, but between incompatible desires of one man at different times, or even at the same time. Even a solitary, for example, like Robinson Crusoe, is bound to realize that he has many desires, each of which is stronger at one time than at another, and that, if he acts always upon the one that is strongest at the moment, he may defeat others that are stronger in the long run. With the growth merely of intelligence there goes a growing desire for a harmonious life, i.e., a life in which action is dominated by consistent quasi-permanent desires. Mr. Russell's theory is an over-simplification, though such an over-simplification is perhaps necessary for clear and compact statement.

The position of John Dewey, as elaborated in *The Quest for Certainty,* is similar to this, though Dewey's statement leaves much to be desired in clarity and precision. Dewey insists that we should not employ the word value for "enjoyments that happen anyhow," but only for "enjoyments which are the consequences of intelligent action." He draws a lengthy parallel between the enjoyed and the enjoyable, the desired and the desirable, the esteemed and the estimable, the satis*fying* and the satis*factory*.

101

The difference between the first and the second member of each of these pairs is that the first is a mere report of an already existent fact while the second is a judgment of the importance and need of bringing a fact into existence. "To say that something satisfies is to report something as an isolated finality. To assert that it is satis*factory* is to define it in its connections and interactions."

As I say, this discussion is not wholly adequate. The definition of values, for example, as enjoyments which are the consequences of intelligent action, seems to me circular: for "intelligent action" must be defined as that which brings enjoyments which are of genuine value. But no one has stated more forcibly than Dewey the inevitability of values and their naturalistic basis: "Affections, desires, purposes, choices, are going to endure as long as man is man; therefore as long as man is man, there are going to be ideas, judgments, beliefs about values. Nothing could be sillier than to attempt to justify their existence at large; they are going to exist anyway. What is inevitable needs no proof for its existence."

We may reject finally, then, the notion that values need religion as a "technique" to "validate" them. It is true that we need to direct and harmonize our affections, desires, and purposes, but we can learn to do this through knowledge and good-will. We may dispense with supernatural sanctions.

102

I. A. Richards' account of value is again very similar to Russell's, but as Richards is dealing with the relations of morality to art, his analysis is in some respects more subtle. Anything, he holds, is valuable which will satisfy an appetency without involving the frustration of some equal or more important appetency. As our various impulses are constantly conflicting, as one must be satisfied at the expense of another, some coördination of his impulses must exist in every individual, and those individuals are most fortunate who achieve the widest and most comprehensive organization of their impulses—one that allows them a maximum of varied satisfactions and involves a minimum of suppression and sacrifice. In *The Principles of Literary Criticism,* Richards defines the problem of morality as "the problem of how we are to obtain the greatest possible value from life," which "becomes a problem of organization, both in the individual life and in the adjustment of individual lives to one another."

It is on the basis of the general principles laid down by these writers, I am convinced, that we may finally arrive at a more satisfactory hierarchy of individual and social values. One of the reasons that makes Humanists secretly or openly antagonistic to science is their belief (a) that science involves a denial of values, and (b) that the only way of establishing values is by dogmatic fiat. Both beliefs are false.

The first results from a confusion between science as a whole and the particular branch of it called physics, and from a misconception of the function and aims of physics. Physics is "material" simply because its subject matter is the "material" universe. It does not deny values; it simply finds them irrelevant to its particular purposes. Considerations of value would only confuse and complicate its problems; therefore it *abstracts* from value, as it does from scores of other factors. Even a schoolboy of seven knows enough to do this when you give him a problem in arithmetic. "If John gave you three apples and Mary gave you two, how many apples would you have?" He knows that the answer is five, and he knows that it makes no difference whether it is apples, pears or marbles, or who gave them to him, or what they cost, or what his respective preferences are among them. He knows that these factors are all irrelevant to his problem. The physicist merely carries on this abstraction on a more elaborate scale. One would not think there could possibly be any confusion on so elementary a point did one not find otherwise intelligent men constantly falling into it.[8]

[8] See the muddled discussion, for example, in the last pages of Aldous Huxley's *Jesting Pilate:* "The generation of Arnold and of Tennyson sat uncomfortably on the horns of what seemed an unescapable dilemma. Either the materialist hypothesis was true; in which case there was no such thing as value. Or else it was false; in which case values really existed, but science could

Physics, then, can never be made into an explanation of the universe. It can never be more than the solution of certain specific problems, solutions arrived at by abstracting rigidly from the full rich reality before us. It solves its problems without prejudice to value. But this does not mean that problems of value must be left in the hands of ignorant sentimentalists or dogmatists. It does not mean that the results obtained in the physical sciences do not affect our scales of value in an incidental and indirect manner, as all fresh knowledge must. It does not mean that *other* sciences cannot take values as their special province. This, indeed, is what other sciences actually do. Economics is concerned with economic values, ethics with moral values, esthetics with values in literature and art. Neither ethics nor esthetics has yet become a "science," and even the claims of economics are frequently denied. But we can at least approach these various types of value with a genuinely scientific attitude, the attitude of patient, open-minded investigation, which recognizes the infinite complexity and delicacy of its task, and does not attempt, like Humanism, to close the door on inquiry by arrogant catchwords and subtle appeals to prejudice.

not. But science manifestly *did* exist," etc. And "Our sense of values is intuitive. There is no proving the real existence of values in any way that will satisfy the logical intellect."

Pupils of Polonius

I HOPE that you who do me the honor of reading what I am about to say here will forgive me if I occasionally fail to observe in this paper the cardinal virtues of the Humanist, as those virtues have been enunciated and agreed upon by both Professor Irving Babbitt and Mr. Paul Elmer More and nodded to affirmatively by all their eager and wistful young followers in America (about sixteen in number, according to the latest census, including those who cannot make up their minds for fear that they may limit their market for book reviews) who are at that happy stage where they think that something should be done about the situation right now, immediately, in fact the day before yesterday, or, at the very latest, twenty years ago when Professor Babbitt published his *New Laokoon*. Those virtues are: decorum, moderation and common sense.

I ask forgiveness for failure to observe these virtues on the same ethical principle whereupon it was long ago established that duellists should use the same weapons. It is manifestly unfair (as we have understood the *ethos* of the situation since the little affair between Saul and David) for one antagonist to use a sling-shot and the other to use a spear, or for one to use a machine gun and the other to use a broadsword, or for one to walk to his firing position at the count of the referee while the other sprints off to one side and takes a pot shot at him before he has had a chance to turn round and address himself to his antagonist at the command, "At arms!"

The *code duello* has always been hypothetical and rarely adhered to by both contestants in actual practice. Messrs. Babbitt and More do not observe the code; they do not observe the Humanist virtues of decorum, moderation and common sense. They write grimly of these virtues and one seems to see them slap their chests with that same maudlin avowal of these virtues which one overhears at the bar of a New York speak-easy when some poor devil, fortified by drink, begins to tell those around him what a man of moderation, decorum and common sense he is in comparison with his idiot of a boss who has just called him on the carpet for failure to land some order which no human being could possibly land because the price set by the boss was several points higher than that of the next lowest competitor.

Life is quite trying at times; and as I read with a tear in my eye the intimate letters of the late Barrett Wendell and the late Stuart P. Sherman, I realize that even in the shades of *academe* there are contentions and competitions and office politics which must trouble and harass the minds of any member of the faculty who possesses imagination and conviction and who is at the same time articulate.

110

(I make this last point because many aspirants for a full professorship in a college so thoroughly exhaust their energies in acquiring the requisite Ph.D. that thereafter they suffer from a sort of permanent amnesia and respond only to cross-references, paradigms, and pedagogical routine. And as teachers they are complete failures. There was one man whose work on the philosophy of religion I had read in a small town library at the age of sixteen and at whose feet I had made up my mind, come weal, come woe, some day to sit. I was fortunate enough to get a class under him in my freshman year, by some finegeling with the junior dean, and day after day I sat in the front row expecting him to say something which would open up the gates of wisdom for me and all I got was a list of books for "required reading" and some questions now and then as to whether, if your sister and mother were both drowning at the same time which one would be the proper one to save providing you had an equal opportunity to save either. I answered these questions with such soul-searching seriousness that I barely made a passing mark; and then, one day, trudging along at the heels of my reservoir of wisdom while he was in ardent colloquy with a senior dean, who probably didn't like him, I heard my oracle boast with proud and vehement assurance that he had "quite taken a reef in her sails" in the last issue of the *Journal of Philology*. He was

111

boasting to support his ego like my salesman friend in the speak-easy and on slighter grounds; for it did appear to me that the salesman could hardly have got the order if the price set by the boss was higher than that of the successful competitor. And I looked up my oracle's devastating reply and then I looked up her reply—she was a professor at Vassar—and it seemed to me that she had the better of the argument. Unfortunately, as I apprehended it, the argument was not of the slightest consequence. It was a matter of guess-work having to do with what the author had really said in a lacuna of a Greek text which threw some light on the tribal customs of the Hebrews in the preëxilitic period.)

I suspect that life has not been altogether a bed of roses and Rousseau for Professor Babbitt with the Harvard faculty and that Mr. More has had his vexatious moments even in his quiet retirement from life under the elms of Princeton and under the auspices of the trustees of the Vanuxem fund. There must have been hours when it was rather trying to preserve the cardinal virtues of the Humanist, the virtues of decorum, moderation and common sense. At any rate, they have not always displayed those virtues, even when they have retired to the quietude of their studies and have sat themselves down to write.

It is not decorous; it is not moderation; it is not common sense for Professor Babbitt to dismiss Oswald

Spengler, the author of *The Decline of the West,* as a "charlatan" just because he happens to disagree with Spengler, as Professor Babbitt does on page 21 of *Democracy and Leadership.* It is, *ipso facto,* libellous. I have written for newspapers and magazines quite a number of years and during that time I have sometimes been intemperate to such a degree in my remarks about men like Professor Babbitt that they have complained that I was unfair—a "hoodlum," I believe was the word. But if I should ever have written that the author of a book which I had under review was a charlatan the word would have been stricken out by the copy-reader and if it did get by and there was any complaint, both the copy-reader and myself would have been bounced out on our heads. I have been bounced out for lesser offenses against moderation and decorum than that.

It is not decorous; it is not moderation; it is not common sense for Mr. Paul Elmer More to describe John Dos Passos' *Manhattan Transfer* as "an explosion in a sewer." That is not criticism. That is what is known along Broadway in New York as "wise-cracking." Mr. More has considerable facility along these lines and the most interesting passages in his writings are in such wise-cracks where his true originality and sense of style show through. If he had greater facility he might easily get a job conducting a column on a tabloid. But he would also have to learn moderation in his wise-cracks—that subtlety and nearness to

113

the actual truth which gives the wise-crack edge and point. Tallulah Bankhead's characterization of Maeterlinck's *The Blue-Bird:* "There is less in this than meets the eye" spontaneously uttered is much more subtle than Mr. More's "explosion in a sewer," composed with great deliberation in the quietude of a library. Another thing, Mr. More: learn from Ring Lardner how to use slang that will endure and become part of the language. In your introduction to *The New Grub Street* in the Modern Library series you used the words "camouflage" and "intrigue." The word "intrigue" used as a verb has now become the sole property of Theodore Dreiser who has earned the right to be slovenly in his diction. The word "camouflage" has not been used by any one with a sense of style since the word was done to death during the war.

It is not decorous; it is not moderation; it is not common sense for Paul Elmer More to refer to a rival critic, Benedetto Croce, as "an epoptic hierophant of the demonic mysteries" as Mr. More does in *Humanism and America.* I grant you that it is rather a neat epithet; but James Branch Cabell could have done it with better effect and greater grace.

It is not decorous; it is not moderation; it is not common sense for Mr. More to dismiss Professor John Dewey lightly, calling him a "loquacious apostle of sweetness and *darkness.*"

114

It is not decorous; it is not moderation; it is not common sense for Paul Elmer More to label *Ulysses* "obscene rigmarole" nor to select one phase of Robinson Jeffers' work that displeases him and damn the whole as "sadism." It is not only not decorous, not moderation and not common sense to hide behind a label—especially one that has taken on such an ambiguity of meaning and implication, thanks to Freudian popularity, that the use of it (as with all catchwords) forestalls all further argument—it is cowardly.

I beg forgiveness for not having been decorous, moderate nor common sensible—for having displayed none of the virtues of the Humanists—but I cannot be decorous if I am to show that they are not decorous; I cannot be moderate if I am to show that they are not moderate; and I cannot exercise their kind of common sense if I am to point out their lack of it.

II

This Humanism business is one of those terrific tempests in a teapot, which has been stirred up by T. S. Eliot, an American-born young man now a citizen of Great Britain and a resident of London, who has a singular faculty for setting the literati by the ears. Some years ago he brought out a poem called *The Waste Land*, which I happen to believe is one of the great poetic achievements of our time. To me and to John Livingston Lowes, Edmund Wilson, Gilbert Seldes, and a number of other critics it was the poetic epitome of post-war disillusion. To a lot of other people it was simply poppycock. Over that poem a terrific battle waged. Even Harry Leon Wilson, creator of the immortal Ruggles, Merton and Ma Pettingill, who hitherto had taken no part in the critical conversation leaped into print with a statement that he had private information that Eliot had confessed that the poem was a hoax and that the critics who had taken it seriously had made jackasses of themselves. Mr. Eliot indignantly denied that this was true.

Even the modernistic poets were hotly argumentative about the merits of the poem. Louis Untermeyer, who had been a propagandist for the whole free verse movement, let go a blast in a review aimed to destroy any pretensions to art or seriousness the poem had. And I remember being taken off my feet by the late, redoubtable, Amy Lowell who had invited me to dinner at her mansion in Brookline, and who fixed me with her glittering eyes and said, "I hear, Mr. Rascoe, that you think *The Waste Land* is a great poem. I think it is a piece of tripe. I know Tom Eliot—he was brought up around here, distantly related to the Harvard Eliots. But Tom is an intellectual and an intellectual cannot write a poem, which is a matter of heart and emotion." That cer-

116

tainly seemed to settle the matter so far as Miss Lowell was concerned; but I went on thinking and still think that *The Waste Land* is a great poem. And since those by-gone days a number of critics, acting as historians and summarists, have taken it to be indisputable that *The Waste Land* is one of the major poetic achievements of our time. It has been the most imitated and most parodied poem of our generation.

Meanwhile Mr. Eliot, who is nearing forty, has embraced the career of a critic. Feeling, apparently, that a critic must have principles to be used like a yardstick in measuring the merits of literature, he has also publicly embraced Anglo-Catholicism and the New Humanism. J. Middleton Murry, a critic of about Eliot's age, a few years ago came upon Irving Babbitt's *Rousseau and Romanticism* which was published in 1919 and wrote a review of it. From his review it was apparent that he had never heard of Babbitt before, although Professor Babbitt had startled the critical world with his *The New Laokoon* in 1910 and had finally been set down as a man who had delusions of being pursued by an imp with a forked tail called Jean-Jacques Rousseau. At the time Murry and Eliot were editing rival, subsidized critical journals—Eliot *The Criterion* and Murry *The Athenæum*—in London and so friendly was their rivalry that Eliot appeared in Murry's magazine and Murry appeared in Eliot's with articles in which they

117

disputed graciously and tediously. Murry was bereft by the loss of his wife and was looking for a religion to cling to which would take the spiritual place of that gifted woman. He was also looking for critical standards. Having encountered Babbitt late in life he let out a cry "I saw him first!" and claimed Babbitt for himself. He and Eliot had already been disputing over neo-Thomism, neither of them agreeing as to precisely what was the message St. Thomas Aquinas had to give to the modern world to save it from destruction. Indeed, it would appear that neither had taken the trouble to read the *Summa*. (Happily it was not necessary for them to do so: so much has been written by scholastic disputants over the means whereby St. Thomas reconciled [to his own satisfaction] the principles of the pagan Greek philosophers, Aristotle, with the doctrines of the Roman Catholic Church as those doctrines existed in the middle thirteenth century that it is quite easy for any two men, who have nothing better to do, to find points of difference concerning these reconciliatory means over which to write quite a large number of argumentative words. Indeed there is only one living person who has any authority in settling such disputes and that is Achille Ratti, Bishop of Rome.)

Eliot had been a student at Harvard and had been a pupil of Babbitt's, so he claimed a prior right. Then

118

he and Murry began to tear the poor professor's body between them. Eliot, who is the cleverer fellow and a better writer, emerged victorious. Deprived of Babbitt, Murry turned to God and wrote a book about Him. Promptly, as becomes a St. Paul of the New Humanism, Eliot announced his articles of faith: (I) Catholicism in religion, (II) Royalty in politics, (III) Classicism in literature. He was also consistent and logical. Although American-born, he became a subject of King George V; he joined the Anglo-Catholic church; and he brought out a book of essays which has been facetiously referred to as *For Lancelot Gobbo*. The actual title of the book is *For Lancelot Andrewes*, the title essay being about the superb prose style of the sermons of the Right Reverend Father in God, Lancelot Bishop of Winchester who died on September 25, 1626.

III

The whole thing is very silly—or very comical— but there it is. Eliot has already become an Anglo-Catholic convert in the name of the New Humanism, of which Babbitt is the prophet. And yet Babbitt, as a Hellenist, is as much opposed to Christianity as he is to Rousseauism. His special detestation is the Christian virtue of humility—"Decorum is supreme for the humanist even as humility takes precedence over all other virtues in the eyes of the Christian." In the

119

Babbitt definition, Jesus could not have existed at all if Jesus were ruled by the Babbitt Humanism; it was indecorous of Jesus to take a lash and drive the money-changers out of the temple; it was indecorous of Jesus to preach an ideal of the kingdom of the spirit as opposed to the kingdom of the Cæsars; it was indecorous of Jesus to show magnanimity to Mary Magdalene because such an act of kindness is humanitarian weakness and Mary should have been "trained in the appropriate habits almost from infancy."

Babbitt's essential ideas boil down to these:

1. Property is the one sacred fact. It does not matter how that property is attained. With the privileges accruing to the ownership of property go the obligations of "noblesse oblige," that is, of being a gentleman. What those obligations are Professor Babbitt has not specifically defined. He has indicated them in a horrifyingly nebulous way by saying that "in the eyes of a humanist . . . such terms as 'justice' and 'liberty,' and above all (at least in its application to man) 'nature,' . . . is not true virtue." That is, in the eyes of the humanist, the gentleman, i.e., the great property owner or man in power is privileged to exercise the *droits de seigneur,* whip-lash his slaves, and be any kind of sadist and slave-driver he wants to because to the Humanist the terms "justice" and "liberty" have no virtue.

2. That there has been only one writer of true

120

value to the human race—Sophocles—and all the rest, from Homer, Euripides, Shakespeare on down to the present time, have corrupted the human race. According to him Euripides was poisoned by Rousseauism centuries before Rousseau lived. So, indeed, were the scribes who wrote the New Testament. This whole thing boils down to the ancient war between the Athenians on the relative virtues of Sophocles and Euripides. It is a war of snobbery. Sophocles came from a wealthy family—so wealthy indeed that when Sophocles grew old his sons entered suit to have him declared mentally incompetent to administer his finances—whereas Euripides was of lowly birth—so lowly in fact that Aristophanes made fun of him and his mother because his mother was an herb-peddler. It is true that Euripides' poetry is not as exalted as the poetry of either Sophocles or Æschylus and is only a slight remove from good Attic prose, but his dramas had value in the eyes of Athenian audiences of the time and remained for years extremely popular.

3. That the Humanist demands "moderation, common sense and common decency." Against that no one, I imagine, has any kick. Those are, somehow, the instinctive "controls" of all human beings. To show how warped by a fixed idea is the mind of Professor Babbitt, let me quote: "One reason that Rousseau gave for his abandonment of his five chil-

dren was that he had been robbed by the rich of the wherewithal to feed them. The ease with which multitudes have been persuaded to follow Rousseau in this evasion of responsibility puts one on the track of a human trait that one may actually observe in oneself and others, and that gives some positive justification to the theological emphasis on the old Adam." To me all that that paragraph indicates is that Professor Babbitt who is the father of three children has been tempted by the old Adam at one time or another to abandon them. I am the father of two children and never once has such an idea entered my mind. There are no "multitudes" who have been "persuaded to follow Rousseau in this evasion of responsibility" and any one who imagines this to be so has a strange idea of the nature of the average man and woman. Now and then one reads in the newspapers of some child's being left on the doorstep of an orphanage or abandoned to charity by some mother who was no longer able to feed the child—but never once have I read that such an act was taken because the mother had been "persuaded to follow Rousseau in this evasion of moral responsibility." Mothers who abandon their children—usually hoping that somebody will care for them better than they, the mothers, have been able to, never heard of Rousseau. Professor Babbitt would argue that it was the mother's duty to know about Rousseau—and, if she did not, she did

122

not count anyway. Professor Babbitt's doctrine is a compound of snobbery of the kind I find most irritating. Yet it has some elements in it of sense, even if these elements happen to be platitudes which my iceman, cigar dealer, grocer, butcher, bootlegger, garbage man and druggist already know: i.e., that it is best to keep temperate and thrifty, not to let your temper run away with you, not to make a nuisance of yourself, not to get up in the air over trifles, to see that your family gets properly fed and clothed, to pay your bills and not violate the laws. But what is new or Humanistic about that? Not a single person among my personal acquaintance has ever abandoned a child, although quite a lot of them have read Rousseau. Rousseau is unpalatable to me, but so are Æsop and St. Augustine. Æsop's fables seem to me pernicious and immoral and St. Augustine's and Rousseau's confessions reveal to me men of a sort I particularly dislike.

IV

Meanwhile, be it known, that as the author of *The Waste Land, Sweeney Among the Nightingales* and *The Love Song of J. Alfred Prufrock,* as the editor of an English magazine devoted to belles lettres, and as the possessor of a clear, pungent and graceful prose style, Mr. Eliot became the idol of a generation of literary yearners in the academies who had been under the hatches for many years in fear of the whirlwind generated by H. L. Mencken against academic dry rot, feeble dialectics masking as erudition, complacency in American optimism, shams and pretensions of all sorts. Mencken, Lewis, Cabell, Dreiser, Anderson, like Shaw, Wells, Lawrence and Bennett in England, had been silent for nearly two years, or at least had had nothing challenging to say. During the lull, the yearners swarmed out of the hatches like so many cockroaches, all proclaiming themselves New Humanists and proving it by hailing Irving Babbitt as their Allah and Eliot as their Prophet, and by never writing two hundred words without appending footnotes.

Eliot's case is psychologically interesting and an understanding of it makes it all the more comical that his followers in democratic America should seriously espouse his doctrines. Eliot is a sensitive and gifted man who was born in St. Louis, Mo., and was educated at Harvard. There he came under the influence of Ezra Pound and joined the ranks of the young revoltés in poetry. His reaction to the staid environment of Boston and Cambridge was bitter and satirical. He wrote a poem deriding the respectable Bostonian's reliance upon the *Boston Evening Transcript* for knowledge of what was going on in the world. He wrote a poem deriding the Sunday morning parade to Church as a social rather than a religious

124

event; and in clever verse he showed the shell of tradition as empty of life.

Then he went to England where he was employed in a bank. He was profoundly affected by the war and especially by the post-war disillusion and he crystallized his emotions in *The Waste Land*. This seemed to exhaust him and next we find him writing at rare intervals two or three brief and obscure poems about the "dry and hollow men"—carrying further the idea expressed in *The Waste Land* that modern life does not nourish the spirit and that men are parched and impotent.

Like Huysmans, Eliot was almost inevitably headed for the Church from the first. Like Huysmans he had an ascetic's fascination for the lusts of the flesh, and loved to dwell upon scenes in which love is an obscene parody. Apeneck Sweeney, his symbol of coarse male lust, gratifying himself brutally, and the pitiable J. Alfred Prufrock parting his scant hair and wondering whether he should wear his trousers rolled in order to attract the girls, testified to his preoccupation. He embraced the Church, but not Roman Catholicism—and this is significant. The middle-western boy who had had his revolt against Puritan Boston with its Back Bay aristocracy, had become a personage looked up to with respect by Lady Rhonda and eminent British divines. He became a British citizen, testifying to his belief in the sanctity of royalty and he was ready for the Church. But Roman Catholicism is, you know, in England not quite *au fait;* it numbers among its adherents so many low and vulgar people. The Anglo-Catholic Church on the other hand is more aristocratic. He joined that. (See Eliot's remarks on the vulgarity of the Roman Catholic Church in *Humanism and America.*)

It was inevitable that Eliot, now an Anglo-Catholic royalist and classicist, should establish a rapproachement with his old Harvard teacher, Irving Babbitt who, in Eliot's younger days, must have represented so much that he found distasteful. For Professor Babbitt is the nearest thing to an Anglo-Catholic royalist in America.

Professor Babbitt has no interest in literature, although he happens to hold a chair in comparative literature at Harvard. He doesn't know how literature is created: he is even so naïve in this respect that he imagines that all that is necessary to produce great humane masterpieces is to observe the rules laid down by Aristotle in the *Poetics* and "exercise the inner control," be decorous, and be a "gentleman." (See his contribution to the symposium *Humanism and America.*) He has a positive distaste for literature and is interested only in dialectics. In this he differs with his brother Humanist, Professor Paul Elmer More, an eminent dialectician, in that More does like literature in his peculiar fashion. He enjoys reading books of poetry, drama, fiction and essays. But he gets out of all his reading precisely what he brings to it; that is, the mind of a Presbyterian Princeton professor in ample circumstances who believes in the sacredness of property as a first principle and Puritan morals as a second. When More reads a page of Plato or Wycherley he finds not Plato or Wycherley but an image of Paul Elmer More.

A careful analysis of Babbitt's credo and of his ideas expressed in his several books, notably in *Rousseau and Romanticism* and *Democracy and Leadership*, reveals behind the involved and nebulous dialectic simply the ideas of President A. Lawrence Lowell, president of Harvard, whose arrogant stupidity in many matters, notably in the summary discharge of twenty scrubwomen because the State Minimum Wage Commission complained that the university was employing scrubwomen at less than thirty-seven cents an hour, has helped to create more Communist sympathy than perhaps any other agency in America. These ideas of Babbitt are simply those of a Boston Brahmin, holding a university chair, living in academic seclusion from contact with the world of today, happily engaged, like a medieval schoolman, in shadow-boxing with the ghost of Jean-Jacques Rousseau, who epitomizes to Professor Babbitt all of the anarchic, destructive and mistaken sentiments of man.

127

THE FALLACY OF HUMANISM—Tate

The Fallacy of Humanism

I F the necessity for virtue could tell us how to practice it, we should be virtuous overnight. For the case of the American Humanists against modern culture is damaging to the last degree. The truth of their indictment, negatively considered, cannot be denied. But this is not enough.

There is a widespread belief that the doctrines of Humanism are fundamentally sound. It would be truer to say that they are only partly and superficially so, and that they are being rejected for superficial reasons—the Humanists are dogmatic, they ignore contemporary literature, they lack the "esthetic sense." These limitations unhappily go deeper. Humanism is obscure in its sources; it is even more ambiguous as to the kind of authority to which it appeals. And yet believers in tradition, reason, and authority—among whom this essayist counts himself—will approach the writings of Messrs. Babbitt, More and Foerster with more than an open mind; they will have in advance the conviction that

the rightful concern of man is his humanity, his world of value . . . that marks him off from a merely quantitative order;

but, after a great deal of patient reading, they will come away with that conviction—and with no more than that conviction. They will have got no specific ideas about values—that is to say, they will have gained no medium for acquiring them; and such a medium, they will reflect, is morally identical with the values themselves. Values are not suspended in the air to be plucked. They will reflect, suspiciously, that the vague method of Humanism resembles the vague method of the so-called Romantic in the very respect in which agreement or difference is fundamental: the Humanist pursues Humanism for its own sake—or, say, restraint for restraint's sake, or proportion for proportion's sake—and while this is doubtless better than pursuing disorder for disorder's sake, the authority of the worthier pursuit is no clearer than that of the baser. His doctrine of restraint does not look to unity, but to abstract and external *control*—not to a solution of the moral problem, but an attempt to get the social results of unity by main force, by a kind of moral Fascism.

The reader will decide, moreover, that this defect of the Humanist is a central one and that, critically examined, it will turn out to be the philosophical malady of the so-called naturalist. Doctrinal differences in themselves may be negligible; the man who supposes himself a naturalist may practice the Humanistic virtues (Montaigne): the Humanist in doctrine may exhibit the method of naturalism (More). But if the appearance of mere doctrine is deceptive,

132

the operation of a technique cannot be. The Humanists have no technique. How, under the special complexities and distractions of the modern world, they intend to make good their values they do not say; they simply urge them. And this discrepancy between doctrine and method their hardier readers will find adequately described in Book II, Chapter IV, of the *Nicomachean Ethics:*

. . . yet people in general do not perform these actions, but taking refuge in talk they flatter themselves they are philosophizing, and that they will so be good men: acting in truth very like those sick people who listen to the doctor with great attention but do nothing that he tells them: just as these people cannot be well bodily under such a course of treatment, neither can those be mentally by such philosophizing.

The Humanists have listened not only to one doctor but to a great many doctors, and they tell us what they say; but they have not learned, and they cannot teach us, how to take the medicine.

I propose, in the first place, therefore, to analyze the position held by those Humanists in whom the minimum of doctrine appears: I mean by the minimum of doctrine that their thought refuses to exceed the moralistic plane: they steadily repudiate all religious and philosophical support. The Humanists of this type are Babbitt and Foerster. Secondly,

I shall try to discover how this Humanism differs, if it differ, from that of Mr. More, who appears to lean heavily upon religious values. Different as the religious and the non-religious brands of Humanism seem to be, they may turn out in the end to founder on the same reef. At the last, if Humanism shall save itself—that is to say, if it shall find a method—what is the position into which it will be logically driven?

I

The Humanism formulated by Mr. Norman Foerster in the last chapter of his *American Criticism* is actually a summary of the views of Professor Babbitt. The summary is, of course, an over-simplification, and does scant justice to Professor Babbitt's intellectual resourcefulness; yet I think it contains the fundamental scheme of his position. (It omits one of his chief difficulties, which I will bring out in a moment.) The assumptions of Humanism, according to Mr. Foerster, are as follows:

(1) ". . . that assumptions are necessary." Foerster points out the self-deception of the naturalist, or the anti-authoritarian, who thinks he has got rid of assumptions.

(2) ". . . that the essential elements of human experience are precisely those which appear to conflict with the reality explored by naturism. It [Humanism] recognizes, indeed, the service of

134

naturism . . . in showing the power of the natural man's impulses."

(3) ". . . the central assumption of humanism is that of a dualism of man and nature . . . the rightful concern of man is his humanity, his world of value and quality that marks him off from a merely quantitative natural order."

(4) "Finally, humanism assumes the freedom of the will to conform to a standard of values, as opposed to the deterministic assumption of naturism."

From these assumptions Mr. Foerster proceeds to a doctrine which I reproduce in a greatly abridged form:

(1) An adequate human standard calls for *completeness*. This includes "natural" human nature.

(2) But it also calls for *proportion*: it demands the harmony of the *parts with the whole* (italics mine).

(3) The complete, proportionate standard may be said to consist of the *normally* or *typically human*.

(4) Although such an ethos has never existed, it has been approximated in the great ages of *the past*. Foerster looks mainly to Greece, but he includes the Romans, Vergil and Horace; the Christians, Jesus, Paul, Augustine, others; the Orientals, Buddha and Confucius; the moderns, Shake-

speare, Milton, Goethe. (But he has misgivings about Shakespeare.)

(5) Unlike Romanticism, Humanism is true to its Hellenic origin in its faith in *reason*. It seeks to deal positively with the whole of human experience, including those elements of experience that do *not* fall within the scope of what is termed science.

(6) Unlike the conceptions of life that grow out of science, Humanism seeks to press beyond reason by the use of *intuition* or *imagination* . . . the human or ethical imagination, as distinguished from the natural or pathetic imagination, which is below the reason.

(7) The ultimate ethical principle is that of restraint or control.

(8) This center to which Humanism refers everything . . . is the reality that gives rise to religion. But pure Humanism is content to describe it *in physical terms* . . . it hesitates to pass beyond its experimental knowledge to the dogmatic affirmations of any of the great religions . . . it holds that *supernatural revelation must be tested by the intellect* . . . it should be clear that Humanism, like Greek philosophy, *begins with science* and *not* with religion.

Now Mr. Foerster says that human values are those which *appear* to conflict (do they or do they not?) with the reality explored by naturism; and yet Humanism demands the cultivation of all human nature, including "natural" human nature. He says, too, that Humanism rejects the elements of experience that fall within the "scope of what is termed science." However this may be, Humanism puts its faith in reason (because of its Hellenic origin) and it is based upon science, and yet it is unlike the conceptions of life that grow out of science. It demands a dualism of man and nature opposed to the monistic assumption of naturism. But how, it may be asked, is this dualism to be preserved along with that other requirement of a "harmony of the parts with the *whole*"? Mr. Foerster has just denounced the monistic whole. And, further, it may be asked, upon which side of the duality does reason take its stand? If science is naturism, and reason science, the question answers itself.

Humanism is based upon science, which is naturism, and yet it is unlike the conceptions of life that grow out of science. And here it may be asked upon which science Mr. Foerster performs his miracle of accepting rejection? Is it just *science*? Or is it an unconscious attitude whose vision of reality is mechanism, a popular version of genuine science? In this case, it is the quantitative natural order of which he speaks. But how did it get quantified? Is it *naturally* quantified? The only plausible answer is that it was quantified by Mr. Foerster's kind of reason, but that

137

being unaware of this he can, with an effective
"chaser" handy, drink "reason" off neat.

The chaser is the "ethical imagination," which
presses beyond reason. We have seen that he puts his
faith in reason, and it is difficult to see why he wishes
a faith beyond faith, or why he selects this particular
super-faith: he refuses to press beyond reason in favor
of religion.

His desire to go beyond reason is his desire to escape
from naturalism. This conception of reason is disas-
trously contradictory. The mere desire to get out
of jail will not unlock the gate, and you remain a
prisoner: Mr. Foerster remains a naturalist. He says
that "supernatural intuition"—the phrase smacks of
romantic Bergsonism—must be tested by the intellect. It is, thus, distinct from the intellect, not implicit in its acts—a dichotomy that puts Mr. Foerster
into the hands of the nineteenth century Romantics
whose evil he sets out to undo. This is the naturalistic,
eighteenth-century "rationalistic" conception of imagination: irrational constructions of reality which
"reason" (naturalism) may break down and reject.
When Mr. Foerster says that religion and the imagination must be tested by the intellect, he therefore
means by naturalism. For naturalism contains the
only idea of reason that is available to the Humanist.

If this were not true, the Humanist would not be
forced to exceed reason. Mr. Foerster is a century

138

behind the thought of his age: he is a romantic post-Kantian who can find no way out of mechanism but intellectual suicide. This intellectual suicide was the ethical imagination which Schiller found to be the only way out of scientism, and its origin is betrayed by Schiller's description of it as the ideal representation of Causality. The difficulty for Mr. Foerster and Schiller is the question, How is this moral imagination to get moralized? You get nowhere by saying that the ethical imagination is above the reason, the pathetic imagination below; you have first to give them a motive for being what they are; without this you have a logical hypostasy, and the above and the below become "picture-thinking."

Mr. Foerster will have to decide to be scientifically reasonable, or not to be scientifically reasonable, whether he wants the parts to harmonize with the whole, or whether he rejects the whole for a dualism of the parts. He cannot have reason checking the natural and still keep it natural. Unless he can make up his mind, his dualism is merely verbal. He is expecting naturalism to unnaturalize itself—or, in other words, the imagination to make itself moral.

But perhaps after all he has a way out: there is one card remaining to be played, and it may turn out to be an ace. Now, the ultimate ethical principle is restraint or control, and the motivation of the ethical imagination is restraint; or at least it acts under the motive of restraint in order to create the "normally or typically human." This is the ideal towards which Humanism strives, deriving its principles from ancient approximations of the ideal. But, if the ethical imagination is the instrument for creating the typically human, what is its motive for doing so? Is it restraint? Or is it restraining morality? Or is it restrained restraint? This will not do. You have got to go back to certain prior conditions under which an ethical imagination is possible. If the ethical imagination *is* imagination it must deal with images; but the Humanists give us only a digest of the ancient cultures; they leave to abstract inference a conception of the particular culture in which the humane life may be lived. However wicked the personal life of Villon may have been, his imagination, under the conditions of his age, was bound to be ethical because it had a pervasive authority for being so; it could not escape this authority in some form.

It has been pointed out that Mr. Foerster's quantified nature has been quantified by his own kind of reason, and that he is, in fact, a naturalist. This brings me to one of the chief difficulties of Professor Babbitt's position.

Now Professor Babbitt, in order to escape from a passive Rousseauism, constantly opposes to it, notably in *Rousseau and Romanticism,* the ideal of the *man of action "who, as a result of his moral choices based on*

140

due deliberation, choices in which he is moved primarily by a regard for his own happiness, has quelled the unruly impulses of his lower nature." Again, in *Democracy and Leadership,* he writes: *"To be completely moral one must be positive and critical."*

This positive intellect, split off from the harmony of action possible to the unified but not to the deliberately controlled mind, is the very intellect that has supported naturalism throughout its history. It has created the self-seeking industrialist who *is moved primarily by a regard for his own happiness.* Professor Babbitt, of course, sees that this man *goes too far;* yet *how* far is *too* far? He has only the positive and critical intellect to tell him, and the best this can do is to set up an arbitrary limit to its own self-seeking activity—another instance of naturalism trying to unnaturalize itself. The stopping-place is pointed out by a study of the "wisdom of the ages," but it should be remembered that this wisdom must be discovered by the positive and critical intellect, which is supposed to use it against itself.

This, I believe, exposes the negative basis of Professor Babbitt's morality. The good man is he who "refrains from doing" what the "lower nature dictates," and he need do nothing positive. He merely refrains from complete action on the naturalistic level while remaining on that level.

It is clear that this is the source of Mr. Foerster's

141

dilemma—whether to suffer the slings and arrows of outrageous naturalism by "cultivating" it or to reject it altogether. Neither Professor Babbitt nor Mr. Foerster conceives a unified "ethical imagination" moving harmoniously from the center outwards. They hypostatize it as a mediator, as an occasional visitor to the mind to be called in or not, at will. The mind is a mechanical parallelism of moral and natural forces arbitrarily distinct. The ethical force, being the mere negation of the natural, does not positively oppose the supposed enemy because he is really his friend. For this parallelism comes down to an attempt on the part of the natural force to control itself by a law of its own making—a law as various as the individualists who try to formulate it.

Now the moralist in this predicament is not the Aristotelian moralist—and I seem to remember that Professor Babbitt aligns himself with the Stagirite. Professor Babbitt's moral man deliberately undertakes to do, say, four good deeds a day to *offset* his evil impulses, which thus are counterbalanced but not transformed—just as the late Henry Clay Frick collected pictures to offset his transactions in steel. The Aristotelian man deliberately undertakes the doing of "goods" not at all, for to him there are no goods distinct from the performance of his ordinary obligations, such as being polite to his enemies or digging ditches, which become moral goods only in so far as

142

the man is a unified moral agent. His morality is not explicit but implicit in his specific moral acts, which are moral or immoral according to his implicit moral quality. Professor Babbitt's explicit morality is the finger of the Dutch boy in the dyke, or the man sitting gingerly on the keg of dynamite lest it explode. The modern problem is desperate, and Professor Babbitt recommends the police force.

From this position comes an illuminating hierarchy of social values. Men should be materially rewarded for three kinds of labor, and in this order: (1) moral work, (2) intellectual work, and (3) manual work. The intellectual and the laborer are not doing moral work because they do not, while attending to their specific jobs, strive to propagate an explicit morality! Thus moral work is not qualitative but quantitative, and can be measured; it should be measurably rewarded. Doubtless it should; but meanwhile the honest laborer may be doing as much moral work as the professional moralist, and with considerably less self-righteous snobbery. Professor Babbitt's unshakable belief in the "war in the cave," interpreted through a categorical rather than a functional psychology, dooms us forever to a kind of Manichean ill-breeding.

The conditions that should underlie the ethical imagination are by no means fulfilled by Mr. Foerster's doctrinaire summary of Sophocles, or of Vergil, or of Augustine, or his summary of these summaries, taken alone. You cannot get out of them a philosophy or a religion; literature is no substitute for philosophy and religion. It is this vague understanding on the part of the Humanists of the nature of philosophy, it is their lack of an exact logical and philosophical discipline, which betrays them, not only into the muddy reasoning that we have just seen; it leads them to expect to find in literature, ancient or modern, an explicit philosophy sufficient unto itself—a philosophy, in short, that does not already exist in some purer instead of a derived and literary form. They ask us to burn the *Summa*, and to study Aquinas, as *Aquinas*, in Dante.

The belief held at various times since the Renaissance that the ancients are models of attitude and value is innocent enough; and it was useful so long as the classics could be assimilated to a living center of judgment and feeling. But, without this center, you get eclecticism—you get Professor Babbitt. And the sole defense of eclecticism is naturalistic—that is to say, it assumes the capacity of the mind to combine mechanically upon a *tabula rasa* a variety of unlike elements into a unity. We know that mechanical interaction, were it possible, could not yield a whole, but an aggregate. Humanism, lacking a center, is an aggregate. It expects Sophocles to fuse with Vergil without an agency of fusion. The Humanist conception of literature is mechanical and naturalistic.

144

This is because its ingrained habit of mind is mechanical. This is the decisively important thing. The way one uses a method is, in the end, the doctrine, and not the literal significance of the doctrine's terms. The Humanistic method, its ingrained habit of mind, is fundamentally opposed to its doctrine, and the sole condition under which this doctrine could be made good would be a center of life philosophically and morally consistent with it. Until this center is found, and not pieced together eclectically at the surface, Humanism is an attempt to do mechanically—that is, naturalistically—what should be done morally.

Its idea of the past is infinite regression. When it is asked for "authority," it is constantly driven back from one position to another. We arrive at last at the "wisdom of the ages"—but can this wisdom be taken in and evaluated by a mind that has no way of knowing that it is wise? Professor Babbitt is a learned and distinguished man, and he may be wise. But for this we have only his word, since his morality, as we have seen, is only an arbitrarily individualistic *check upon itself*: his wisdom is a naturalistically historical recovery of the past.

The idea of infinite regression to authoritative judgment inheres in the thought of Foerster and Babbitt (and of More, too, as we shall see), and it is probably the subtlest fallacy to which Humanism is committed. It takes all the *time* out of the past and all the concreteness out of the present. This fallacy is due to an unconscious transformation of the idea of an increasingly distant temporal past into the idea of a logical series which is quite timeless. This is another pitfall of picture-thinking: time is confused with logical succession which, of course, may run in any "direction" or all directions at once. The Humanist thus convinces himself that his logical series is a temporal past, and as such affords him a stopping-place—some fixed doctrine or some self-contained wisdom of the ages. But there can be no absolute in a logical series because all its terms are equal and it never ends. Now the logical series is quantitative, the abstraction of space. The temporal series is, on the other hand, space concrete. Concrete, temporal experience implies the existence of a temporal past, and it is the foundation of the religious imagination; that is to say, the only way to think of the past independently of Mr. Foerster's naturalism is to think religiously; and conversely, the only way to think religiously is to think in time. Naturalistic science is timeless. A doctrine based upon it, whether explicitly or not, can have no past, no idea of tradition, no fixed center of life. The "typically human" is a term that cannot exist apart from some other term; it is not an absolute; it is fluid and unfixed.

To de-temporize the past is to reduce it to an abstract lump. To take from the present its concrete

146

fullness is to refuse to let standards work from the inside; it follows that "decorum" must be "imposed" from above. Thus there are never specific moral problems (the subject matter of the arts) but only fixed general doctrines without subject matter—that is to say, without "nature."

The "historical method," says Mr. Foerster, rose in the age of naturalism, but he wishes to keep it as a valuable adjunct to Humanism. This may be due to his fallacy in the concept of reason; or it may be that he does not wish to embarrass the American academic system, to which he belongs. His hope, however, that Humanism may rise upon its own débris is the miracle of naturalism unnaturalizing itself. Men cannot be naturalists with one half of the mind, Humanists with the other; or does Mr. Foerster desire the growth of two coöperating classes—naturalists and Humanists? The convictions of the one class are bound to undermine those of the other. The "historical method" has always been the anti-historical method. Its aim is to contemporize the past. Its real effect is to de-temporize it. The past becomes a causal series and timeless; and as a quantitative abstraction (as Foerster himself sees) valueless. Are we to infer that, after the historical naturalists have done their work, the Humanist will intercede and evaluate? This is the Victorian and naturalistic illusion all over again— that good may somehow be the "goal of ill."

147

Professor Babbitt has acutely charged the experimental moderns with not being experimental enough —they have not, he says, questioned the assumptions of their time, but swallowed them whole. He himself continues to experiment, but, as Mr. Eliot has pointed out, we cannot go on experimenting indefinitely. The reason why Professor Babbitt remains an inveterate experimenter is that he, in his turn, has not been philosophical enough. He constantly repudiates "esthetics," which he believes to be a trivial decoration of moral doctrine; but it is actually *philosophy*. The dilemma between an externally imposed decoration and externally imposed morality is false, and Professor Babbitt merely prefers the pot to the kettle.

The Socratic method, which he and Mr. Foerster after him apply so ably to contemporary society, is a method only, and it may be used by the Humanist and his critic alike. Torn out of the Platonic Dialogues, it is an instrument for the exposure of contradiction; it brings with it no motive for the exposure; it yields no absolutes. This will be made clearer in an analysis of the Humanism of Paul Elmer More.

II

If Professor Babbitt's Humanism is eclectic, Mr. More's is equally so—but the apparent synthesis takes place on the religious plane. Humanists like Babbitt

148

and Foerster have to meet the problem of access to truth beyond the personality: it is obvious that Babbitt is a sound man, that his views are sound because he is; but there is no other guarantee of the soundness of his views. He is a "personality," and there is nothing to do about personality but to feel that it is sound or unsound. Mr. More, however, compels us to answer the question: Is his religion as a source of moral authority sound or unsound?

The problem is harder than that of personality, but in the end it is the same. What, in the first place, is Mr. More's religion? Is it Christianity? It is possible that it is. He has written time and again about the insight afforded us by Christian writers, and to them he has brought no inconsiderable insight of his own. There is also, according to Mr. More, a profound insight in Plato—perhaps the profoundest. Again, his studies in the Hindu religions and philosophies have stimulated him to some of his best and most sympathetic writing: the Hindus teach a deep religious dualism. Mr. More's *Studies of Religious Dualism* is a kind of breviary of the good he finds in half a dozen or more religious attitudes. The question remains: which of these religions is Mr. More's? The answer to this, I believe, is: Mr. More's religion is Mr. More's.

Now one of Mr. More's apologists has justly called the five volumes of *The Greek Tradition* an "original

149

and profound work"; yet does its originality and profundity bear upon the question of religious authority —the sole question that I am putting to Mr. More's religious writings? However, Mr. More's defender indirectly attempts to answer this very question: he says: *"The Christ of the New Testament* [contains] an exact and unmistakable explanation of his [More's] acceptance of the historic Christian revelation." I have read this explanation in addition to the rest of Mr. More's religious writings; yet what "acceptance" means is not clear, for Mr. More's Christianity excludes belief in the Miracles and the Virgin Birth. There is a detailed analysis yet to be made of Mr. More's religious books; still I think that my conclusion will be found to be correct: the historic revelation that Mr. More has accepted is largely one of his own contrivance. It is revelation on Mr. More's own terms—revelation as revealed by Mr. More. It is a reconstruction of the historical elements in a pattern satisfactory to the needs of Mr. More's "independent faith," the authority for which is to be found solely in his own books.

He has written a good deal on religion, but it is not easy to put one's finger on his idea of it. Because of the discrepancy between the individualism of his religion and the dogmatism of his judgments his explicit statements on the subject tend to be vague— something like pulpit rhetoric. And yet he does have

150

definite ideas. Their most significant expression is in incidental remarks, when he is off his guard. About twenty years ago he took to task an interpreter of the Forest Philosophers for trying

to convert into hard intellectualism what was at bottom a religious and thoroughly human experience.

Is intellectualism hard (or soft) incompatible with religion? If the experience was thoroughly human, was it also religious? Mr. More thinks that it was. If intellectualism has no place in religion, where does it belong? Mr. More's reply to this is undoubtedly Mr. Foerster's conception of reason: reason is the exclusive privilege of what the Humanists call naturism. Religion is an indefinite, unutterable belief. Mr. More, as well as Babbitt and Foerster, cannot get out of this notion of reason. Now, if religion is not allowed to reason, what may it do? Shall it be contented with visions? I think that Mr. More would say no; but he could not rationally say it. Mr. More repeats implicitly the dilemma of Babbitt and Foerster—and it is very different from a dualism. You have on the one hand scientific naturalism: on the other, irrational belief—the "illusion of a higher reality" that is only an illusion. It is the familiar doctrine of the *philosophe,* that the religious or ethical imagination is an aberration of the intellect, of naturalism. Mr. More would say that the religious and

151

the human join in opposing the natural. But if the religious and the human combine in the present state of Mr. More's religion, which is individualistic, he is opposing naturalism with opposition, or in other words with itself. You cannot overcome naturalism with an illusion of higher reality or an individualistic faith; the illusion and the individualism are properties of the thing to be overcome. In spite of Mr. More's religious attitude, most of my criticism of Babbitt and Foerster apply to him.

Mr. More's dilemma is implicit throughout *Christ the Word*, the most recent volume of *The Greek Tradition*, and it becomes explicit in an essay entitled "An Absolute and An Authoritative Church" (*The Criterion*, July, 1929). Harassed by the demon of the absolute, he tries to find religious authority apart from the Protestant claim of infallibility for the biblical texts, on the one hand, and, on the other, from the Roman claim of absolute interpretation of these texts. The solution of the problem seems to lie in the Eastern and the Anglican Churches, which offer "the kind of revelation which neither in book nor in Church is absolute, but in both book and Church possesses a sufficient authority." The merit of any particular church is beside my point, but Mr. More's idea of authority is very much to it, and he fails to make it clear. He admits that his authority may bring "the reproach of uncertainty," and the reader must conclude that the uncertainty is rooted in his persistently independent faith. The new essay is a summary of Mr. More's religious thought, and it is forthright and fearless; but it ends in vague appreciation of tradition tempered by individualism. The dilemma of absolutes remains untouched because Mr. More seems to lack the philosophical impulse to think himself out of it.

He gives us, in the first chapter of *Studies of Religious Dualism,* something of his religious history up to that time (1909). He had repudiated Calvinism. He was drifting, but suddenly he found a book that initiated him into the "mysteries of independent faith"—the kind of faith, one observes, that the romantic, the naturist, the Rousseauist, has supported all along. Calvinism, it seems, was not independent enough or too independent. Now just how much independence was necessary? Mr. More had to make his decision individualistically, and he had, like Professor Babbitt, no way of knowing when he came to more than a personal stop.

His critics have accused him of a defective "esthetic sense"; he has seemed to be preoccupied with the content of literature; he has little to say of style, almost nothing, except what he says impatiently, of the craft of writing from the point of view of the writer. With Professor Babbitt, he never permits us to forget his conviction that the problems of craft

153

are secondary and "esthetic" and that, if the writer is virtuous, the writing will take care of itself. The reply to this is not that such confusion of thought is unworthy of Mr, More—which it is. It is not enough to oppose to it an equal confusion—that his is due to a lack of esthetic perception. His failure to understand the significance of style is a failure to understand most of the literature that he has read. It is his intention to extract from any given book the doctrine that coincides with his own. We have just seen that it is difficult to find out what Mr. More's doctrine is. With what is literature, then, to coincide? Mr. More entertains false hopes of literature; he expects it to be a philosophy and a religion because, in his state of "independent faith," he has neither a definite religion nor a definite philosophy prior to the book he happens to be reading.

In his most recent volume, *The Demon of the Absolute,* he remarks somewhat complacently, that he is not concerned at the moment with artistic means; only with "results." This distinction runs all through Mr. More's writings: he is not concerned with the letter of religion or of literature—the means through which it exists and is preserved, the religion or the literature itself. Religious results, separate from religious means, become—if they become anything—independent faith. Literary results, that is the moral paraphrase of a work of literature, become independ-

154

ent morality. In either case the full content of the literary or religious text is left behind. When Mr. More tells us that a writer has a sound moral attitude, he may be right, but there is no reason to believe that he may not be wrong. His judgments, for us, are thus neither right nor wrong: strictly speaking they are meaningless. He cannot cite his independent faith because he has no text outside himself; it is rationally inarticulate; there is no way to communicate it.

Nevertheless, Mr. More evidently supposes that he is conveying it; else he would not continue to write books. His reasons for this supposition not only command attention; they are of great interest in themselves. Mr. More is, among other things, a Platonist. What is a Platonist? Is he a man who believes what Plato believed? Or is he a man who uses the Socratic method for the exposure of contradiction? If he is the latter, to what end does he expose contradiction? Since Mr. More obviously believes things that Plato did not, he is, if he be a Platonist at all, one by virtue of his use of the Socratic method. But why does he use it? There is only one answer: for the support of independent faith. He is a Platonist only in the sense in which all men are said to be either Aristotelians or Platonists.

And yet he constantly draws upon Plato for quotations and analogies (he has written a book on the subject); he has the air of delivering his opinions from quoted authority. But owing to the distracting influence of the other authorities—Christ, the Forest Philosophers—which compose his independent faith, it is difficult to ascertain just how authoritative, at a given moment, Plato is. The real authority at all times, of course, is Mr. More. I need hardly point out that Mr. More logically drives himself into the position of spiritual exile and, if he speak at all, of arrogance to which he has consigned the romantic enemy.

The belief in the authority of Plato when More is the actual authority explains the poor quality of his literary judgments. Moral judgments are never more irresponsible than when the judge deludes himself into thinking that the high and mighty of the past are behind him. Mr. More is a man whose critical habits are not subject to the purification and correction of specific external standards, and the delusion that they are only increases their irresponsibility. In the name of restraint he is able to evoke the limit of his personal distastes.

Mr. More's fallacy is identical, as I have said, with that of the non-religious Humanists. Because he cannot find an adequate conception of concrete tradition (experience) in terms of authority (reason), he gives us abstract, timeless, rootless, habitual ideas that closely resemble, in structure, the universe of the naturists; authority in More becomes the spectral sorites of infinite regress. There is no conception of religion as preserved, organized experience; you have a mechanism of moral ideas. Take this passage by Mr. More:

> True art is humanistic rather than naturalistic; and its gift of high and permanent pleasure is the response of our own breast to the artist's delicately revealed sense of that divine control moving like the spirit of God upon the face of the waters.
> So far I seem to see my way clear. If you should ask me by what rhetorical devices or by what instrument of representation one poem . . . appeals more successfully than another to the higher faculty within us, how, for instance, Milton's *Paradise Lost* accomplishes this end better than Blackmore's *King Arthur*, though *both poems were written with equally good intentions* [italics mine]; I would reply frankly that the solution of this problem of the imagination may be beyond my powers of critical analysis.

The first part of this passage is a fair example of the pulpit rhetoric into which Mr. More plunges when he speaks of the relation of literature to religion, and the reason why his thought is vague is that, like Professor Babbitt, he has not been philosophical enough; he has not examined his own assumptions. It is difficult to distinguish, in the above quotation, any reason why true art is Humanistic; for the "high and per-

157

manent pleasure" and "the divine control" are only
pleasant ways of saying mechanical habits of thought.
Mr. More has never philosophized his ideas into ulti-
mates—those fixed yet interpretative flexible positions from the viewpoint of which the ghost of naturalism and the otherwise disembodied spirit of
morality become, not things, but descriptions of
experience in the life of man. As Mr. Eliot
has pointed out in the case of Babbitt, More ignores
the conditions out of which a book emerges. These
conditions alone realize the author's ideas; they alone
contribute morality, not an abstract, but a specific
morality in terms of experience, to the work of literature. More cannot tell us why Milton is superior
to Blackmore because his sole idea of the mind is
that of a mechanism of moral ideas. The intentions
of the two poems being equally good, he cannot understand why their equal morality does not moralize
the pieces into an equal excellence; because moral
ideas are *things* they ought to be as efficient one place
as another. Mr. More conceives literature, first, as a
mechanism of ideas; then, as a mechanism of books
themselves; literature is a timeless, self-perpetuating
machine set in motion in an infinite past which is no
past at all. To be another Dante you have only to
believe that his ideas, his "results," are good, and
to identify them in some undefined sense with your
own moral habits. It is fairly clear that the

158

problem is beyond the power of Mr. More's analysis.

Mr. More's doctrine is morality for morality's sake, and if art for art's sake has always been an outrage upon reason, his position is no less so. There is little rationally to choose between them.

His view of style as rhetorical devices is, then, perfectly consistent: they have no necessary connection with what is being said; like morality, they simply exist. Morality being automatically moral, moral values are moral before they are communicated; the style merely dresses them up. But how can there be abstract results apart from the means—apart from the medium which, under *temporal* conditions, fixes the values in experience? Style—the way values are apprehended—is the technique for validating them. Mr. More's theory logically ends in never uttering another word.

Because he cannot take the philosophical view he sees naturalism as the worship of instinct, license, self —all the things, in fact, that a respectable citizen of the United States, for reasons of social habit—would not permit himself to do. This is admirable enough —but it is not philosophical. No one in his senses would deny that François Villon was a person of instinct, that he was pitiably engrossed in his own self, that he was a licentious fellow; no one in his senses would call François Villon a naturalist. The point at issue lies where Humanism cannot take hold of it.

159

The anti-naturalist is still a naturalist, if he cannot get off his naturalistic plane. More is one because he presents a mechanical view of experience. A doctrine is not a method, and until it can be made one, the Humanists are "flattering themselves they are philosophizing and that they will so be good men."

III

How shall we know when we have values?—a more difficult problem than the mere conviction that we need them. There is no such thing as pure value, nor are there values separate from the means of creating and preserving them. There are certain definite ways in which men have had access to value in the past (the Humanists tell us that Dante had values, but not how he got them); but our problem is, Have we any of those ways now? If we have, how may they be used? Is there a condition or are there several conditions that must be met before we may use them?

We have seen the assumptions of the Humanists. The assumptions of this essay are that Humanism is not enough, and that if the values for which the Humanist pleads are to be made rational, even intelligible, the parallel condition of an objective religion is necessary. There should be a living center of action and judgment, such as we find in the great religions, which in turn grew out of this center. The act of "going into the Church" is not likely to supply the

160

convert with it. Yet, for philosophical consistency, this is what the Humanists should do. It is clear that this essay urges the claim of no special church, and it is in no sense a confession of faith; but the connection between the Reformation and the rise of Naturalism, and what I conceive the religious imagination to be, define the position that the Humanists must occupy if they wish to escape intellectual suicide. The religious unity of intellect and emotion, of reason and instinct, is the sole technique for the realization of values.

The virtue of religion is its successful representation of the problem of evil, for no metaphysical system has been able to account for evil in a unified world. We have seen how Mr. Foerster, wishing at once to cultivate natural human nature and to reject it, could not decide how far he wished to go in either direction. This was because his dualism was verbal; there were no really opposed principles; there was simply an infinite number of points on the same scale. And thus his opposition between Quality and Quantity was verbal too; it was Quantity versus Quantity, presided over by rootless Restraint, the referee who checked nothing but coherent thought. The Humanists tell us that somehow we have to do with Quality, yet since, for them, nature is the quantified nature of scientism and the mind is a quantified machine of moral ideas, it is difficult to see where Quality

161

comes from. The Humanists seem to use the word to mean something "better" than something else— the philosophical level at which the fashionable tailor uses it. For Quality in itself is neither good nor bad.

There is, then, a preliminary question to be asked: What is the source of qualitative experience? Both horns of his dualism being reduced to Quantity, the Humanist cannot tell us; and that is why much of his criticism gives you the feeling that he expects you to pluck values out of the air. Since the Humanist has not been philosophically hardy enough to work out of the naturalistic version of nature (which he naïvely accepts), since, in fact, he cannot root the concept of nature as Quantity out of his mind, his idea of Quality is irresponsible, foot-loose, highly transcendental in a kind of Concord sense.

The source of Quality is nature itself because it is the source of experience. It is only by holding to an idea that leaves nature an open realm of Quality that experience is possible at all; and, conversely, experience alone is the road to Quality. If an American zoölogist sees a certain Philippine cobra he doubtless says, "*Naja samaransis*"; the snake is merely an instance of the quantification of nature. The headhunter, however, has a more vivid feeling for the unique possibilities of the particular cobra; it may bite him; it may give him the evil eye—both richly qualitative experiences. For the Humanist, *opposing*

162

Quality to nature, has got it on the wrong side of his duality. Pure Quality would be pure evil, and it is only through the means of our recovery from a lasting immersion in it, it is only by maintaining the precarious balance upon the point of collapse into Quality, that any man survives his present hour; pure quality is pure disintegration. The scientist says, *"Naja samaransis"*; Mr. More, a cadence of the same theme— "Immoral"; Quality is quantified before we ever see it as Quality; and nature becomes a closed system of abstraction in which man is deprived of all experience whatever and, by being so deprived, reduced to an abstraction himself.

The religious attitude is the very sense (as the religious dogma is the definition) of the precarious balance of man upon the brink of pure Quality. But if you never have Quality, never have the challenge of evil, you have no religion—which is to say, you have no experience either. It is experience, immediate and traditional fused—Quality and Quantity—which is the means of validating values. Experience gives the focus to style, and style is the way anything is done. Rhetorical device is our abstract term for properties of style after style is achieved; they have never of themselves made one poem better than another.

Religion's respect for the power of nature lies in her contempt for knowledge of it; to quantify nature is ultimately to quantify ourselves. Religion is sat-

163

isfied with the dogma that nature is evil, and that our recovery from it is mysterious ("grace"). For the abstraction of nature ends, as we have seen, with the destruction of the reality of time, and immediate experience being impossible, so do all ideas of tradition and inherited order become timeless and incoherent. It is the indispensable office of the religious imagination that it checks the abstracting tendency of the intellect in the presence of nature. Nature abstract becomes man abstract, and he is at last condemned to a permanent immersion in pure and evil Quality; he is forever condemned to it because he can no longer see it for what it is. The protection of religion is the abstraction, not of nature, which so conceived would be the abstraction of abstraction, but of experience. It proposes a system of Quantity *against* nature; it is a quantitative version of the encounter between the head-hunter and the cobra; but it says nothing about the cobra-in-itself. The organized meaning of the encounters of man and nature, which are temporal and concrete, is religious tradition, and religious tradition is not exclusively the Church, but necessarily implies a way of life historically protected by the Church. The dogma acts for the recoil of the native from the snake: it is his technique for finding out the value of the encounter. Every such encounter is rich and unique in Quality: it is the temporal, never recurring focus, the new triumph, the re-affirmation of

164

the preserved experience of man. The modern Humanist, because of habitual reactions, recoils, but he has no reason for doing so, and his recoil is without value. He and the snake are one: Quantity versus Quantity; nature against nature; snake against snake; or, for that matter, man against man.

It is the failure of the Humanist to get out of this dilemma which makes his literary criticism feeble and incomplete. Mr. Foerster says: "It is best to face the issue in all candor"—the issue being Shakespeare. This poet merely "presents" life; he does not "interpret" it. If I had never read Shakespeare and had not read the rest of Mr. Foerster's book, his distinction would sound plausible; but having read his book, I know what he means, which is something very different from what he thinks he means. He means that the mind of Shakespeare was not a mechanism of moral ideas. The Humanists quarrel with literature because it cannot give them a philosophy and a church; but they keep turning to literature because they cannot find these things elsewhere. You cannot have the sense of literature without the prior, specific, and self-sufficient sense of something else. Without this you expect too much of literature; you expect of it a religion and a philosophy; and by expecting of it the wrong thing, you violate it, and in the end you get from it less than it is meant to yield; you get neither literature nor religion, nor anything that is

165

intelligible. You destroy literature without constructing a religion.

For, as M. Ramon Fernandez has recently said, with Aristotelian tact, Humanism should not pretend to be a "body of Doctrine"; it is "a resultant situation."

The American Humanists have tried to make the resultant situation its own background, because they lack the resultant situation itself. Humanism is too ambitious, with insufficient preparation. (I do not mean erudition.) It tries to take a short-cut to the resultant situation, and ignores the social difficulty of making or reconstructing an appropriate background. It ignores the philosophical difficulty of imagining what the background should be; it is an effort to imitate by rote the natural product of culture; it is a mechanical formula for the recovery of civilization. It is the cart before the horse, and because it gets the "philosophy" in the wrong place, it invites philosophical attack. Humanism should be culture, but it may be a little untamed in the Humanists until, as the digging of graves in the grave-diggers, "custom hath made it in them a property of easiness."

THE ALLIES OF HUMAN-
ISM ABROAD—BURKE

The Allies of Humanism Abroad

THE men whom the New Humanists in America recognize as their colleagues in France are advocates of Catholicism. Mr. Eliot in England, however, stands midway between the French position and the American attempt, under Mr. Babbitt, to consider Humanism as an independent moral technique. Being influenced by both M. Maurras and Mr. Babbitt, he effects somewhat of a synthesis, by showing how humanism hovers on the edge of religion, and how the social utility of humanism and religion may differ. Thus, in grouping these men, we come uncomfortably near to discussing several things at once. And there are sufficient divergencies among the various Humanists for us, in disagreeing with one of their number, to be in agreement with another. This fact makes any general refutation of their tenets impossible, and undesirable. The present notes on the Humanists abroad are offered, therefore, more as comment than as polemic.

I am in sympathy with other writers in this volume who have been wrathful. I feel that Mr. Paul Elmer More, for instance, is something to be wrathful about. His article in *Humanism and America* is not the article of an inquirer, but the article of a debater. Consider how, to make an analysis of modern art, he chooses as one of his texts a little nursery rime by Louis Aragon (who has written works of great talent), a casual jingle about *la réa, la réa, la réalité,* and bears down upon it with all the wisdom of the ages. Mr. More scores a victory, a positive triumph, which no sane observer could hope to deny him. But the men I am about to discuss, and particularly Mr. Eliot, win battles less overwhelmingly.

I

Charles Maurras, an ardent polemic writer, prominent in the *Action Française,* finds many social ills— declining population, abandonment of the farms, deforestation, revolutionary agitation in the industrial centers, desiccation of local life, centralization, and increasing control by the State. At the same time, however, he holds that "the development of industry, commerce, and agriculture, under the encouragement of science and machinery, the enormous economic translation which they instigated, the resultant soaring of finance, the general activity which it represents, the extension of life, the multiplication and growth of fortunes, particularly personal fortunes, are facts of the highest quality. We may distrust them for one or another of their possible consequences. But the more we examine these facts in themselves, the less cause we find for blaming them."

M. Maurras has not, to my knowledge, ever discussed specifically why the vices listed above are not attributable to the same cause as the virtues. Though he feels that the vices all "flow from a single historic source," he does not believe that the virtues come from the same source as the vices. To some persons the vices and virtues might seem of a piece, obverse and reverse of the same factors. Certain of the great fortunes he admires, for instance, must have arisen out of deforestation, or their development must have had integral bearing upon disorders in the industrial centers. It is no mere accident, however, that M. Maurras chooses to find different origins for our modern vices and virtues. For he proposes to attack the vices at the roots, and did the vices and virtues have the same roots, by destroying the roots of the vices he would necessarily destroy the roots of the virtues. On this matter, highly important to his system, he does not enlighten us. His doctrine, which we shall call the doctrine of divergent genesis, is taken for granted.

Following his own line of reasoning, we must leave the modern "virtues" to flourish of themselves, while we turn our attention to his genesis of the vices. The vices are our inheritance from the French Revolution, and stem with great consistency from the pages of Rousseau, Kant, and Hegel. Essentially the trouble lies in the emphasis which Rousseau and subsequent romantics place upon the individual will. American Humanists, who accept M. Maurras as one of their own number in France, attack romantic literature on the grounds that it minimizes the will, but M. Maurras situates the romantic error in the stressing of it.

By the coarsest part of Rousseau's public, the German, his doctrines were accepted to the letter: what had once been considered ignorance, imperfection, and weakness, could now lay claim to a barbarous freshness, with corresponding superiority over the aridity and exhaustion imputed to every instructed, cultivated, and mellowed race. Arts, letters, science, tradition, the past, in short everything that was *finished*, no longer counted. Pure nature led immediately into the divine, and it alone could address the world in the infallible words of the future. Under this subversive ideology, one looked for guidance to ignorant men and backward peoples. Henceforth, in verse and prose, philosophy and the novel, you find "this newborn principle of the absolute sovereignty of will and human nature, and of conscience, which is the most arbitrary of sentiments."

M. Maurras pictures France after the Thirty Years' War, entering the great period of its genius and thought, the apogee of its order and nature—a monarchic State, a Catholic religion, and an art to express this fair season appropriately. In their times, he says, Ronsard, Malherbe, Corneille, and Bossuet defended the State, the king, the fatherland, property, the family, and religion. But the romantics attacked the laws or the State, public and individual discipline, the fatherland, the family, and private property. Their success seemed almost wholly a matter of pleasing the opposition and working towards anarchy.

How different are things under the romantic decay! Indeed, in reading M. Maurras' picture of the monarchy, and his plea for another king, one is at a loss to explain how the Revolution ever got under way. It seems to have arisen as an act of perversity, a gratuitous development in literary style. Could a movement go so far unless its slogans were needed? I grant that many of these slogans now seem absurd. The doctrine of the innate goodness of man, of man born good and depraved by society, becomes meaningless in the light of recent psychology (particularly in the light of those Behavioristic theories which the Humanists despise), as likewise does the theological doctrine of original sin. But diseases are cured by poisons; one error is canceled by another. Whatever the doctrine of natural goodness was as the statement of a fact, in its function as a working principle, a slogan, it acted as the neutralization of a formula which no longer served. It was a plus sign to balance the old minus sign and allow one to start at zero. Yet I am willing to grant that it did damage, since I don't know of any principle that didn't. Under both systems, people have burned.

M. Maurras matches the actual republic against his

173

ideal monarchy. Consider, for instance, his advantage in comparing the financial condition of the monarchy with the financial condition of France between 1789 and 1799. Further, consider the great war which Rousseau caused in 1914. I have never understood the reasoning about this war. Messrs. Maurras, Massis, and Maritain, and our own Mr. Babbitt, would give the impression that war is a new thing. None of them, to my knowledge, has distinguished between this war and wars of the past. Owing to vaster populations, and greater scientific improvements, and the survival of religious feelings in patriotism, the war was exceptionally big, but I have not seen the Humanists distinguish it in principle from previous wars. Possibly this particular war, in its particular form, would have been avoided had religious feelings remained religious feelings without being deflected into patriotism, and had the Church been a power for economic unification, though we have the example of the Crusades to remind us that Catholicism can make wars of its own. Our hope for the future avoidance of such disasters lies greatly in the further weakening of the religious, of the respect for authority as moral authority survives in its secular form of patriotism—but this hope must be deferred until there are fewer men like M. Maurras in the world. For he openly conceives of his country's glory as an efficiently warlike glory, condemning a republican

174

State because it tends to let its army and navy languish in times of peace, and pointing to the Treaty of Versailles as a proof that a republic "does not know how to prepare, or conclude, or exploit a peace." Because France was a republic, it could not keep its grip on the Ruhr, the Emperor of Germany was "practically released from all pursuit," and the standing army was decreased. Or going further back, because France was a republic the guilty Dreyfus was released, by a violation of Article 445 of the Code d'Instruction Criminelle.

A patriot, and a royalist, but also an agnostic, M. Maurras comes to embrace Catholicism for purely political reasons. As a political credo he adheres to "the learned cortège of councils, of popes, and of all the great men of the modern élite," nor will he turn from these to place his confidence "in the gospels of four obscure Jews." His religious affiliations on these terms have been embarrassing to the Church, and in 1926 Rome called believers away from any allegiance to this dangerous and brilliant man.

A monarchic system, he tells us, would avoid the constant "civil war" of political factions, a breach which weakens a nation's "furious movements of anger and enmity" against a foreign government by creating intestine broils. Religious dissension, we learn in passing, would be eliminated. Since "a democracy must rely upon the votes of its citizens," a

175

democratic administration is "less free than any other form of government to ignore what is going on in the hearts and minds of those who are its masters." It "must depend upon their votes, and thus indirectly, upon their feelings and thoughts." The democratic state cannot consistently hold any one spiritual doctrine, any one philosophic, historic, or moral theory. Since the State was more decentralized under earlier monarchies, he holds that monarchy would enable similar decentralization again, though he does not explain how this would come about in opposition to the purely industrial factors which seem so powerful a factor in causing centralization to-day. Universal suffrage now being a fact, he will not insist that it be abandoned. We need but diminish the "competence of the vote." The people, that is, might elect representatives, who would voice their hopes to the king, and the king would be at liberty to hear them. Given a king, democracy would be "limited, balanced, corrected, tempered by another principle which is not drawn from itself. For to right one election by another election is like regulating the rainstorm by the tempest." The king would also serve to offset the power of plutocracy. As for artists, who are now at the mercy of wealth, they are invited to shift their allegiance to the monarch, since this would be a nobler allegiance, and one under which they flourished in the past.

176

II

With M. Massis, who has reversed himself, and turned from an opponent of Maurras to a fierce disciple, the cause of the ill is broadened. He finds the welfare of the Church Militant endangered by the Orient. We may oppress Asia with our armies, but Asia is a still greater menace to us—she threatens to disintegrate us with her philosophy. Romanticism and Rousseau here become secondary—it is the Buddha that threatens us. The philosophy of the Buddha is creeping over Europe, and undermining our healthy realism, our philosophy of absolute values, our belief in the individual person. We must distrust the "Hindu Brahman and the Chinese ascetic"—particularly, I might add, since certain American Humanists have been tricked into welcoming these influences. M. Massis reconstructs for us the ideal Occidental: "The Christian is the runner in the stadium, the man who aims ever higher, who tirelessly propels his whole being towards that which is outside himself, in advance of himself, and which he will not reach until the end of his action, in a struggle in which defeat is rewarded with more than death. The heaven to which he aspires is not proposed to him as the annihilation of nirvâna, but as something to be taken by force and violence. *Quantum potes, tantum aude.*" It suggests, among other things, the Spaniard in Mexico.

Let us consider, however, what this Christian soldier has to fear. The Buddha imperils him thus: "Those who do me hurt and those who give me joy, towards all I am the same. I know neither inclination nor hatred. In pleasure and in pain, I remain unmoved; in honor and the absence of honor, everywhere I remain the same." Safety for safety, the Christian warrior seems too well armed; a dissenter might hope to fare better under the Asiatic system.

The *Defence of the West* is a vast *argumentum ad hominem*, justifying the "truth" of the faith on the basis of its past profits. Furthermore, the Church is taken as the *cause* of our civilization, not as one of its modes, though the logical reasons for this assumption are not given. If I choose to hold that Catholicism was merely one of the many conflicting ways in which the genius of our civilization manifested itself (often in conflict, for instance, with our science) but was not necessarily a prime mover, M. Massis has provided no refutation. He has assumed that concomitance is identical with cause. He happens to have chosen the Church as a cause. But some non-humanist economists, noting that machinery was absent in the Middle Ages and is prevalent to-day, have by the same *post hoc, ergo propter hoc* method of reasoning concluded that machinery is the source of our difficulties. M. Massis' argument for Catholic religion, when reduced to a syllogistic form, must run

178

somewhat like this: we reached a more satisfactory state of civilization in the past: *and* we had a strong Church in the past; therefore the Church was the cause of the more satisfactory civilization. Some might choose to say that the satisfactory civilization was the cause of the Church. Let us, for the moment, assume that the past *was* more satisfactory, though M. Massis has gone to no great pains to prove it. And let us even assume that his syllogism is cogent, that the Church was the cause of this more satisfactory past. This would still not prove that the Church could be the cause of a similar satisfactory condition in the future, since so many other factors have changed. To prove that a Church was needed for a medieval system of society does not prove that it is needed for ours.

M. Massis' refutation of anti-realistic thinking is in keeping: "If the concept of being has no real existence, then there is no absolute knowledge or objective truth. The universe is without causality and without finality; life is purely 'phenomenal'; the notions of good and evil and the idea of liberty are at once destroyed; . . . our body is nothing more than a 'colony of souls,' an 'aggregate of divergent tendencies and instincts,' and the *self* nothing more than a stronger instinct that prevails over the others." Here the basis of his cogency is: this notion is unpalatable, therefore it is wrong.

179

He does not discuss the possibility that a civilization like ours, which has changed so radically from the time when the Church flourished, might need a new philosophy if it is to adjust itself to these new conditions. With our present multiplication of power, whereby a very slight effort can do enormous mischief, and the unemotional pressing of a lever can, in a few seconds, cause an amount of damage which once required the sustained wrath of hundreds of men, perhaps we need precisely some element of Oriental passivity if our civilization is not to be endangered by its own energy.

III

With Jacques Maritain we pass into a much calmer territory. This subtle dialectician is a pleasure to read, if only through delight in the processes of his mind. Well equipped in the methodology of the scholastics, he has devoted himself to the reapplication of Thomist philosophy to modern conditions. He is not a pamphleteer, a player upon fears and resentments, as are our two previous "Humanists" who, even if they were right, would only too often be winning us to their cause for the wrong reasons. He is fighting under difficulties—for to-day relativism is easy, and absolutism is hard—so one can better admire the sportsmanship of his struggle than its results. His most characteristic trait is his tact. Like Mgr. De-

180

ploige in his *Conflit de la Morale et de la Sociologie*, he works to prove that the system of Saint Thomas had taken care of practically everything that could happen; he shows that all significant modern tendencies were either refuted in advance or admitted in advance; and he makes his pages both entertaining as performances and innocuous as conclusions.

Consider, for instance, his attack upon Einstein. Admitting himself incapable of discussing Einstein as a physicist, he grants the validity of Einstein's physical theories, then advances to attack Einstein as a metaphysician. Whatever the physical world may be, he insists that by the Thomist nomenclature a realistic world is preserved as a metaphysical reality. It is delicate work, deftly accomplished, but metaphysics is saved at the expense of its importance. If a non-Einsteinian metaphysics grants that it cannot refute an Einsteinian physics, we can only say that it has gracefully retired.

Essentially, M. Maritain seems to preserve his absolutes by the Platonic system—they are turned into relatives so far as the world of our experience is concerned, but they exist as pure, as absolutes, in God, and can be handled as such by the processes of reason. I have wondered why our pragmatists do not begin by granting their opponents the existence of absolute truth, beauty, and goodness. For so far as the experimentalism of the world goes, we handle these

181

things only in their relative aspects, and therefore all our judgments are the same whether the absolutes exist in heaven or not. (I omit now the unarguable and unprovable doctrine of divine revelation by which the saint could presumably see the absolutes as absolutes.) Indeed, a complete systematization of beauty, for instance, would still leave room for endless controversy as to whether a specific work satisfied the requirements of the scheme.

Whatever one may think of M. Maritain's findings, there is an inspiration in the spectacle of his meticulousness. The mere suavity of his work restores our faith in the culture of his religion, where the vigor of Messrs. Maurras and Massis arouses misgivings. More enterprising esthetically than our American Humanists, he can respect the "rules of art" while holding that one can observe these rules by breaking them—and he suggests that Aristotle would, for this reason, enjoy the music of Erik Satie. Similarly with the argument as to the "unmorality" of art, he contrives ably by holding (a) that the artist, as artist, is entitled to be unmoral, that his ends are sufficient to themselves, but (b) that the artist, as a man, must adapt his work to the prescriptions of morals. M. Maritain shows us the inclusive side of Catholic thinking, that aspect of the Catholic method whereby more could always be let in if it had to be (Saint Thomas, at least as interpreted by M. Maritain, seems

182

to have avoided anything as rigid as, for instance, the Protestant doctrine of predestination, by which definite inclusions and exclusions are made once and for all). The new inclusions are not creative, to be sure—M. Maritain shows that the Church can often find ways of quieting the stormers at its doors by admitting them, but these stormers must come from without.

IV

We turn to Mr. Eliot, who recently announced that his "general point of view may be described as classical in literature, royalist in politics, and anglo-catholic in religion." However, when one recalls the nature of Mr. Eliot's verse, and the consternation which this verse has caused to some of our leading American Humanists, one quickly realizes that, as his own examples of classicism could appear in the *Little Review,* perhaps his royalism and Anglo-Catholicism will be equally a development rather than a simple reaction. On this score we are still left greatly in doubt, however, as the "three small books in preparation . . . will not be ready for a considerable time." So far we have only some very conscientious technical criticism of English divines, and three articles on Humanism which have presented some difficulty for masters of Humanist thought.

Mr. Eliot is probably nearer the historical meaning

183

of humanism than the American Humanists in that he emphasizes its purely skeptical or negative aspects. He sees humanism valuable as a corrective of other excesses, a discourager of fanaticisms, be they the fanaticisms of "naturism" or of religion. In his way he parallels M. Maritain's (or Saint Thomas's!) inclusiveness by recognizing that we must have humanistic skepticism to undermine bigotry, and must have bigotry to counterbalance the quietism of the skeptical. Like making a saint of Judas, he even holds that the Church is kept pure by the attacks of its heretics.

To what extent the "inner check" formulated by American Humanists becomes an "outer check" of conflicting parties, Mr. Eliot has not yet made clear. Democracy has at least the self-contained dualism of balancing election by election (which has been described as "bloodless revolution"). In M. Maurras we found this system condemned as needless conflict. M. Maurras seems to be tending in his monarchic system towards political monism, whereby the benevolent monarch (he is always assumed to be benevolent) would be able to apply the requisite social remedies without the interference of party maneuverings; yet M. Maurras does have the hint of a counterprinciple, a dualism, since he seems to imply at times that the interests of plutocracy and those of the monarch would differ substantially—or again, we will

184

recall, he sometimes considers his king as a "check" upon democracy.

Returning to Mr. Eliot, we find that he has not yet made clear to what extent skepticism (humanism as he sees it) and fanaticism (religion, naturism) must coexist in the individual, whether they function as mutual checks within the individual or tend to manifest themselves as party strife between "pure" skeptics and "pure" fanatics. Perhaps either attitude corrodes the other, so that the outward struggle has its inward parallel.

At the present time, however, we can only say that, if Mr. Eliot is the link between the self-styled Humanists of America and the neo-Catholics of France, he has served to imperil the value of American Humanism as a "secular religion." The moral imperatives of Humanism he sees as a survival of religious imperatives. For Humanism in America is not built upon the cult of esthetic sensibility as was the humanism of the Renaissance; it advocates a "will to refrain," not on the hedonistic grounds that we must refrain from indulgence in one pleasure the better to indulge in another, but because of some categorical respect for a "will to refrain" in itself. There are only two kinds of sanctions: deductive sanctions (metaphysical, theological, "consensus omnium") and inductive sanctions (utilitarian, pragmatic). And the "will to refrain" is sanctioned deductively, as an "ought,"

185

and not as an instrument for personal advantage. It is, as Mr. Eliot holds, a survival of religious certainty —and accordingly, if Humanism is to accept it as a base, Humanism must accept religion as its source. By being in itself an attenuated form of religion, Humanism must then have at hand a flourishing religion in order that new generations of Humanists may have something to attenuate. American Humanism is thus placed before these alternatives: either it must drop the "inner check" as a moral imperative, or it must found this "inner check" on religious sanctions. Mr. Babbitt, in trying to save his cause, has written:

"In his attempt to show the inadequacy of humanism apart from dogmatic and revealed religion, Mr. T. S. Eliot has painted a picture of the humanist exercising in a sort of psychic solitude self-control purely for the sake of control. It is evident, however, that the real humanist consents, like Aristotle, to limit his desires only in so far as this limitation can be shown to make for his own happiness."

The limitation of one's desires "only in so far as this limitation can be shown to make for his own happiness" would involve very delicate distinctions if it is to be kept different from the hedonistic scheme of canceling one desire by another. I do not mean to imply that I find anything reprehensible in such a hedonistic scheme; but the Humanists, with vested interests in the "inner check," have necessarily attacked it, since a simple recognition of conflicting appetites would leave no room for an inner check. One must refrain from gluttony because of a will to refrain, they would contend, and not merely because he desires an athletic body. This inner check has a suspect history. The Greeks found that moderation was a serviceable instrument for satisfactory living; in this they were doubtless accurate; but with their customary hypostatizing methods, they erected moderation itself into a kind of entity, a spiritual *thing*, so that it became looked upon as something to be attained rather than a means of attaining something; and thus, having been made a purpose, it now requires another means, the "inner check," for its attainment. Restore it as a means, which it unquestionably can be, and there is no place left for the "inner check."

v

In conclusion, what objection could one possibly have to M. Maritain's Church? It is innocuous, it furnishes elevated topics of discussion and a deft method for discussing them. It is doubtless some such gentlemanly Church that Mr. Eliot has in mind when casting his important vote for Anglo-Catholicism. Could Messrs. Maurras and Massis have remained silent, we might readily have thought that the militant aspects of orthodoxy were gone forever, and have easily been won over to this calm and ineffectual

187

body. But the two bellicose champions remind us of the secular tasks to which a vigorous religion can always be put.

I grant that there are many unsatisfactory elements in our society at the present time. I grant that many things are in a decline. Yet we are always in the decline of something, and merely because historians happen to choose certain manifestations of culture for their topics, let us not assume that there is an *absolute decline* when we find that some of these manifestations are declining. Even a decline of "ideals" is no reliable test of impoverishment. It is a prevalent habit, for instance, to rate American civilization as inferior to Russian on the grounds that the American system is without ideals, whereas the Russian reformers bring great moralistic zest to the handling of their problems. Looking further, we find that much of this moralistic zest is expended on the effort to obtain some such efficiently functioning system of distribution as exists in America already. When trains run on time, good train schedules must necessarily disappear as an "ideal," and similarly the nobler ideals of coöperation can vanish from our vocabularly. We may find much evidence in the disparateness of feudal barons to justify a contention that the ideal of Catholic unity and order flourished best when such unity and order were socially nonexistent. In one respect we may all be followers of

Rousseau—all victimized by the hypertrophy of a critical vocabulary, all finding ills because of the growing nomenclature for ills, and mistaking our discovery of these ills for the growth of them. And we tend, among other things, to make no distinction between a loss of liberty and a rise of traffic regulations.

But even if the unsatisfactory elements in the life of to-day were proved unmistakably attributable to Rousseau, and to romanticism, and to the humanitarian theories which the Humanists attack as the corollary of the doctrine of man's original goodness, we should still not be forced to conclude that an anti-Rousseau, anti-romantic, and anti-humanitarian policy is required for righting these unsatisfactory elements. We can still assert that these excesses are capable of refinement within their own terms, that every romantic deviation merely forms the basis of its own classicism once the process of maturing and revision through successive generations has been completed. The loss of authoritarian principles, so decried by the Humanists, may be a "healthy" process, a stage in readjustment, admittedly an impoverishment in itself, as with the razing of an old structure, but necessary to new building. The humanitarian "gospel of service" which Mr. Babbitt sees flourishing at a time when we have in America an opportunity for a Humanistic "education with the idea of leisure enshrined at its very center," does not seem on the face of it so in-

189

nately wicked. There is cause to believe that it can develop into something more intelligent and socially more advantageous than its present industrial counterpart of mere increased production. The desire for leisure in such form is, after all, no exclusive possession of a Humanistic code. And its tenets can arise as well out of mass production as out of the minimum production attitude which seems to have preceded the machine age. Indeed, the "problem of unemployment" can be looked upon as the first crude emergence of universal leisure; and humanitarian policies would be enough to make leisure generally attainable by leading to the redistribution of unemployed hours, dividing them among an entire group of workers rather than heaping them upon some and requiring others to work overtime.

This brings me to the real danger which seems to me to lurk at this time in the focusing of our interests upon such indirect or "cultural" cures as religion or Humanism. The issues to be faced are confused by the introduction of alien terms. To ask for the restoration of religion in order that religion may in turn restore society is to focus one's exhortations upon indirect remedies. For if religion were successfully restored, we should then have to begin studying the application of religion to these specific social problems. It would be too much like getting stick to beat dog to bite pig to make it jump over the stile. Also, it

190

seems to be about as enormous an undertaking to get religion back as it is to handle our secular problems on a direct secular basis. Though it is probably true that ninety people out of a hundred would still pray in an earthquake, this tendency to bargain with the Father is not much on which to reërect an all-pervading structure of faith.

There are two ways of reaching a satisfactory adjustment between the individual and his environment. He may change the environment to suit his desire, or he may change his attitude to suit the environment. We must have a reserve of subjective changes to fall back upon when the objective changes prove beyond our power, but let us never resign ourselves to an ache by recourse to philosophy until we are sure that the ache cannot be removed. Bad hygiene in the East bears witness that the subjective adjustment can be made too soon. We need not call our present system good. We need merely recognize that it is undeniably present and that, like a fire, it must be met in its own terms. We must reserve our nobler manner for less homely issues.

Dignity? Yes, there seems to be a thirst for personal dignity. There is a trace of the hysterical, the devious, in this need of dignity. Dignity belongs to the conquered; one leaves the room with dignity when he has been routed; the victor can romp. Dignity is a subjective adjustment. It is objectively unpliant;

it is unbiological, a dignified man could not run from a lion. One meets facts objectively without dignity. One sacrifices his authority, first asking what mean task the outside thing demands of him. Dignity is Ptolemaic, indignity is Copernican. The development of man in Europe, some one has said, has been a loss of personal dignity in proportion to his mastery of nature.

HUMANISM AND THE FINE ARTS—Hitchcock, Jr.

= HENRY-RUSSELL HITCHCOCK, JR. =

HUMANISM AND THE FINE ARTS

> To sum up, Art is more exclusively intellectual
> than Prudence. Whereas Prudence has for subject
> the practical intelligence *in so far as it presupposes
> the right will* and depends therefrom, Art takes no
> account of the proper good of the will, and of the
> ends which it follows along its line of human ap-
> petites; and if it supposes a certain rectitude in the
> appetite, this is still in relation to some ends prop-
> erly so-called. As a Science it is rivetted to an ob-
> ject (object to be made, it is true, not to be con-
> templated). It is only accidentally that it uses
> the roundabout way of deliberation and counsel.
> Although it produces individual acts and effects,
> it does not judge, except accessorily, from circum-
> stantial contingencies; so, less than Prudence, it
> looks at the individuation of actions and the *hic
> et nunc*. In a word, if in the way of its material,
> which is contingent, it runs with Prudence rather
> than with Science, *according to its formal ratio
> and qua virtue*, it runs with the Science and the
> *habitus* of the speculative intelligence rather than
> with Prudence: *ars magis convenit cum habitibus
> speculativis in ratione virtutis, quam cum pruden-
> tia*. The Scientist is an Intellectual who demon-
> strates: the Artist is an Intellectual who does
> things: the Prudent Man is an intelligent Volun-
> tary Agent who acts well.—From Maritain's *Art
> et scolastique*, translated as *Philosophy of Art*, by
> REV. JOHN O'CONNOR, pp. 26-27.

OUR conception of the artist is an inheritance
from Romanticism. Murger's heroes remain
the type of the artist, however doubtful we
may be of the quality of their art, and Murger's heroes
were certainly in no sense Humanists. It might be

195

possible to recast our conception completely, to deny the validity of the dominant artistic type of the past hundred years, as the Humanists deny the validity of the dominant literary type. We should then have to deny as well the productions which, to avoid begging the question, must be called the most typical, the most characteristic, rather than the greatest of the same period. Our attitude toward the age of Romanticism and the succeeding age, which the Humanists are inclined somewhat indefinitely to label as that of Modernism, might, in other words, resemble that of the humanists of the Renaissance toward the Middle Ages. It was the Romantics who reaffirmed the validity, cultural and artistic, of the Middle Ages, refusing more and more to believe in a Dark Age even of very brief duration. Curiously enough the Middle Ages to-day provide an important source from which the more syncretistic Humanists draw some of their strength. Without the architecture of the Middle Ages in their armory they would leave to their opponents too strong a weapon in the field of the Fine Arts, and the guild training of the artists receives their whole-hearted approval, however much their Aristotelianism may differ from that of Saint Thomas.

Oddly enough our conception of the artist has received increasing sanction from the study of the history of art, an activity in its present breadth of scope largely Romantic in origin, but capable nevertheless of non-Romantic and even of anti-Romantic treatment. It is hardly disputable that in all ages in which artists have had existence as individuals and not as mere hands working for a superior and completely dominant extra-artistic will, the study of the *œuvre* and the correlation of the *œuvre* where possible with the biography, displays in the majority of cases that, consciously or unconsciously, drastically or compromisingly, the artists of pre-Romantic times fulfilled our own conception of the artist. This discovery resembles the discovery of the picturesque and in a particular sense the discovery of nature. There is endless testimony that the appreciation for the picturesque, as for Burke's sublime, existed previous to Romanticism but that appreciation was, as we should say, uncritical, and not isolated by analysis. The appreciation of nature by the Western European man previous to Romanticism, was possibly more fitful and individual, but the discovery of nature is not therefore the less valid. But Romanticism in its analytical disintegration of the Baroque—or if the term be objected to as unduly weighted by connotation—the post-Renaissance-world, went always too far, failing for the most part, from the enjoyment of its specific discoveries, to relate them to the esthetic or to the cultural whole. Thus the picturesque degenerated into the anecdotal and the appreciation of nature became a cult of which the most extraordinary result artistically was perhaps the rise to dominance of landscape art in painting—which had begun during the Baroque—and the subordination of architecture to gardening. Similarly the Romantic discovery of the artist as a type led to an exaggeration of the characteristic at the expense of the universal, making possible the phenomenon that for the study of Rimbaud knowledge of the years after his literary production ceased entirely is as important for the understanding of his *œuvre* in the broadest sense as analysis of his actual writings. But it is of course not my intention to stray into the field of literary criticism, difficult as it is when the leaders of Humanism have so largely restricted themselves to its consideration. Nor is it profitable to repeat what Mr. Mather has done so well for the Humanists in "The Plight of Our Arts" and indicate in what fashion social and economic changes in the nineteenth century came to cast out the artist from the general body of society, destroying his common function and further emphasizing his unique and peculiar position. For there is nothing specifically Humanistic in regretting with Mr. Mather the breakdown of the pre-nineteenth century system of training the artist; nor does Mr. Mather support the illusion which was so dear to the later Romantics that that particular system can ever be built up again. Mr. Mather, however, remains too consistently in the mood of regret and fails, perhaps,

198

completely to balance possible gains against certain losses. He is inclined to imply that the building up of a new system lies largely outside the scope of the artist with which one can well agree without admitting that the artist could regain a satisfactory relation to society only if that society, by diligently following Messrs. Babbitt and More and their like, were to become at least effectively, if not universally, Humanistic.

Mr. Mather is not a very helpful ally to the Humanists. He does not castigate very sternly the manifestations of Romanticism and Modernism in the arts and possesses, temperamentally rather than rationally, a catholic, if somewhat conservative, taste. A Babbitt come to judgment in the fine arts would find very much to do, the importance of which Mr. Mather seems not to have realized, either from a propagandist or an historical standpoint. The question of what are the manifestations of Romanticism in the fine arts, of when they began, of how they developed, of the forms in which they were continued into what the Humanists call, in literature and general ideas, the era of Modernism, he all but entirely omits. Except for remarks of a very incidental nature he makes no attempt, moreover, to correlate the Romantic movement in literature with the coeval movements in art, or to estimate how far the manifestations in art were independent and parallel, and how

199

far they were the direct carrying over from literature of the ideas of Rousseau and the English poets, of Mme. de Staël and Goethe, of Chateaubriand and Victor Hugo. Of course there is here labor for half a lifetime; but it is possible to embark upon it, to do for painting, let us say, something I myself have elsewhere begun to do, however inadequately and tentatively, for architecture. For this a mood and a documentation not wholly dissimilar to that of Mr. Babbitt was of assistance; but less so than that of many more objective studies in the general field, as diverse in subject matter and point of view as Christopher Hussey's *The Picturesque*, Kenneth Clark's *Gothic Revival*, Daniel Mornet's *Romantisme au 18ᵉ siècle* and Pierre Gaxotte's *Revolution Française*. Instead of embarking on such an enterprise, for which the Humanist standpoint in art would seem to have the utmost need, for Mr. Babbitt has not damned in literature with the full vigor of his vituperation matters that he has not at least inspected and correlated whatever may be his body of information with regard to more contemporary phenomena, Mr. Mather in his *Modern Painting* has been content for the most part to fill in again the outline of the minor movements since the mid-eighteenth century according to the definitions left by the succeeding generations that produced them. He has found little bad in each phase that was not conspicuous to those who immediately followed it

200

with a minor rebellion, and little good that is not a mere dilution of the claims of contradictory generations of laudatory critics. That he has done this, as the Humanist should, with moderation and urbanity, with grace of phrase and scrupulous politeness, cannot make that which is intellectually slight more than slight, nor that which merely summarizes a past epoch, the opening of a new epoch in the criticism of art. The comparison of such a work with the *Art et scolastique* of Jacques Maritain, whom Mr. Foerster at times would appear to claim most unjustly as an ally of the American Humanists, is a sufficient indication of the difference there is between the true application of an ideological system to the fine arts—in the case of Jacques Maritain, Catholic Neo-Thomism —and the retelling of a familiar tale with largely extraneous obeisances to a group of literary critics. It is far from my intention to attack the writings of Mr. Mather. They are distinguished in a field which tends to forget the graces of good writing and to become falsified by the exaggerations of the specialist, and by excellences of moderation in dealing with error for which anti-Humanists more than Humanists may be truly grateful. I would only with all respect suggest that the Humanists have not in Mr. Mather a very vigorous bearer for their "tiny banner."

II

Mr. More, with more energy and enthusiasm if infinitely less experience and depth of appreciation, has also entered the field of the fine arts. But he has approached the problem of Romanticism from the wrong end and attacked with all the energy of which he is capable the esthetic of Croce and the painting of the Expressionists, matters which many who oppose the Humanists would consider as the mere reduction to the absurd of Romanticism and Modernism—to use again that peculiarly offensive and ambiguous term to which the Humanists almost alone among respectable critics have given currency. But Mr. More is not at all, as Mr. Mather in his history is so often, a half repentant impressionist. He could not encompass that extraordinary sequence from mild but full praise of Sargent's mural decorations to mild but equally full praise of Cézanne, which others beside myself must find extraordinary in Mr. Mather's *Modern Painting*. Unfortunately he is even less familiar, it would appear, with what the Expressionists paint than with what Mr. Joyce writes; and although the Demon of the Absolute in the guise of spontaneity is an admirably ringing phrase for the art of Klee, Kandinsky and Mirò—at best but a very small fragment of the whole of even twentieth century painting—it must fail to satisfy those who have studied

202

their work and that of other contemporaries with any thoroughness, particularly as the tendency of modern painting for at least fifteen years has been quite as much away from as toward the absolute in all guises.

The Suprematists and the Elementarists, it is true, aim at an absolute the reverse of spontaneous but they are no longer of great intrinsic importance nor are they particularly influential upon the younger painters. The Surrèalistes represent the cult of spontaneity; but they have bestowed their approval on many painters in whose work there is very little of it. Mirò alone among their major men seems to justify to the full Mr. More's tirades; and even among his limited group of admirers Mirò finds few if any imitators. The difficulty with the absolute is practical rather than critical. As you approach any absolute the field narrows, a very few paintings exhaust the possibilities and it is increasingly difficult to distinguish one from another. If you have, for example, reached the point of painting a black circle upon a black field, as Lissitzky is said—probably falsely—to have done, painting has little more left for you in that direction, or indeed for any one else! But if you are a Lissitzky, it is possible that typographical design may pose for you, extra-esthetically, innumerable problems which, with the training of abstract painting, you can handle with extreme success. In a far

203

less extreme form of abstractionism Le Corbusier has
been, and indeed remains, a minor master. His painting will never be other than secondary to that of
Ozenfant—a master incidentally already far on the
return voyage from the absolute—but the training his
painting gives him has found its full fruition in the
brilliant qualities of design in the *machines à habiter*
he builds as an architect.

To attack the cult of the absolute in modern painting is already almost as useless as to attack the time-
of-day art of Impressionism as developed in the later
work of Monet, which must be equally offensive to
the Humanists as a prime manifestation of Naturism
in art. The manners of spontaneity and of geometry
may continue to be practiced through the lifetime of
certain artists now in early middle life. But historically speaking they are over, and their immediate
effect—regardless of critical approval or disapproval
—is bound to be and has already begun to be, a reaction as I have pointed out in an article in *The Arts* on
"New Painters of Mystery and Sentiment." It is perhaps possible to canalize or to mold that reaction; but
it is silly merely from the wrong side of the fence—
from never having been over the hurdle in experience
—to attempt to batter it down. It will fall down
surely as rapidly as did the Versailles decorative manner after the death of Lebrun.

I have devoted an inordinate amount of time to a

mere incident in Mr. More's writing and I am compelled therefore to postpone consideration of Mr. Babbitt's partial consideration of the fine arts in *The New Laokoon* to a concluding note. The attention these two leading minds among the Humanists have given to the fine arts is at best very incidental. Mr. Foerster neglects them even more completely. He has an irritating habit, in those magical formulas of his which read like the inscriptions on public libraries, of mentioning the name of Phidias. If this name is to be taken as anything but a resonant rallying cry, I suppose it refers to the mind that directed the execution of the Parthenon friezes, pediments, and possibly of the entire building. For surely even the layman can hardly be much impressed with what we are able to reconstruct of the chryselephantine Athena Parthenos or the Olympian Zeus, from coins and statuettes. An impressionist critic it is true might be carried to enthusiasm by the mere word chryselephantine, but surely not a Humanist. But even the knowledge that Mr. Foerster approves the frieze and the pediments of the Parthenon and doubtless the building itself would do little to guide a young sculptor or architect desirous of following the Humanistic path, and almost nothing at all for a young painter.

Before attempting to establish for ourselves an outline of a critique of the arts from the dicta of the general Humanistic theory, something must be said of the writing, if not of the art, of Mr. Kenyon Cox to whom the posthumous honor has come of having his books entered, with those of Mr. Mather and Mr. Brownell, upon the brief list of Humanistic writings on the fine arts. Mr. Cox does much, curiously enough, to establish the fact upon which we have earlier insisted, that the majority among the important artists of the European past were artists according to the Romantic conception of the term. He makes this particularly clear with regard to Michelangelo. "In a word, Michelangelo was a great *Romantic* genius." He says no less explicitly of Rembrandt that he "was one of the greatest Romantic painters of all time."

The case of Humanism in art is presented chiefly and most effectively through consideration of Raphael and Rubens, and most clearly in a comparison of Veronese with his two contemporaries and compatriots, Titian and Tintoretto, who are regarded as less balanced and therefore inferior to him. Considering that Mr. Cox was a mural painter active in that abortive American Renaissance which grew out of the World's Fair of 1893, his preference for Veronese is easily understandable. Even the one painter who, every one admits, was a Romantic of the letter, Delacroix, turned to Veronese as a model when he was called to decorate buildings of classical inspiration. Mr. Cox's criticism is that of a professional decorator

206

and perfectly sound as far as it goes, in the same way that the preference of a mosaicist for the Byzantine style would be. But it is nothing very deep ideologically nor more relevant to the art of the period in which Mr. Cox wrote than as a skillful defense of his own work and that of his friends against the shift of general taste toward Impressionism.

The treatment of Raphael is rather parallel although less fully developed, but here it is easy to see that Mr. Cox is so carried away by the greatness of the Romantic Michelangelo that he can only defend somewhat coldly him whom Sir Claude Phillips with maudlin but Humanistic sentimentality used so often to call the Bee of Urbino. So also Rubens, as obviously a decorator as Veronese, wins more measured but less heartfelt praise than the Romantic Rembrandt. Strangely enough Poussin, the most clearly Humanistic in the sense of Messrs. Babbitt and More of all European painters, is not mentioned at all. He received, however, more than his due from Mr. Brownell, whose book on French art was first issued in 1892, long before there was any reason in America for capitalizing Humanism.

III

Since it is my purpose here to consider specifically the relation between the capitalized Humanism of the last few years and the Artist—who might be equally granted the honor of the majuscule to make discussion more sonorous—it seems expedient now that the ground has been somewhat cleared of Mr. Mather and Mr. Cox, more than competent enough among the general run of critics of Art, but feeble champions of Humanism, to embark directly on the vital question: What would happen if the Artist were to devote himself seriously as Mr. Mather gently but firmly recommends to becoming a Humanist? It will be sufficient, I think, to study the latest and most succinct pronouncements of Mr. Babbitt as they appear in *Humanism and America,* neglecting those of his prophet Mr. Foerster, who has done so much to change Humanism from an intelligible attitude into an increasingly fixed creed, and of other humbler disciples. Much of what Mr. Babbitt sets down has clearly no applicability to the Artist as such, but much on the other hand the Artist might apply to his work, if he so desired, without need of translation of terms.

"Nothing too much" may be referred directly to Mr. Cox's conception of a balanced art, such as that of Veronese. But Michelangelo, Rembrandt and probably all the Primitives as well, were less balanced, as Mr. Cox admits. If they were less great in their art, all well and good; if they were equally great or greater, then balance is a virtue so little cardinal that its lack may be compensated for by the abundance of

208

others. The young Artist therefore, considering the claims of the Humanists on this point, would have little reason for following them. There have been great Artists who were balanced—Raphael in some of his work to the point of mediocrity—but the balanced Artist is a type which has achieved in the long run no greater success than types that have been overbalanced in one direction or another: toward form or toward content, toward color or toward design, toward the dynamic or toward the static, toward finish or toward bravura. Greek art was heavily overbalanced toward form and away from content, away from color, and in the period previous to Hellenistic Romanticism, toward the static and away from bravura.

The art of the twentieth century has preserved in all its versatility a sort of interior balance, since strong emphasis in any given direction has almost always been paralleled at the same moment by equally strong emphasis in an opposite direction. Eventually, even perhaps shortly, fusion, re-synthesis of elements which after Romantic or Modernist discovery by analysis have been developed in isolation, will almost certainly occur. But the Artist so ill-advised as to attempt it self-consciously and alone would find himself, not in the class of Poussin but in that of Delaroche, or at best of Chasseriau. Chasseriau, had he

209

lived, might conceivably have been the greatest French figure painter of the first half of the nineteenth century through his balancing of Ingres and Delacroix. He died too young, however, to be more than a painter of great promise, and only the Ecole des Beaux Arts continued his experiment, with how little result the state-purchased collections in French provincial museums plainly show. Even Couture, who attempted somewhat later much the same thing as Chasseriau, does not receive from Mr. Mather very fulsome praise for his venture. Mr. Mather, indeed, implies that thus consciously to combine opposites was to lose the specific virtues of both Ingres and Delacroix without substituting, as Courbet or a Manet were able to do, some new—and I fear equally Romantic—virtue of one's own. Fusion to be effective must, as the development of Italian Baroque painting illustrates, introduce some element or elements as new as were provided at the end of the sixteenth century by the art of Caravaggio.

The law of "Nothing too much" in its workaday form of decorum need trouble the artist even less. Mr. Edmund Wilson has elsewhere displayed how inapropos is the mention of Antigone's immediate perception of "laws unwritten in the Heavens, not of to-day or yesterday," in this connection. The history of art makes it clear enough that decorum is generally of yesterday or at the latest of to-day. There have been exceptions: an external and artificial decorum was partially established in the Renaissance by humanists, contemporaries of the first scientists in art; and in the Classical Revival by Romantics—even if before the letter—contemporaries of Rousseau.

In this connection it is worth introducing the specific testimony of Maritain. Despite the fact that he has written with extreme effectiveness on the *Primautè du spirituel,* certain American Humanists have had the extraordinary temerity to claim this Catholic Neo-Thomist as an ally, which he certainly is not as regards matters esthetic. Had they ever read *Art et scolastique,* they might have discovered that in his discussion of esthetic questions, based on Saint Thomas and fortified by frequent quotations from such Romantics as Baudelaire and Delacroix, as well as from such Modernist contemporaries as Gide, Cocteau and Max Jacob, he has rather, for Catholics, disposed so completely of the attitude of the merely prudent toward the arts, that even those who are not of the Faith can find in his book acceptable answers to almost every Humanist contention.

Elsewhere than in *Art et scolastique* Maritain,[1] has gone so far as to write that far from remaining primarily decorous the Artist must be ready if necessary to make a scandal of his art in the same way that the Saint must be ready to make a scandal of his

[1] In *Réponse à Jean Cocteau.*

devotion. The Artist no more than the Saint need seek the scandal, but if in the pursuit of his ideal of beauty the existent decorum of art is in his way, he has not only the right but the duty to break through that decorum. But Babbitt makes a general concession which as others besides myself have realized weakens, if it does not destroy, the entire Humanist case. The Artist is safe here if his final appeal may be that of the Humanist: "not to any historical convention but to intuition." If the "normal has come to have less appeal than the novel," one must ask on the basis of intuition: What is the normal? And has not the entire history of art illustrated exactly the same truth: that what has become normal has in so doing lost its original creative force, that the Artist must repeatedly seek in his art not a fixed beauty, but a new analogue of a beauty perfectly attainable only by angels? Such an analogue will in all probability be very different from the analogue that has just become normal and whose inadequacy is for that reason become most conspicuous. Revivalism provides occasionally a partial novelty. But a revival has virtue only as it departs from the preceding established norm and since that which it revives is but another analogue of the beautiful, it comes no nearer to universal validity than another novelty. Indeed since the greatest attainable perfection of each analogue of the beautiful is reached well before it has become normal, a revival can ordinarily only go on from where its original—that which it revives—left off. It is, in other words, further beyond the point of greatest human perfection than the completely novel is on the near side of it even when it is first proposed. The attempt to arrive at a new analogue through the search for what is novel, and its development may fail; but the attempt to revive is an attempt to revive that which for being past already has gone through success into failure.

Intensity, uniqueness, which Mr. Babbitt indicates as the false goals of Romantics and Modernists, are as clearly to be found in the poised and unspontaneous art of the mythical Phidias or of Poussin as in that of Rembrandt or of Paul Klee. Indeed, as I have previously suggested, the fault of the absolutists in modern painting has been exactly that they could no longer remain sufficiently unique, either themselves or their individual works, and that therefore their works soon came to lack intensity. A group of works by Impressionists or by the Cubists of before the War has not only fewer intensities than a group of Poussins or Raphaels, but is probably even as a group less intense.

If "Humanism appears primarily not in the enlargement of comprehension and sympathy . . . but in the act of selection, in the final imposition on mere

213

multiplicity of a scale of values," and if those values are no further defined, then the Modernist Artist and even the Romantic Artist would appear, paradoxically, to conform to Mr. Babbitt's ideal better than the artists who are generally recognized as Humanistic. But Mr. Babbitt is of course addressing the critic and not the Artist. He assumes, moreover, that to broaden the sympathy is to include Negro sculpture and the painting of Matisse, while to select is to select the balanced; that the varieties of modern art are mere multiplicity while a scale of values would reject in varying degrees all, let us say, but the bric-a-brac of Paul Manship. The assumption, as always with the major Humanists, is that all that occurred in Europe before 1750 is familiar and more or less acceptable, and that many things that occurred elsewhere and most things that have occurred since are, *a priori*, of different essence and may be as readily rejected without any serious loss to the total of culture.

Mr. Babbitt lacks the courage to cast out all that is non-European, as does Henri Massis, or to emphasize chiefly the Mediterranean heritage as does Charles Maurras, or even to pare the valid down gradually to the single point of himself beyond which there is nothing, as does Julien Benda. He persists in attempting to broaden his Humanism by a flirtation with the

214

Far East, which Spengler would rightly join Massis in finding unhealthy and dangerous. But his general sympathy and broadmindedness he expends entirely on Confucius and Buddha, whom he knows at a distance comparable to his distance from Aristotle, while orientalism in modern art, I fear, appears to him but as a dread result of expansiveness. It is true that he finds Buddha a very incomplete Humanist sadly overbalanced on the side of religion; but why should he be so gentlemanly and decorous in dealing with him and so intransigent and immoderate in dealing with those Americans of the nineteenth century who were overbalanced on the side of Humanitarianism—is that, by the way, allied against Man with God or with Nature? (it is never made quite clear) — whom Mr. Lewis Mumford has boldly called true humanists? For the same reason, doubtless, that he would find Chinese architecture acceptable and that of Berlage and Wright and Behrens as offensive as that of Walpole or Wyatt. Because in the distance he looks for values and in the near he finds only multiplicity: a defect of eyesight rather than a critical or philosophical principle.

The critic should be as able to bring the far near, to give it its own actuality—which is very different from applying it to our actuality—as to create for the present the proper perspective of distance. To

215

the Artist all but the immediate past may be, and often quite profitably is, applicable to his own actuality—as in the case of Mr. Cox's discrimination between Veronese, Titian and Tintoretto. The Humanist's approach to the past is that of the Artist, but from the present, for all his apparent desire to be constructive, he merely retires in confusion, which he interprets as retirement from confusion. Thus the Humanist is incapacitated for action in the present since he functions as Artist only as regards the past and as critic, which he chiefly essays to be, only in his own particular borderland between the past and the present, which for Mr. Babbitt happens to be the age of Romanticism.

In his attack upon Naturalism, with which Mr. Babbitt apparently confounds all post-Newtonian physics, in the same fashion that Anglo-Catholics confound with the Devil all post-Caroline theology Catholic or Protestant, he makes a most dangerous admission. Upon this Mr. Wilson has already jumped. His two statements: "When first principles are involved the law of measure is no longer applicable. One should not be moderate in dealing with error," opens as in the case of his statement about the intuitional basis of eternal laws, the very floodgates for the Artist. For the Artist, as Maritain makes clear again and again in *Art et scolastique*, the first principles of art are always involved. It may be objected

216

that the first principles of art are not strictly first. It is true that in the final analysis, even of the atheist or agnostic, the first principles of religion come before them. But on the human plane—with which Humanism by definition alone deals—the principles of art have as much primacy within their own field as any other principles, as wisdom or prudence, have within theirs. And in the case of conflict a valuable decision can be made only by recourse to the superior principles of religion. The frequent recourse of the Humanist to the test of happiness or unhappiness is ignoble. The Artist is ready to be unhappy for the sake of his art just as he knows he probably will have to be poor for it.

The distinction between the modern and the modernist which follows, employing terms frequently used in current criticisms of art, might have some application to the arts, although it appears to be used solely as a discrimination between two different metaphysics. In so far as the current use of the terms has achieved exactitude in the criticism of art they refer to the difference between the novel for which the Artist is finally capable of discovering Saint Thomas' *viæ certæ et determinatæ* and thus creating a style that is the normalizable, which is very different from the normal, and the novel which fails to achieve such integration or has not yet achieved it. Clearly, therefore, although the modern is superior

217

to the modernist, only the passage of time can make really certain how the distinction in the case of contemporary art lies, and within any given modern there will be many manners merely modernist, as there are to-day, which have only partial and dependent validity. In this sense the Baroque was for considerably more than a century before 1750 modern while the Rococo, in the strictest sense, was never more than modernist. In the same way the various revivals in the age of Romanticism were modernist while Romanticism itself was modern. Clearly in this conception the modern and the modernist exist merely in the epoch where one is, while for Mr. Babbitt apparently the term post-modern is not nonsense nor even synonymous with Maritain's *anti-Moderne,* a term derived in part from an opposition to Bergsonism at least as strong as Mr. Babbitt's. Now in this particular sense the Artist has for the most part remained *anti-Moderne* from the beginning, owing to the material with which he works which is spatial and not temporal, however much the theories on which he may superficially repose, Futurism or Surrèalisme, owe to Bergson or Freud. But these incidental movements are modernist and not modern— not wholes but parts of a whole and therefore of dependent validity only, never the complete exclusive systems their enthusiasts claim. It is characteristic that the work of a painter like Max Weber who

218

has passed through all the manners more or less has a greater validity as a total *œuvre* than in any particular phase. In this sense a Humanist art to-day could be modernist, but it is excessively improbable that it could ever be modern. The young Humanist is for the moment, indeed, the most aggressive because the latest of modernists. It is my very conservatism which causes me to doubt that a Humanist art will ever be modern, the suspicion that Humanism savors too much of a revival and that revivalism —*pace* Strawinski—seems to have been worn out by Romanticism and thus for a long time discredited beyond repair.

As to the question of the "law for man" and "law for thing" which so disturbs the Humanists, there is, short of metaphysics, no question of the discretion of the two. The Artist is not directly concerned —as the critic may be——with metaphysics. For him the law for thing is studied in order that it may be subordinated to the law for man. This is as true of Eiffel as of Vermeer; it is even true of the Impressionists, although possibly less completely. It is peculiarly true of all contemporary art.

"Humility, conversion, decorum, all go by the board in favor of temperamental overflow." From the religious point of view this may be unfortunate for the Artist as a man; but from the artistic point of view it is more probably an advantage to those who

219

are creative, an advantage exactly compensated for by its disadvantage to the weak. In the case of Michelangelo it is clear that he lacked, as Artist, humility, the temper of conversion, and decorum, though he had them from a religious point of view. But a Michelangelo humble, converted and decorous as an Artist would bulk very small beside the one we know, as I think even Mr. Cox and Mr. Mather would admit.

As to whether the Artist should be in Mr. Babbitt's sense a gentleman—a conception borrowed from Burke who did so much to open the way for Romanticism in the arts by his discovery of the sublime— it is more difficult to decide. If the idea of the gentleman is merely a new form of the idea of decorum the matter has already been discussed; if it be anything more it would seem to concern the Artist as such very little. The conception of the gentleman is distinctly Anglo-Saxon and hence ill adapted to the fine arts in the first place. By any definition it is surely possible to find quite as many major artists who were not gentlemen as others of the same rank who were. It might incidentally be mentioned that the chief difficulty in the way of the development of a new architecture in America lies in the fact that architects are predominantly gentlemen rather than Artists. On the whole, while it is certainly possible, like Baudelaire, to be both an Artist and a dandy. In

220

the frequent conflict between fundamental conceptions the Artist could not consistently be the gentleman without ceasing continuously and wholly to be the artist.

It is a very different matter to be a Christian; more difficult, perhaps, but on a clearly superior plane to that of either the artist or the gentleman. Yet Mr. Babbitt's peculiar difficulties with religious matters should in all probability not concern the artist at all. The artist may often be a religious man, in which case he will look for extra-artistic guidance elsewhere with more profit than to the Humanist—if a Catholic to the sympathetic writings of Maritain or Gill.

As to the "higher will," that central monstrosity of the Humanist Pantheon, the artist might even agree with Mr. Babbitt in admitting it not as a concept but as a psychological fact, but I hardly believe he would as an Artist experience it primarily as an *frein vital*. If the Artist be more of a philosopher he may well find that Mr. Babbitt by opposing Aristotle in the matter of the primacy of the intellect embogs himself in one of the most serious of modern difficulties from which his shift from the word "will" to "energy of soul" hardly saves him. Nor will the Artist find mediation on the Humanistic plane—balance and decorum particularly of the negative sort—the analogue of meditation on the religious plane. The artist

221

may rightly claim that although he makes things his activity is more analogous to meditation than is the mediation of that gentleman; and he may well distrust, even if he be not religious, the adviser who in distinguishing three planes so definitely lays his chief emphasis on the medial, far more than he will distrust the naturalist who fuses two planes or who denies the existence of the superior. As to enthusiasm the Artist can dispense with it no more than the Saint. Without enthusiasm as a sanction the Artist would rightly decide to exercise the *frein vital* to the point of ceasing his artistic functions.

The supreme goal of artistic endeavor is to make things—the Romantic would say create them—which will be right. But for the artist as artist the liking or disliking of the right things is incidental; he must use his critical faculties primarily in the process of making and cannot squander them more generally. Hence his likes will automatically have significance in relation to his own work—as in the case of Mr. Cox's preference for Veronese—while his dislikes will have little direct connection therewith and will be more personal, ephemeral, and casual. The Humanist, whether himself Artist or non-Artist, must primarily achieve taste of the selective, judging, negative sort. Taste, the Artist may completely dispense with except as a positive force within his own work. In a certain sense the Artist creates or at least perpetually modifies taste; not invalidating that which has been accepted already by taste, nor making acceptable that which has been decried—which is for the arts rather the province of the historian—but discovering new matters to which taste has not previously been found to apply, as Le Corbusier and other new architects have done for engineering. This is indeed as true of the revivalist artist as of him who is more absolutely the innovator. The taste of the Renaissance—as in the question of polychromatic statuary or the free use of the vault and the arch—was as frequently contrary to that of the Classical past as synonymous with it even among the most learned.

From his consideration of religion Mr. Babbitt comes to a very general laudation of the "will to refrain" as a prime Humanistic virtue. This is to the Artist, except as a human being in mere terms of conduct, so utterly contradictory to his inner function as to be a denial of his existence. In practice the "will to refrain" has meant only to the Humanists refrainment from the practice of literature as an art so that they might use their not inconsiderable talent and intelligence solely for ethical exhortation. To the painter or architect such a course would be suicidal, since the criticism of those arts is in no sense a part of them, but as in the case of literary criticism a part of literature in the widest sense. In my own case to refrain from the practice of architecture be-

223

cause it is impossible to be a humanist under modern conditions—which would not be my own explanation of my act—is to cease altogether to be an architect and to find as critic or historian the artistic function of my activity equally denied by Humanistic theory.

Mr. Babbitt's final plea for a surrender of education to the Humanist, for what amounts to a complete domination of the young—a Behavioristic idea —by his followers, is as intolerable to the Artist as would be the Communistic control of education, more intolerable by far than the Catholic control of education which leaves the development of the artistic *habitus* almost entirely to the individual. Such fragmentary Humanistic education as we have had in the last decade has produced critic after critic and not one major writer; indeed in the person of Mr. Eliot it has perhaps made impossible the full fruition of a talent of high order. However much we may be oversupplied with Artists, however much too readily the artistic vocation is assumed to-day, such a sterilization in the field of the fine arts could not but be unfortunate. It is exceedingly true that we need not more artists but better ones. But as the appeal of Humanism—to its credit it must be said—is to an élite, its increasing dominance would remove from the field not those certain never to attain major rank, but those of most promise.

It is the misfortune of the Humanists—of Mr. Babbitt in particular—that beginning with the negative and on the whole valid criticism of a period of the past, that of Romanticism, they have extended the particular antitheses of that cultural episode both forward and backward. Entering the lists of the present primarily as critics in the carping sense and finding themselves heeded, they have sought to derive from their negations a constructive program of affirmation. While in the fine arts they might have handled with effectiveness and profit a thorough critical examination of Romanticism, their attempt to apply their program to the arts of to-day reveals at once the predominantly negative character of their idea. Neither Scientism nor Catholicism is a mere system of negations. An intermediate and purely esthetic program hospitable to the ideas of both could be both affirmative and constructive.

IV

It remains to conclude this essay with a few words on the Artists of to-day. What is needed is not an anti-Humanist program (since that would be as negative as their own anti-Romantic or anti-Modernist platform) but some indication how the reaction from the absolute in art, the diminution of radical experimentation, the return in the broadest sense to order, might be strengthened and integrated without benefit of Humanism.

225

In the first place the Artist may be expected to come to some sort of terms with society as he finds it and not with a past or future ideal society. The Artist is vowed to the ideal, but to the ideal within his art, and it is fundamentally more important that he should function than that he should attempt the modification of the social terms of his functioning. To the painter this means that he must submit with grace to the dealer's contract system and find in it the contemporary—if one will the democratic—equivalent of traditional and humanistic systems of patronage. This for the easel picture. For illustration, for typographical design generally, for mural decoration, he must submit to the material, non-esthetic conditions that the world offers and to the printers and architects with whom he collaborates, competing on equal economic terms with those non-artists who fulfill materially the same functions and supplying something outside the scope of the printer or the architect. Or if he refuses these conditions, and the Artist's temperament is likely, and quite justifiably, to find them irksome, he must not complain that he is thwarted or that society does not appreciate him. The thwarting is of his choice and it is he who does not appreciate modern society. If he be economically independent —and those who practice the arts like those who are tempted to become Humanists in America frequently are—he must take particular advantage of his amateur standing, working in those forms particularly for which neithed dealer nor publisher nor architect has use, not considering himself superior because the material conditions of his art are less stringent but in a different and indeed more difficult category. He is in a sense client and patron as well as Artist, as were, for example, in the last century, Corot, Manet, Mary Cassatt and Cézanne.

For the architect the way is the same. First, complete command of the tools, the métier, as it has been completely remade to-day by technology; then within those practical limitations the extremest devotion to an extra-material ideal toward which he approaches in the same mood as the builders of Beauvais but along an entirely different road. The fact that that road is of concrete instead of being a cart-path makes it no easier; but because the cart-path once pushed incredibly far toward the unattainable mountain of the beautiful is no reason for leaving the turnpike to-day for the pleasant side lanes which lead nowhere. Greater speed is possible on the high road but the distance to be covered is now greater—since art no longer includes all the *factibile*—and the addition of the burden that the rules of the road shall be derived not from the new and inherent difficulties of its straightness and smoothness and opportunities for speed, but from the rules for muddy cart-paths and stone paved roads as well, is to make advance

227

toward the mountain not only impossible but ridiculous.

With regard to the problems of his personal life the Artist may turn either to the priest or to the psychiatrist. There is no particular reason why he should turn to literary critics who are not even in the ethical field specialists and who are devoid of external authority as much as they are devoid of any internal authority that all men do not possess. For the problems of his art the Artist is himself the specialist and he may have the deepest respect for earlier specialists such as Rembrandt and Poussin without finding that he has anything specific to learn from either, since so many of the great qualities of one are clearly as contradictory to the great qualities of the other as in the case of Chartres and the Parthenon. The integration which the Artist of to-day rightly desires may be in part synthetic—that is it may lie in a combination of those elements of the esthetic whole which Romanticism and Modernism have discovered and isolated by analysis. But it must be at least as much a wholly new order, a culture form of which the whole is indefinable until the parts, in themselves for the most part perhaps known, have grown little by little together, and not been fused self-consciously by compromise and rules of artificial balance. Humanism is for the artist of to-day the snare, the trap, the false synthesis offered ready-made, and established briefly

228

by the denial of the values that have been incidentally discovered in the analytical disintegration of the past century and a half since the Baroque. The Artist calls for bread and the Humanist offers him the stone of renunciation. Bread he must make himself, perhaps indeed with the Romantic yeast of Mystery and Sentiment, now fresh again.

NOTE

I offer the following as a concluding note both because it was written after the body of my essay and because only a desire for thoroughness necessitates its inclusion.

Mr. Babbitt in *The New Laokoon* promised an essay on confusion in the Arts. Actually he restricted himself almost entirely to the confusion of *genres* within literature and the confusion of literature with the other arts. He restricted himself as well to a period including the Renaissance and the Baroque, which he calls the neo- or the pseudo-classic, and to the succeeding period coming down to the present day which he calls with more justice that of Romanticism.

In the first quarter of his book in which he deals with the pseudo-classic confusion of the arts he mentions but one artist in the text, Reynolds, and then refers not at all to his work but only to his criticism. Nor does he appear to realize what Christopher Hussey makes so clear in his study of the picturesque that

229

Reynolds was in his theory very frequently a proto-Romantic, particularly in his sympathy for irregularity in architecture. It is the more extraordinary that he makes no mention of Poussin, the one major painter who seems to have taken seriously the Horatian *ut pictura poesis* and the Aristotelian theory of imitation in the correct form with which he is chiefly concerned. Bernini, it is true, is mentioned in a footnote where, under material for a wider survey of the type he attempted is set down the one matter that might have been, from the point of view of the fine arts, of interest: those aspects of the Baroque and Rococo styles which illustrate the pseudo-classic tendency to confuse the arts formally and objectively. Mr. Babbitt is concerned solely with critical theory, and what is more, theory of a type which hardly influenced the practice of art at all before the coming of Romanticism and the combination of Canova and Thorwaldsen, Mengs and David. Reynolds, one suspects, is mentioned because he was a friend of Dr. Johnson.

In the rest of the book there are perhaps a score of comments which are concerned directly with the fine arts, and the mention of somewhat over half-a-dozen artists, among whom only Rossetti, Böcklin and Rodin belong to the period with which he is dealing. He quotes the incredibly imbecile statement of Hazlitt—a literary critic—that Raphael could not paint

230

a landscape—Raphael the climax of the Umbrian school, the prince of space painters! Again he quotes an opinion of Hazlitt which amounts to saying that Titian is more Romantic than Claude—a more than debatable position—and confirms it himself. Du Fresnoy, Reynolds, Lessing: Theirs is at least criticism of some historic importance in the field of art, but Hazlitt is surely quite insignificant.

Babbitt disturbs himself over *Einfühlung* and Croce, but with less vehemence than More. He states that Rousseau's pastoral mood found expression only in the landscape of Corot and neglects the obvious remark that this was true only of the inferior, one might almost say that decadent, work of the artist, whereas his earlier work was almost anti-Romantic in its sternness, its strength, and its solidity. He protests temperately in the midst of his attack on Romantic tendencies toward expressionism, that for a certain type of neo-classicist beauty resided almost entirely in mechanical symmetry and proportion and suggests no third alternative, except the vague recommendation that symmetry and proportion should be vital—which has a naturalistic enough ring. He remarks and approves the fashion in which the best Greek sculpture fulfills Aristotle's conditions and fails to indicate whether any comparable artistic quality has been achieved since. He finds that Rodin's "Belle qui fut heaulmiére" is not shapely (desirable?) and

231

suggests not very profoundly that he had gone too far in the direction of painting: a truth which all his great followers have long since taken only too much to heart with their massive torsos and hewn reliefs. As regards architecture he is particularly unsatisfactory. He quotes Schegel's "Architecture is frozen music" with deprecation and practically leaves the matter at that, although this is very probably the key to the whole problem of Romantic architecture. He mentions the Parthenon in connection with Renan's Prayer and he compares generically the skyscrapers of lower New York unfavorably with the Place de la Concorde, which masterpiece he finds insufficiently subtle in its symmetry. Save Bernini he mentions no architect by name nor any other buildings—except Cologne Cathedral as the subject of a Schumann tone poem. Lest this résumé seem too drastic a demonstration of the degree of his competence, the amount of his interest and the tenuousness of his ideas on the fine arts it should be remarked that actual works of literature or music do not receive much more frequent mention. Contemporary literature is represented specifically by the mention of Bernard Shaw, Peter Pan, Babes in Toyland—and a novel by Bettina von Hutten!

Mr. Babbitt, it is true, was in 1910 kinder than he has since become to anti-Newtonian science, speaking kindly of non-Euclidian geometry and Henri Poincaré. But on the whole the meat of the book lies in that condemnation of Rousseau and those eternal exhortations which cause, in their application to the arts, a *mélange des genres* more appalling than even the program music of Claude Debussy and Richard Strauss, matters now sufficiently reacted against by a whole generation of excellent and quite definitely anti-Humanistic musicians.

Since the Humanists appear quite unaware of that excellent if no longer applicable book, Geoffrey Scott's *Architecture of Humanism*, I have made no previous mention of it. A word may be said of it in conclusion. Although Geoffrey Scott could hardly have known when he wrote it in Florence before the War of the distant activities at American universities —with which in his Boswell work he later came into contact—it is a presentation of a humanistic, rather than Humanistic, point of view in one art, that is more appreciative, more sympathetic, deeper and sounder than any of the American writing that has been discussed here. Time has answered his contentions in architecture, not by controverting them but by posing the problem in a form he hardly conceived. But he took in his day more answering than anything that the Humanists have brought up since in connection with the fine arts.

233

THE DISCIPLINE OF
HUMANISM — Blackmur

The Discipline of Humanism

HUMANISM is supposed to be a discipline, based upon the law of measure and upon the dualism of the higher and lower natures, which is applicable to every kind of life and art. "Humanism,"—says Norman Foerster—"Humanism does wish to emphasize discipline, whenever, as to-day, it needs to be emphasized. . . . It does desire to show that the quality of all life is higher or lower according as our power of vital restraint is exercised." Etc. I think it will be agreed that all fifteen contributors to *Humanism and America* subscribe to this intention; and I hope that none of them will object if some uninvited but willing guests coöperate with them a little in their great labor.

It is so great a labor—this matter of achieving a discipline—and they have so far begun it, that we should take from them our inspiration. Since, unfortunately, none of the Humanists achieves his discipline in terms of creative art, or in original work of any kind, all are bound at this time to express the notion of discipline only as it affects the work of others—in the criticism of the arts, philosophy, and science. So we must, on our part, observe what discipline they recognize and what lapses from it they condemn. Then we may understand, perhaps, something of that mysterious discipline they draw from the higher will, which gives them their courage to write and their ardor to judge.

The evidence in *Humanism and America,* and elsewhere so far as Humanism has dealt with contemporary art and thought, is peculiarly unsatisfactory; it is made up almost entirely of adverse criticism of various literary works. This adverse criticism never refers to the kind of discipline in which the artist is interested—the discipline of his subject-matter—but chiefly examines that discipline which involves a view of life or the apprehension of the higher will; discipline, that is, in which the artist need not be directly concerned at all. Humanism has refrained, and no doubt this is an admirable instance of vital restraint, from all that a novelist or poet would mean by literary criticism. There was nothing to compel it to refrain, so that it must have been an act of choice; either Humanism is not interested in the content of literature and the problems surrounding it, or it has had no experience therein. Or, positively, it may be that Humanism intends to deal, and has enabled itself to deal, only with that one significance of the arts which may be transformed to the Humanist ideal. Certainly the bundle of Humanist tracts contains many stray sentences which suggest as much. For instance, there is Mr. Foerster's comparative condemnation of Shakespeare (in his *American Criti-*

238

cism) because he only mirrored life rather than Humanistically transcended it.

But before we decide among these interpretations, —thus deciding upon the actual value of the Humanist discipline as the standard of criticism—we should, lest haste mistake us for Humanists, examine in a general way some of the particular judgments the Humanists have made. Mr. Babbitt, Mr. P. E. More, and Mr. G. R. Elliott condemn modern literature wholesale on the grounds that it is naturistic, realistic, mechanistic, monistic, and romantic; also because it is pessimistic—a ground which I separate from the others, since I think it is only because the Humanists misunderstand themselves and their position that they include it. What these gentlemen mean by the application of such adjectives is this. In the novels and poems which they have scanned, certain ideas and certain points of view, some actually present in the works and others only present by strenuous implication, have struck them as violently antipathetic to their own scheme of an ordered society. A similar prejudice led Plato to banish the poets from his Republic; and I suspect that if they were "historically minded" enough, the Humanists would agree with Plato in his judgment of the Greek poets. And that would save our ears from many a gratuitously ennobled reference to Sophocles.

239

This is the judgment of the masters. The younger men—younger at least in Humanism—are more naïve; they risk immediate contact with particular persons and works. They apply with the disingenuous frenzy of converts the principles of their elders. Mr. Thompson sets up a theory of tragedy in the word admiration, a theory of which the chief virtue is that it lets Shakespeare in. He then proceeds to show that because of our naturalism we have lost the talent for admiration. Hence, every nine-pin topples almost before it stands: Hugo, Rostand, Ibsen, and O'Neill being prominent among the pins. In relation to O'Neill, Mr. Thompson makes the following remarks: "Indeed, he seems to find no man whom he can whole-heartedly admire; he can exalt no character or cause, and thus does not gain the elevation of heroic tragedy. He finds life a muddle; he leaves it a muddle." Mr. Thompson appears to believe that modern art fails because of its naturalism. "So long as he [an author] thinks of man as in no way superior to the outer world, or different from it, he is subject to the naturalistic point of view." To the Humanist, he says, it seems that art must deal with ethical laws. "Romantic art as recreation is a blessing to jaded mortals; and naturalistic art at its best is, within limits, penetrating. But to the Humanist it seems that both types of art have failed in dealing with ethical laws." Since Mr. Thompson has himself

240

pointed out that O'Neill presents in his plays the problems of extreme conduct, it must be merely that he is not satisfied with O'Neill's philosophy, or lack of it. That is, the plays do not come to Humanist conclusions.

Mr. Shafer, in order to explain Dreiser's mind, uses ten pages to sneer at that novelist's life and loves. With the sneer to prompt him, he pronounces Roberta Alden, in *An American Tragedy*, to be without importance. Her grievous distress, he observes, takes on "the same significance as the squirming of an angle-worm, impaled by some mischievous boy—no less, but certainly no more." As to the book as a whole, I select two sentences. "Eight hundred and forty pages devoted to the unconscionable prolongation of a mere sensational newspaper story! . . . The more successful he is, the more insignificant his work becomes." Between these two sentences appear references to Æschylus, Sophocles, and the Moral Law (the capitals are Mr. Shafer's). We observe that Mr. Shafer grants Dreiser neither his life, his subject, his knowledge, nor his treatment of these; because he fails apparently to observe Mr. Shafer's Christian notion of the Greek Moral Law in Sophocles' plays.

In Mr. Clark's résumé of American fiction, I find this highly indicative hiatus. "Let us skip the realism of the later nineteenth century, most of which is essentially arid, and approach such a figure as Floyd Dell." Mr. Clark proposes to skip Stephen Crane, which is his own loss, although it amounts to skipping a heartbeat. Mr. Clark proposes to skip Henry James. That is, for the sake of making his Arcadian monstrosity perfect, he skips, as essentially arid, the most dignified, the most disciplined, and, I should have supposed, the most humanistic of American masters. Let us see where his skipping and hooping leads him. He is looking for a literature which, "ministering to all the higher needs of the mind and spirit, yields the greatest delight and the greatest beauty." The one example, presumably the best he knows, which he can bring himself to name, is Dorothy Canfield's able but vacuous novel, *The Brimming Cup.* There he finds the higher will, the will to refrain from experience, with a vengeance; he also finds an "exalted human happiness." He does not find such matters in Hawthorne, Melville, and Mark Twain; they have not an Emersonian aspiration, and hence are evidently not the right sort of writers.

Thinking of T. S. Eliot, Mr. Chase releases the following summary of contemporary poetry. "Love-making carried on with an accompanying sense of its futility and ridiculousness, an acquaintance with art and poetry which serves only to confirm misgivings as to their relevancy for us to-day, the employment of religious symbols to arouse a poor mirthless mockery

242

—in such experiences our young intellectuals find
mirrored the age and body of their time." Mr.
Chase's paper is called "Dionysus in Dismay," but I
think it is Mr. Chase who is unconsciously dismayed;
like many a more learned man, he is bluffing without
knowing it. There are an insufferable patronizing
reluctance, a dullness of sense, a weak weariness about
his disapprovals, which are worse than the immoderate ecstasies of Babbitt, More, and Shafer. It is
possible that Mr. Chase is really a humanitarian in
villainous disguise, and not a Humanist at all.

Mr. Munson does not here cry Mahabharata, nor
even Mahabracadabra; he is perforce restrained, since
he is dealing with critics, to the less stringent vocables,
Babbitt! More! and a final, ghostly Arnold! Arnold!
. . . with perhaps as a prevalent echo of equivalence
the faint "susurrus of his subjective hosannah." He
combines misjudgment of and insight into certain
living critics, and omits all mention of the half-dozen
men, aside from T. S. Eliot, now actively engaged
in literary criticism; he comes finally to the conclusion that nobody writes like Babbitt or More, and
that we ought to write like Arnold. It is difficult to
take a serious view of the sensibility of a man who
asserts that, "Objectively considered, literature may
be found to have been in decline, not just for a century and a half or just for six hundred years but almost from its classical sources and from the Scriptures

of ancient lands." Mr. Munson is, just now, a free-lance Humanist; I do not think a real one needs so great an antiquity to promote his arrogance.

The passages selected for quotation and comment should make plain in themselves what sort of discipline the Humanists exercise; every one of these gentlemen is working to suppress, to prohibit, to censor such literature as does not fulfill, in the most obvious manner, the notion of a Humanist society. And in view of the fact that all the evidence here collected of disciplined judgment is drawn from the essays of teachers of literature, there is something profoundly sad about Mr. Richard Lindley Brown, a last year's senior at Bowdoin. Mr. Brown believes that, "The teacher of literature may well turn out, in the end, to be the sole means by which society and literature can be raised from their present depression." The sadness lies not in the truth or falsity of his faith, but in its objects. There is no choice between natural depression and elevated vacuity.

Oh, well, we have seen the drama, the novel, and poetry go by the board, and if Mr. Mather has his way, and a hundred Humanists be born to-morrow, we shall see the arts of the future similarly disciplined before they bud; providing the Humanists have their way. But we may be grateful to the Humanists that by their own principles we may save ourselves. Not one of the judgments quoted above but can be set

244

aside. Not one of these judgments stands firmly upon its own feet, not one of them is imposed through such a discipline as the Humanists profess. In fact, we may begin to imagine that the Humanists have no discipline at all, and further that they do not know what it is; that they are possessed by principles they have not the knowledge, the subtlety, the life, to apply to an actual instance. They have only the fanatic's notion of moderation, an arrogant love of the golden mean; and without moderation no principle can be intelligently acted upon: discipline becomes merely a pejorative, a censorship, or a prohibition.

II

Here is a deep distinction, among many, between Humanism as it is and Humanism as it intends to be. The contributors to *Humanism and America* undoubtedly intended to discipline their contemporaries. They have succeeded in writing as if they were censors, and the tone they have taken towards present-day literature is very similar to the tone of the supporters of prohibition, another example of *frein vital*. It is to be assumed that all authority, all light and truth, is on their side: human nature must be as they assert: any difference is wishful thinking, or the illusion of disillusionment; and further, every difference must be ruled out, so that what remains will be right and healthy, even if what remains is infinitesimal.

245

Their writings, and their decorum, would have been very different had they honestly bent their attention to their chosen task. An intellectual discipline, their avowed instrument, is that routine of thought, that activity of mind, whose principles so fit the subject-matter in hand as to promote the clearest understanding, or the finest expression, as the case may be, of that subject matter. An emotional discipline, likewise, is a routine or faculty for the delicate recognition or expression of feelings in oneself or elsewhere so as to permit their finest adjustment to the subject-matter. Great knowledge, obtained by great labor, of the particular subject is necessary. Discipline inherited or already acquired, is an aid to the particular discipline only when the necessary knowledge is had and the labor performed. Any application of discipline in general, or discipline *per se,* can result only in some form of censorship—a decidedly malicious and far from equivalent substitute. It is in a connection like this that T. S. Eliot's converse of the biblical maxim is most apt: "The spirit killeth; the letter giveth life."

Put the other way round, the censorship which I think the Humanists so often inadvertently substitute for discipline, is the judgment of a mind whose principles do not fit the subject matter, because they were gained *à priori,* accepted as a rigid body of arbitrary doctrine without reference to the material they were

246

intended to judge. It is a distinction between form and formalism, between experience, raised in the individual mind to principle, and principle taken whole as a pill or purgative, and intended to substitute for experience. Principle of this second order, when absolute or formalized, is invariably heretical: that is, it may not pronounce truth without vital exaggeration or distortion. So I think that the principles of Humanism, as they are held, cannot avoid heresy; they do not arise out of individuals—out of a sensibility, a civilization, a religion, or a generalized experience of any sort—but only from the notions of these. It is obvious that such principles prevent what they aim at: deep penetration and right judgment of human nature and art. They cannot penetrate, they cannot judge, because they must exist and move without data—that is without experience of the work in hand.

Another way of getting at this same difficulty between discipline and censorship is to import, fairly loosely, an analogue from the courts. In the common law there is a broad distinction between *malum in se* and *malum prohibitum*, the first being an act inherently evil, and the second an act evil only by custom or regulation. The law deals with these different kinds of evil differently—*malum prohibitum* being always subject to extenuation, *malum in se* only circumstantially or conditionally so. We see the Hu-

247

manists listing the errors to which man is subject, confusing the two, and more often than not treating every activity of the mind and of the feelings which they disapprove as action evil in itself. A notorious example is their general, thorough-going condemnation of every act, thought, or desire which springs from or ends in expansive emotion. As Edmund Wilson has pointed out, the need of most of us to-day is just these expansive, easy emotions; and their condemnation is an excellent case of *malum prohibitum* assuming the absolutism of *malum in se*. It is a case which arises whenever the leaders of a community become afflicted with the legalistic spirit to the detriment of intimate knowledge and sympathy. In the instance of Humanism, such legislation and such judgment occur when the law of measure and the interpretation of the higher will, to mention two main tenets, are strictly applied to the contemporary scene in terms of some other scene. We have the condemnation of Dreiser, O'Neill, *et al.*, and the elevation of Dorothy Canfield, noted above, *and in the language and for the reasons there given*. And we have Babbitt making a gigantic and exhaustive study of nineteenth-century romanticism, and then proceeding to castigate what he calls the naturalism of the twentieth century as if the evil were in both cases the same. Though there may be a superficial resemblance in effect, the experience, the feelings, which produce it

248

are very different. The fact is that the notion of measure and the law of higher will cannot be treated as if they were rules of conduct, rigid in nature and inevitable in application, but must, to be useful, be understood as convenient myths, susceptible only to such applications as the times demand. As for Babbitt, we shall be able neither to understand nor to answer, if that be necessary, his judgment of modern literature, until he shows us something comparable in length, care, and knowledge to his study of Rousseau or Pascal. At present he but preaches, and his prophecies hang in the thin air of inspiration, a pretty pyrotechnic.

III

Now, I think it is worth inquiring how a movement so genial, so broad in inspiration and history, could come in our day to seem so arrogant and narrow. There are two explanations: first, the solitude in which that social creature, Humanism, is confined; and, second, the great stress it lays on its dualism as an active principle of practice.

When I say solitude, I should perhaps rather say isolation, in the vacuum of formalism, from every immediate perception of life and art; for such an isolation seems the positive condition of every effort witnessed by the Humanist symposium. Who could say, for example (except some weaker Humanist),

249

that Mr. G. R. Elliott's essay, "The Pride of Modernity," has touched at any critical point the modern sensibility? Mr. Elliott would have us believe that among the failures of contemporary literature is its failure to express the tragedy of pride, its inability to conceive some driving force in human character approximate to the Greek *hubris*. One example of just such an expression, just such a conception of human nature, worked out with as much pity and terror and honesty as most of us can stand, is James Joyce's *Ulysses*. Ample proof of this is found in two recent essays, those of S. Foster Damon and Edmund Wilson; but that Stephen Dedalus is struck down by an overweening pride should catch an earnest reader by the throat. Another example could be shown in a four-volume novel of which I think Mr. Elliott must have heard, Ford Madox Ford's tetralogy about Tietjens. Something of the sort is at least implicity present in the works of that anathema of Humanists, Dreiser, and in O'Neill's *Strange Interlude*. Mr. Elliott's difficulty is that he has taken his principles so much to heart that he can understand only Greek and Christian pride, which it appears that he and all Humanists who deal in pride have unwarrantably confused. Our ethos is neither Greek nor Christian, but only our ethics—and this is but the thinnest formal superficies to the feelings and events which are the substance of both life and letters.

Mr. Elliott is not alone in isolation; his brother symposiasts share it. What they have done, with the exceptions of T. S. Eliot and Bernard Bandler II, the first of whom undermines and the second modifies Humanism, is very simple and very stultifying. They have taken principles and notions once embodied in Greek civilization, medieval Christianity, and perhaps the French seventeenth century, and made them their own without embodying them in the civilization of to-day. They have conceived a tradition which cannot move except by imitating itself, by remaining static and duplicative—which is not, therefore, and cannot be, a living tradition at all, but merely the dry intellectual shell of once vivid sense. They have so equipped themselves with these principles and this tradition, that they can admire only Sophocles, Dante, and Racine—and them only in a Humanistic way; so that when they come to deal with moderns, they cannot get inside them; they have no discipline in their minds suitable to their substance, but rather a foreign and irrelevant discipline which acts in the way of a censorship. It is not objected that they admire Racine, but that they condemn Dos Passos and Dreiser because they do not do what Racine did; and that they prevent themselves in advance from reading Dos Passos and Dreiser. And it is not only in dealing with their contemporaries that the Humanists fail. Mr. Babbitt's marvelously exhaustive condemnation of the Romantics succeeds largely because he separates what cannot be separated without decimation, the ideas from the poetry which alone permits the ideas to flourish.

What is there in American Humanism which seems to compel its isolation from its own subject matter? I think it is that higher will on which it claims to depend. Certainly, to an ordinary mind, the distinctive intonation with which all American Humanists rehearse their ritual is that of their dualism. It is an article of faith, this assertion of a higher will characteristic of man and foreign to the rest of creation; and since it is an article of faith, the mystery of its nature and workings may not be questioned; it requires merely the complete assent of the individual. By this higher will he is governed. With it as a standard he will criticize the arts and actions of this world. Both for the individual and for society as a whole it is the source of discipline and the end of life. Here is Mr. Babbitt's latest definition: "Positively one may define it as the higher immediacy that is known in relation to the lower immediacy—the merely temperamental man with his impressions and emotions and expansive desires—as a power of vital control (*frein vital*)."

This would take a good deal of consultation and stretching and private interpretation to make it intelligible; so we had better leave it what it is, a cathe-

252

dral statement, and assume that it means something explicit. But there are some points that may be indicated as descriptive of any will superior to that will which expresses, in relation to mundane and passionate affairs, a continuous intense intention, the opposite extreme to velleity. Higher will has usually been associated with religion, and in Christian terms has been usually known as the will of God; its professors have been saints or mystics. We may notice that in the degree that the saints or mystics kept their knowledge of the will of God on good terms with their general body of doctrine and feeling, it was intelligible and useful; and to the contrary, that in the degree to which their notions escaped the terms of general faith, they became unintelligible excrescences. The Humanist is not a saint; and for him the higher will may be a useful hypothesis, whatever character he may assign it, only when it is connected at every point with the infinite area of common experience. Then it may suggest a sound poetic report of human nature in terms of the hypostatic imagination; and its character will vary with the flexibility of its object— the needs of man at the time. The great difficulty is to prevent that which the Humanist does not prevent but rather proclaims, the transformation of the higher will from sound myth into a set of principles. It has little to do with any type of conduct except as an ideal reference. Certainly it has nothing to do

253

with either the making or meaning of art in general; and it cannot be a source of discipline upon worldly things of any kind. It is avowedly either supernatural or ideal. If it is ideal we must admit that every object and every life expresses it differently. If it is supernatural, it is a mystery we can only recognize, not expound. It is the last weapon we should use in criticism or judgment.

The Humanists themselves show us very clearly what happens when an inconstruable mystery is adopted as an instrument of understanding, order, and discipline. It promotes a dualism which is merely a kind of double life in the mind: such a double life as that of a shadow successfully pretending to substance. For that is what dualism does; it divides life into the material and the spiritual, the lower and the higher wills, and asserts that the spiritual, the higher will, is the meaning of the material. The Humanists, lacking either the dogma of Christianity or the body of Greek civilization to infuse the spiritual with the nourishment of earth, tend to divorce their higher will from experience altogether, and to employ it, so divorced, as a standard by which to judge others' experience. It is no wonder, then, that what the humanists call their insight, their imagination, their discipline, should seem to us their arrogance, their blindness, and their censorious ignorance.

DRIFT AND MASTERY IN
OUR NOVELISTS—CHAMBERLAIN

DRIFT AND MASTERY IN OUR NOVELISTS

THE peculiar domain of literature, say the New Humanists, should be the normally and typically human, or what is most richly and typically human. The second fiat we may ignore, for no one with any sense of scale can confuse what is most richly human with what is typically human, except by perverting either one adverb or the other in the orthodox Humanist manner. As for fiat number one, I would certainly endorse it to this extent: that literature should not refuse to take into account what is typically human, provided one is sure what it is. And one would endorse a statement of Alan Reynolds Thompson to a similar extent. When Mr. Thompson says that "literary art, dealing as it does with human actions, must deal with ethical laws, which are the foundation of conduct," one feels like answering: "Of course, provided we have a society whose actions are predicated on ethical laws." But given a society on the make, whose symbol is the Public Relations Counsel (who earns his living out of salesmanship without reference to value), one turns from the New Humanists to men whose interests lie outside the field of literature for information and encouragement, or to literary critics who do not treat art as something that exists in a vacuum. One turns from the New Humanists because they want to make the poet, the

257

novelist and the dramatist bear the burden of the philosopher, the reformer, the social engineer and the critic of society, a confusion of métiers that may be said to constitute our newest Laokoon.

One parts company with the New Humanists for reasons connected with the common sense and the humility which they are so fond of invoking. For it is extremely difficult to see, except in moments of wishful thinking born of a despair that steals the clarity from one's judgment, just how literary art is to be changed by fiat. It has not ceased to be axiomatic with me that great art is always socially based, both in the sense that it must inevitably draw its material or impetus from the existing social order, and in the sense that it must depend for elbowroom on a state of society that will support the artist to some degree. If it doesn't draw either material or impulse from the existing social order it will lose vitality, as one may discover by reference to any literature at any period. And if it has no elbowroom, it will be stifled; the artist cannot live in an atmosphere of perpetual scorn for all that he is endeavoring to do, as the history of this country between the Civil War and 1915 so well demonstrates.

It is precisely because of the social basis of art (and this may be stretched to include a metaphysical basis, for every society makes its fundamental assumptions) that one turns from the gestures of the New Human-

258

ists to the critics who have dispensed with the ivory tower. If modern tragedy is in a dilemma, it can only be brought out of that dilemma by social criticism, by a drive to create a condition of society that will permit and encourage people to work from other motives than those of acquisition. And only social critics can help create such a condition; the esthetic and technical critics become effective *after* the existence of such a milieu is assured. Not only can the social critics help bring about a salutary state of affairs in the future; they have already succeeded to some extent, in the past fifteen years. They have succeeded because of a highly courageous frontal attack on what was the *status quo* fifteen years ago. The frontal attack must be sustained because it can never win more than a partial victory, and a relapse in its energy would mean a cancellation of gains.

When one contrasts the year 1915 with the year 1930, one endeavors in vain to discover any reasonable grounds for the animus of the New Humanists against such social critics as Van Wyck Brooks, Walter Lippmann, Lewis Mumford, Randolph Bourne and others. No one can deny that the state of the literary life in America is much sounder to-day than it was fifteen years ago. Certainly a much more genuine interest in the arts is shown by the generations born this side of 1900 than can be found in any of the earlier generations. This interest struggles bravely, and often futilely, against the onrushing material interests of America; but it at least makes its battle. We may lack our geniuses; we may, for instance, have no one of the native endowments of Mark Twain; but there are a number of writers who, at the moment, are managing to sustain their careers without either compromising or going under, or without being marred to the extent that, I believe, Theodore Dreiser was marred by a view of life borne in on him during his younger days in the cut-throat environment of Pittsburgh's steel kings. When one thinks of Elizabeth Madox Roberts and Glenway Wescott, both of whom give every indication of retaining their integrity as artists, one realizes that the labors of Brooks and others have borne fruit. Certainly we are getting a number of younger critics whose guns will not easily be spiked. This body of critics (spiritual offspring of the older men who have been disposed of by the cavalier Mr. Munson) should make possible the hope of seeing Mr. Brooks's gloomy pronouncement that the sustained career in literature is not to be found in America, become a statement with an historical interest only. If the sustained career does become a common phenomenon, it must be kept in mind that Brooks's diagnosis, when made at the opening of the decade, was absolutely valid. It must also be remembered that he, more than any

260

other single critic, has made possible the cultivation
of a sense of free will among writers, even among
writers who know of him only by hearsay.

One is disappointed in the writings of the New
Humanists because they fail, in their mock humility,
to credit the accomplishments of the social critics.
They overlook the gains made by the men already
named, and by the politically-minded Mencken, the
later Edmund Wilson, and a score of lesser men who
contribute to the more liberal journals. One is disappointed because they scorn ground work in favor
of debates staged over what must seem, in the last
analysis, to be mere figures of speech. (What
earthly difference does it make, for example, whether
man differs in kind or degree from the animals—or
the lower animals? To say that belief in difference
in kind has a more salutary effect on the ego is to confuse explanation with valuation.) Finally, one is
disappointed because (with the possible exception of
Professor Babbitt) the New Humanists have no political program, no social program that takes into
account the tools whereby social change may be
effected, no religious program that is intellectually
respectable, and no educational program that could
possibly take root in our age. Lacking any positive
line of attack, how are they to rehabilitate certain
ethical laws that might, in turn, rehabilitate modern
tragedy? How are they to rescue what is most richly

261

human for literature? Or what is most normally and typically human?

II

What the Humanist calls the normally and typically human is, if we may guess, something that is no longer of the norm. What has been normally and typically human in modern society has been the will to material profit, as it takes no man with superior perceptions to discern. In the literal sense, the answer to the Humanist demand for the typically human is —the complete works of Ring Lardner. Because we have been, to a great extent, a nation of shufflers in the realm of what is ethically justified—or, to use a more polite term, a nation of pragmatists—it follows logically that our literature is not of the sort to please Mr. Thompson in his desire for art based on ethical laws, or Harry Hayden Clark in his wish for literature that deals with the "central" facts of human experience. Any sensible person may regret that this is true. But to condemn our novelists for dealing honestly and openly with what exists, or what has existed, in American life is another matter. To rule Dos Passos out of court, as Mr. More has done, because he writes a novel, *Manhattan Transfer*, around a number of people who do not live by ethical laws of past eras, is to advocate putting an unseemly gloss upon the status quo, to suppress the evidence (surely

262

an unwise thing to do), and to put the hope for any change into an even more infinite distance than it is at present.

I am not arguing that the literary artist should not concern himself with values. He should be concerned with this realm. But he is not to be blamed for an inability to create values; for, as Allen Tate has somewhere pointed out, he is doing his part when he puts them into circulation. He should be concerned with values only to the extent to which a novel or a story should deal with "what is" from a point of view that implies a philosophical judgment in the mind of the artist; only to the extent that it is fair for the novelist to introduce characters who will, as the phrase goes, body forth potentials, and show, by their contrast to the blacker sheep of the novel in question, that the author has a hierarchy of values to set forth in fleshly dimension.

Before 1925 some of our contemporary fiction was undertaken from a definite and positive point of view, some from a nebulous and groping point of view, but more of it was created out of the confusion of a popular nihilism that was upheld proudly. A good deal of it, we may admit with the Humanists, was devoted to the record of sensation, or to the record of behavioristic patterns of action. It was a literature of "drift," not "mastery." Dreiser, of course, took a great deal of color from philosophers who had

263

created a system which denied the ability of the human organism to free itself from an absolute mechanical fatalism. The will, not as a metaphysical toy, but as an attribute of the organism (Herbert Read calls it "the practice of courage," which is certainly an observable practice when it is in evidence), was conspicuously absent from the general run of fiction. Scores of novels born of such records as *Sinister Street* were published. We had the definitely non-philosophical novel. *This Side of Paradise,* which remains the most charming novel of the time, was wholly non-philosophical; it was a record of sensation; and ideas, when present in it, were treated more or less as delightful playthings. Our artists were very much wrapped up with problems of personality that were distinct from social problems. Amory Blaine, for example, ended by saying, "I know myself, but that is all." An individual was an individual, not a member of a community, a society, a nation, a world. Society was something to be shunned. To cope with it in any stay-at-home way was to be crushed beneath the juggernaut. The mood of Anderson, our most sensitive, poetic and humane writer of the period, was a definitely escapist mood; he was called a "realist" because, at the time, it was considered that his marching men were escaping into "real" life, not from it. The standard Anderson hero was the man who, overwhelmed by aridity, by bleakness, by vul-

264

suspicion of malaise in the fiction of the Anderson-Dell school. But they are only correct in the suspicion; they have done no more than hold up their hands in the face of the malaise. They fall back on literature that would be an organic impossibility in this age, and by their disdain of the present they break the stream of continuity between generation and generation. More damaging to their pretensions to discernment has been their failure to deal with the late 'twenties, a period much more encouraging than the first half of the decade. It is the Humanist's blindness to what is actually beneath his nose that makes him such an impotent, such a feeble guide to literature. In fact, it is illuminating to note that the one contributor to Professor Foerster's Humanist symposium who has been interested in the actual quotidian product of our literature is Gorham B. Munson—and he, by his own proclamation, is not an orthodox Humanist.

The second half of the decade is more encouraging because there has been an increasing tendency, among younger novelists, to conceive the problem of the individual in terms that are much less naïve than the terms of Anderson, Cabell, the Hergesheimer of *Cytherea*, and the writers of documents that are undertaken with the simple idea of photography. There is, of course, a great deal of overlapping: the older mood has been perpetuated, for example, by Conrad Aiken,

who took to fiction *circa* 1925 and produced a novel
which, however much it was distinguished for its
brightness of language, was content to record the flux
of sensation as graven on a brain that is never very
purposive in its thinking. Ludwig Lewisohn, who
might have been expected to write a novel in the
dominant mood of the early 'twenties, provided the
counter-balance to Aiken by surprising a good many
people with *The Island Within*. It was a distinctly
new note, ethically speaking, in contemporary American fiction. For Lewisohn's Arthur Levy was no
moon-calf, seeking a refuge from the ills of life, but
a practicing psychoanalyst (and a respectable one)
whose one great aim was to force himself into a chan-
nel that would be morally acceptable to his own nature. He solved his problem in a way that would
only suffice for a Jew who is also an impassioned
Zionist, but he solved it, and the method of solution
made good drama. Many Jews call *The Island Within*
an escapist novel. It is hardly that, unless the act of
getting the sort of work one believes in can be called
an escape. It is true that Arthur Levy sailed for Europe at the close of the book, but not with a view to
expatriation at the tables of the Dome.

Lewisohn, however, is an older voice, and it is a
question whether he will ever work into another satisfactory theme. The really noteworthy thing about
the second half of the decade is the emergence of

268

Glenway Wescott, Elizabeth Madox Roberts and
Thomas Wolfe. Thornton Wilder may be included
for the sake of those who consider a literature incomplete without its stylist who distills pleasurable books
from greater books. Edmund Wilson's *I Thought of
Daisy* is encouraging, not necessarily for its merits as
a novel, but for its ideas, and its distinct contrast to
This Side of Paradise. Stark Young's *River House* is
interesting because it dramatizes life in the South in
dynamic, purposive terms, not in the mechanistic
terms of Dreiserian fiction. Hemingway's *A Farewell
to Arms* shows a distinctly hopeful departure from
the Hemingway of *The Sun Also Rises,* for it is evidence that its author will not always content himself with themes in which human volition is either
hopelessly weak or entirely absent. Of the "new
primitives," we can do without an increase in the
crop. John Herrmann, Josephine Herbst, Morley
Callaghan and the rest are merely the complements to
the flow-of-sensation school. Instead of recording
the stream of consciousness, they are content to record
the flow of observed action. They follow Watson instead of Freud or the introspectionists; the major intellectual impulse behind their work is, whether they
know it or not, behavioristic. Volition, the will as
an attribute of the organism, is left out, and the absence of will, or the power to put on pressure to gain
ends that exist in the future, means, inevitably, a loss

269

of dramatic reach, a drying-up of the springs of the imagination.

The return of the concept of volition to fiction in America will hardly please the New Humanists, and for this reason: Wescott, Miss Roberts, Wolfe, Edmund Wilson and the others do not part company with the materials presented to them by their sensibilities. So far, Miss Roberts and Glenway Wescott have solved their problems by dealing with a way of life still observable in the regions of Kentucky and rural Wisconsin, but bound to disappear with the spread of urban civilization and mass production. The moving pictures, I gather from Wescott's preface to *Good-bye, Wisconsin*, are already working their insidious mechanical will on the younger generation of farmers; the old life, with its mixture of "Greek tragedy and idyll," is passing. Miss Roberts has dealt almost exclusively with the Kentucky that is heir to an eighteenth-century mode of life, the Kentucky that was a part of the agrarian democracy, or slavocracy, of the old South. Just what Wescott and Miss Roberts can do with material that is, roughly speaking, more modern, is still conjectural. One may be sure, in any case, that neither one would close the eyes, as Andrew Carnegie once advised Charles M. Schwab to do in the steel mills, to "what is."

Purposive thinking has made its appearance in Wilson's *I Thought of Daisy* because it has made its appearance among literary and intellectual people. The "I" who "thought of Daisy" is a young writer who has caught a glimpse of a life lived with reference to ethical values, as well as esthetic values, from a knowledge of the ideas of a philosopher and scientist who bears a remarkable likeness, in his intellectual occupations if not in his physical lineaments, to Professor Whitehead. The protagonist of Mr. Wilson's book, when compared with Fitzgerald's Armory Blaine, is a rapidly maturing personality. His sense of responsibility would qualify him as one imbued with Mr. Lippmann's psychological equivalent of high religion, for he is not content to let himself drift with every passion until his soul is the Wildean stringed lute on which all winds can play. One contrasts *This Side of Paradise* and *I Thought of Daisy* because the two novels set the tone for the beginning and end of the decade, respectively. The contrast gains piquancy because Fitzgerald and Wilson are from the same college, because each novel is, obviously, autobiographical, and because the authors have lived very much the same sort of life. *This Side of Paradise* was preoccupied with drift; *I Thought of Daisy* makes efforts towards mastery. Neither novel is first-rate fiction, for Fitzgerald's lacks form, and Wilson's is underdone on the dramatic side; but they are extremely illuminating. The New Humanists might gain a

271

clearer insight into actualities if they would read them in succession. Whether Mr. Wilson's protagonist has achieved a philosophy that is tangible enough for the majority of people in a democracy is not the question; the author has done his part by choosing an observable type to serve as the character for a novel. In a land of advertising run mad, of the public relations counsel, of business men who continue, and who probably will continue for a staggering number of years to come, to make quantity their desideratum, Mr. Wilson could hardly do more than he has done, for the number of people who live by humane ideals has not changed greatly in the past two decades. We still honor the wrong sort of efficiency, by and large. We still secretly admire the man who knows the joys of making successful contacts that will serve friendship and profit together. We still honor trivial gods by electing the wrong man to the presidency. We are still, many of us, shufflers, and being what we are, the only sort of literature that can issue from us is of the sort that will continue to annoy those who are cranky because the millennium is not upon our necks. The best we can do for those who want a literature about responsible human beings is to make of ourselves the instruments for social change, and if we do that we may be sure that Mr. More and others will condemn us as Rousseauistic radicals, and libertarian anarchists.

IV

In writing of the reappearance of volition in our fiction I have passed over the challenging figure of Dos Passos, whose *The 42nd Parallel* illustrates the dilemma of the artist who would bring ethics—which depend upon the sense of personal responsibility—back into the novel. Dos Passos's career has been an effort at passage from one concept of fiction to another. When he began writing, the older concept was pretty firmly entrenched. It was the concept of the novel as a reflection of life. The contrasted type of novel, as this survey must have brought into focus by now, may take one of two forms in its final fictional embodiment: it may be shaped so as to bring out the author's point of view, his vision of the world in philosophical terms that are more than agnostic, or it may rest content with dramatizing that point of view through the activities of a favored character. The latter form is, of course, on the borderline; it is often mistaken for its lesser brother, the novel that is a reflection of the world. Dos Passos began, in *Three Soldiers*, as the novelist who reflects life—but who, at the same time, wishes to do something more virile than serve as a camera eye. The Humanists, undoubtedly, would push *Three Soldiers* to one side as "naturalistic." It is naturalistic; but it is also a trifle more than a document, for the favored charac-

273

ter, John Andrews, with his preoccupation with the John Brown of popular mythology, implies a purposeful point of view. Uncertainly, flickeringly, Dos Passos lets a vision of the possibility of a different, an improved, social order, shine through his work. His novels of American cities are not undertaken merely to describe our urban civilization; they are written to indict its more unpleasant, its more blighting, aspects. If they do not go much beyond Dreiser (whose work is, in its effect, an indictment without vision as well as a transcription) they do strain at the possibility of visualizing a set of human beings who are able to cope with their surroundings in the effort to improve the conditions of existence.

Dos Passos's latest work, *The 42nd Parallel*, promises more, perhaps, than his previous fiction, for it is shaped with an idea towards making a philosophical judgment rise positively out of the record. For this novel, Dos Passos has looked about him and, try as he might, has found no common type in industrial America that will illustrate anything save a career devoted to what Count Keyserling, in one of his more lucid intervals, has called the service of the animal ideal. Mr. Dos Passos's people are authentic; they are wobblies who get aboard the I.W.W. band wagon for the thrill, dollar-a-year men who help promote profitable wars, secretaries who don't know what they want from life, sailors who knock around for want of anything better to do, interior decorators very much on the make—in general, the common run-of-the-mine American. Such people have been the stock in trade of the novelists of the 'twenties who have discovered the American world for themselves; they and their spiritual brothers and sisters appear in many a book devoted to the hobo's jungle, the career of the gangster, the profession of the prize-fighter, the rise of the bootlegger. From one of them, Fitzgerald made a superb novel, esthetically considered, in *The Great Gatsby*. But Dos Passos is not content to record the actions of such people; he must let the impact of his own volition, his own will to a different order of affairs, shine through his testimony. He has by no means achieved perfection in *The 42nd Parallel*, but he may succeed in his aims when the trilogy, of which I am told it is a part, is completely in our hands. In any event, Dos Passos is experimenting in the right direction. He, too, is unwilling to run ahead of his material. Because of his unwillingness to do this, he has incurred the hostility of Mr. More. Such is the penalty of common honesty.

v

It is difficult to speak of the future in any heartening prophetic terms, for there is not likely to be any great change in the dominant ideals of western civilization. We may expect good work from Thomas

Wolfe, who has written, in *Look Homeward, Angel*, an autobiographical novel of provincial life in the South that has neither the self-pity of the moon-calf school, nor yet the hopeless desire to escape the obligations of this planet which the characters of Sherwood Anderson have evinced. Mr. Wolfe has humor, an interesting temperament, and he is not afraid of the resources of the language. If Miss Roberts turns to urban themes (which might be disastrous), we may be certain that she would not lose her own special quality of bravery. Hemingway should grow because he has too much of a zest for life himself to permit him to stay by characters who impart their own ineffectuality and frustration to a novel. We may expect something from Fitzgerald if he will cease to scatter his gifts. Of the hold-overs from an era that preceded the 'twenties, Willa Cather should continue to satisfy some of us with her stories of older Americans. We have had enough of the satire of Sinclair Lewis, not because Mr. Lewis's own work is to be decried, but because continued repetition of an easy thing to do will only serve to take the edge off what has already been done in *Babbitt*. And if the quality of life in our novels and short stories fails to please the Humanists, we must remember that toning up that quality is the province of social criticism, of editorial writers of the dimensions of Lippmann, of educators of the Meiklejohn type (who do not re-

276

gard the English teacher as the sole repository of wisdom), and of philosophers who work with minds that are hospitable to the developments and methods of science, whether it be "pretentious" science or not. We must remember that literature cannot be cured by exhortation. If it could, any pulpiteer would be able to father a renaissance the like of which would stagger Pericles.

PAUL ELMER MORE AND THE EXTERNAL WORLD—Bandler II

PAUL ELMER MORE AND THE EXTERNAL WORLD

> *Phædrus:* I always wonder at you, Soc-
> rates; for when you are in the country,
> you really are a stranger who is being led
> about by a guide. Do you ever cross the
> border? I rather think that you never
> venture even outside the gates.
> *Socrates:* Very true, my good friend;
> and I hope you will excuse me when you
> hear the reason, which is, that I am a
> lover of knowledge, and the men who
> dwell in the city are my teachers, and not
> the trees, or the country. Though I do
> indeed believe that you have found a spell,
> with which to draw me out of the city
> into the country, as hungry cows are
> led by waving before them a bough or
> a fruit. For only hold up in like manner
> a book before me, and you may lead me
> all round Attica and over the wide world.
> And now having arrived, I intend to lie
> down, and do you choose any posture
> in which you can read best. Begin.

PAUL ELMER MORE, student of Socrates, Plato, the Indians, the Poets, and comparative religions, at the beginning of his career, displayed few of the Socratic virtues. Though he has been critic, scholar, preacher, and sage, he has been these almost accidentally, and not as a result of a definite purpose.

[1] The editor of this volume has asked me to write a note to explain my anomalous position of appearing both in *Humanism and America* and *The Critique of Humanism*. As I understand it the discussion is about ideas, not words, personalities, or parties: both groups favor humanism, but differ in their inter-

His criticism has not been directed to any particular end, nor addressed to any particular public; yet, as he is chiefly a moralist, he cannot have been writing for his own edification. He is a prophet without a people, and his message, lacking any practical intent, is vague and diffuse. He considers himself a follower of Socrates; but though he may agree with many of Socrates' conclusions, in his life and writings he has ignored the methods which Socrates employed and the medium in which he worked. Knowledge, Socrates taught, was to be found in the city; his teachers were men; and by intercourse with them, not by meditation in the country, or the study of books, he learned to know himself. Further, Socrates had a method. He began his conversations by considering some instance of courage, or friendship, or piety, which prompted his inquiry into their most general meaning. Moreover, he never relaxed his hold on the aim of the person questioned: knowledge insured correct vision; and with its object clearly discerned action would be firm and conclusive.

The *Shelburne Essays* open with "A Hermit's Notes

pretation of it; both believe in thought, in order, and in discipline; but whereas the academic Humanists believe that these can be introduced into modern life from the outside, the contributors to this volume seem to agree that these must issue out of modern life itself, taking what form the materials of the contemporary scene permit. Since the two volumes are complementary there is no need to explain an apparent change which does not exist.

on Thoreau." On the first page More confesses that "having found it impossible to educe any meaning from the tangled habits of mankind while he himself was whirled about in the imbroglio, he had determined to try the efficacy of undisturbed meditation at a distance. So deficient had been his education that he was actually better acquainted with the aspirations and emotions of the old dwellers on the Ganges than with those of the modern toilers by the Hudson or the Potomac. He had been deafened by the 'indistinguishable roar' of the streets, and could make no sense of the noisy jargon of the market place. But—shall it be confessed?—although he discovered many things during his contemplated sojourn in the wilderness, and learned that the attempt to criticize and not to create literature was to be his labor in the world, nevertheless he returned to civilization as ignorant, alas, of its meaning, as when he left it." To the same volume he had affixed as motto the remark of Lowell's, "Before we have an American literature, we must have an American criticism." But nowhere in his published writings has More attempted an analysis of that statement! [2]

[2] Nor has Norman Foerster, who uses the same remark for his *American Criticism*. Does he believe that More has given us an American criticism? Why, then, does he duplicate the achievement? Does he believe More has failed or is inadequate? Why, then, does he not say so, and point out the deficiencies in More's work?

Now what is the explanation of this state of mind that admits ignorance of its fellow countrymen and the American scene and yet wonders at its inability to understand them, and that would remedy its ignorance by retreating for two years to the Maine woods? What is behind the horror of New York, the emotional search for the meaning of civilization, the vague acceptance of Lowell?

No one can object to More's retiring to solitude for study and meditation; many people have left the world to understand themselves better, to discover their vocation or to commune with God; but More retired with conflicting and vague purposes which his subsequent writings will illustrate. Many of his statements on first reading appear wise and profound and only when analyzed and studied in the context of his total work does their indefiniteness and lack of any precise meaning become apparent. Consequently it is impossible to grapple with More's interpretation of people or movements, or with his ideas on any philosophical plane; his thought spins around and eludes one, so that the sole method for a critical analysis of his writings is that of quotation. If I quote extensively from an early and little known book it is not to ridicule a man for whom one can have the greatest personal respect, nor to ridicule his more mature writings, but because that book contains the key to More's

284

attitude towards life and the essential doctrines of his philosophy.[3]

More had published three volumes before the first of the *Shelburne Essays*: *Helena*, a book of poetry, *The Great Refusal, A Romance Told in Letters and Verses*, and *A Century of Indian Epigrams*, translated from the Sanskrit. The verses of *Helena* tell the story of a rustic courtship and Helena's refusal of her swain. The poems are often charming, filled with pleasant conceits and precise observations. *The Great Refusal, Letters of a Dreamer in Gotham* repeats the story of the poem: but the melancholy of the hero's mind has replaced the open countryside. A young man of studious interests, "a monk at heart, ensnared by the toils of skepticism," is required by his parents to enter into active life; he teaches Latin for a year; but "the nervous strain was too great for his sensitive nature"; he retired to his study and later withdrew from the world. While teaching school he met the sister of his favorite pupil, whom he had seen in a vision outside of Trinity Church. The romance consists of the letters and verses he addressed to her. Lady Esther, judging by his letters and verses, decided

[3] It may serve to prevent misunderstanding if I mention that I had twice read through More's works before I came to *The Great Refusal*. That book proved so helpful to me in understanding a development and an attitude that were otherwise baffling that I believe it will prove equally illuminating for other students of More.

wisely in refusing him: she thinks his moods untrustworthy, she protests that they are foreign to her thought, and considers him unfitted for life. Evidently the hero never expected to win her. "Too well I have known from the beginning," he writes, "that I could touch your imagination but not your heart. It is the heavy penalty I must pay in that I myself look out upon the rest of the world as upon fingers moving through a dream, scorning to feel for them in my heart." In the same letter he mentions the "reality of my passion"; but for that there is no evidence, and the reader can well doubt it, as he can doubt the reality of Lady Esther, of New York, and the philosophers and mystics so frequently quoted.

Of Lady Esther there is scarcely any description. Of New York we read, "The men of the street upon whom I looked out seemed in some way the cause of my mental torment. It was to satisfy their ideal that the dream life of my soul must be roused into painful activity. Their factitious world of daily routine and sordid cares bound my spirit as in an iron chain. I began to hate them. As always happens with me, my vision was affected by my emotions, and the stream of faces that flowed past became like so many diabolical apparitions, distorted, grimacing, threatening. The rumor of their voices and footsteps became like the noise of a tumultuous, victorious army charging over me."

For here within these city walls
No sound of laughter ever falls,
No tread of home-returning feet
Resounds along the melancholy street.

On either hand tall houses rise
With dead or heavy-slumbering eyes,
With dusty doors that never turn,
And smokeless chimneys where no fires may burn.

Within these walls no soul may be,
No soul of all humanity;
And all these mansions ranging dumb
Stand always ready, yet no tenants come.

For when the spirit enters there,
Like smoke 'tis scattered in the air:
Only their sighs that reach no ears,
Only the misty vapor of their tears,

Only the sobs of voiceless grief
Of this sad people past relief,
Remaining, cloud the air with pity,
Like fogs that overhang a human city.

And the dark sorrows of each heart
That with his life will not depart,
Here as a guilty thing abides,
And wanders wailing with the phantom tides.

And of philosophy we read, "I live not in a world of faith but in a world of imagination; and the sublime enunciations of St. Augustine or the vast dreams of Erigina may have more reality to me than to many a good member of the orthodox fold. I measure such ideas by their intrinsic beauty and not by any meager standard of revelation or dogma. . . . I revolt from substituting an intellectual creed for the beauty of mere hope."

The world of friendship, love, combat, art, religion, and philosophy, in which the Greeks so freely moved, exist only as they are reflected in the dreamer's mind and are colored by his feelings. The interest of the book does not lie in any drama of the dreamer's spirit, his gradual disillusionment, and his renunciation of the world; he was never attached to the world, and so there is no movement, no increase of insight; the sole interest lies in the exposure of the dreamer's mind. He reads the Indians and suspects that there "must lie the consolation of those who find our Western religion superficial and our philosophies mechanical; for here is taught in its purest form the method by which the individual soul, shaking off the trammels that bind it, may mount upwards into true communion with its infinite source." Soon he enters "into the more abiding fullness of renunciation, for love is crucified within me, and henceforth I listen only to the divine voice speaking from the infinite

288

realm of the heart." He discovers that "Brahma and Atman were but different names of the one Spirit. This conception of the inner and the outer Self, and their essential unity, is undoubtedly the ultimate achievement of thought. And this is clearly to be distinguished from a philosophy that would exalt the infinite Ego of a man. For the *Ego* says within us, *This is I! This is mine!* and is but a fiction of the brain rising and perishing with the body; but the Self is precisely that within us which is least individual, which suffers not nor enjoys, which knows neither birth nor death, which is not a portion or an emanation of the Eternal, but is that eternal Self."

A Century of Indian Epigrams contains More's most distinguished writing; but these, being translations, need not detain us, except for a passage in the introduction, written while he was at Shelburne. "The forms of the Greeks have passed away with their civilization, and cannot be revived or imitated. . . . We cannot to-day—it is better so—reproduce the literature of Greece; we should shudder at the Roman sternness; to call ourselves disciples of Buddha, or believers in Brahma—as some unstable minds are prone to do—would be superstition and not spirituality; yet to each of these peoples we may turn for strength and confirmation; nay, we must turn to them if we would fortify our isolated life with the virtue and dignity of experience."

289

II

The *Shelburne Essays* add nothing to our knowledge of More. His ideas are not developed; they are freed from many of their emotional overtones, although as T. S. Eliot observes, the mystical impulse "occasionally gets out of Mr. More's hand"; they are repeated, and are often introduced as mechanically as song cues in a musical comedy; and they are stated more authoritatively. The fear of New York is still upon him, of "the deep cañon of Broadway, between those vast structures, beautiful but sinister, where one feels depressed by the mere sensation of enormous creative life without sympathy and of unresting power without pity." This in 1905, when More was in his forty-first year! In *The Great Refusal*, the artist is described as "one who in his own way would likewise escape from the trammels of earthly things"; in the *Shelburne Essays* the function of the poet is "to beguile us into forgetfulness," to give us a "largeness of release from the fretful constraints of circumstance," to "break down the walls of this narrowing individuality and to bestow on us the illusion of unconfined liberty." In an essay on Dickens, More gives us one of his few reminiscences about Shelburne. "One day, being hungry for emotion, I started on these volumes; and read them through— read as only a starved man can read, without pause

290

and without reflection, with the smallest intermissions for sleep. It was an orgy of tears and laughter, almost immoral in its excess, a joy never to be forgotten." Literature was to fill the spiritual void, it was to replace experience and not to sharpen it, it was to corroborate and fortify his early conceptions. "Only, perhaps, when the hope of love (the *spes animi credula mutui*) and the visions of ambition, the belief in pleasure and the luxury of grief have lost their sting, do we turn to books with the contented understanding that the shadow is the reality, and the seeming reality of things is the shadow. At least for the critic, however it may be for the 'creative' writer, the final deliverance from self-deception would seem to be a necessity." This is in an essay on Sainte-Beuve.

The antipathy to metaphysics, theology, and exact thinking, in favor of some incommunicable personal experience and private beliefs becomes increasingly pronounced. More does not bother to refute philosophers and theologians any more than did a dreamer in Gotham; he dismisses them and on the strength of his authority assures us that "those questions that touch man's deepest moral experience are not capable of logical solution; indeed, they lose all reality as soon as subjected to dogmatic definition." While for most of us religion without content and without an object, without beliefs, dogmas, and institutions, is meaningless, there is "one man here and there, who

291

can rise to the clear vision of faith unsupported by belief in God." "Religion is the voice of faith uttering in symbols of the imagination its distrust of the world as a scene of deception and unreality." And More leaves us in no doubt as to what he means by faith: "It is that faculty of will, mysterious in its source and inexplicable in its operation, which turns the desire of man away from contemplating the fitful changes of the world toward an ideal, an empty dream it may be, or a shadow, or a mere name, of peace and absolute changelessness." From this vision of "one who stands apart striving in his own small way to live in the serene contemplation of the universe" it is easy to see that "Zeus and Apollo, the nymphs and driads, may retain their appeal as symbols of the religious imagination, when Jehovah and Jesus, Allah and Mohammed, have been dethroned as false gods and denounced as priestly impositions"; it is easy to "retain a reverence for traditional religion as for one of the illusions without which mankind would sink into the slough of the senses," for "he will know on what foundation of his own soul to build his hopes when myth and dogma seem to be crumbling away." No wonder that the Oxford movement meant to More "a kind of epicurean vision of holy things" and that he wrote of Newman, Newman who spent his life fighting emotionalism, the efforts of Protestants to maintain a religion without dogmas, institutions and authority, Newman to whom God was an ever-present reality, never doubted because never absent, that "his inability to find peace without the assurance of a personal God answering to the clamor of his desires is but another aspect of that illusion of the soul which has lost its vision of the true Infinite and seeks a substitute in the limitless expansion of the emotions."

At the end of the eighth volume of the *Shelburne Essays*, appropriately named *The Drift of Romanticism*, More has written some definitions of dualism. There we have the essence of his philosophy: they sum up the principles implicit in his earlier writings; and they underlie his interpretation of Plato and the Greek tradition. The author of *The Great Refusal* quickly eliminates the external world. "By the word desire is here not meant the intelligent want of a definite object, but the mere outreaching of vital energy." "Happiness is a feeling that accompanies the governing of our impulses by the inner check." "Whatever is recognized as remaining in the self after the separation of the phenomena of nature is called the soul." "Self-recollection is the quiet and deliberate gathering of the mind from the many to the one. Prayer is the same and directed to the one imagined as the infinite, eternal God. A great need of mankind is for more recollection of prayer. Therein shall a man learn to know the truth of his own being and see with

293

open eyes the infinite consequences to himself of that truth; and from thence he shall go out into the world armed with power and assured in peace. Through the distractions and trials of life he shall carry with him the secret possession of religious philosophy which has been called the *amor dei intellectualis;* rather to him belongs the praise of Plato, 'Show me a man able to see both the one and the many in nature, and I will follow in his footsteps as though he were a god.' " The quotation is from the Phædrus and we have seen what method Socrates employed to discriminate between the one and the many. If we consider the Laws, we can see what methods Plato employed. They hardly resemble the Greek Tradition. They are perhaps the most thorough work ever conceived by man on the minute and practical government of a state; they are the fruit of long reflection on Greek life and long experience in it; they do not thrust us into an impoverished, sterile, inner world, but into the world of the Greek city and its enterprises; they do not discuss impulses but the proper way and time to drink; they do not exalt an inner check but the golden cord of reason which connects man with the gods and demonstrates their existence.

III

Of the Greek tradition one can repeat what a dreamer in Gotham said of Albertus Magnus: he

294

"seemed to bring the hard intellectual faculties of the brain into the service of the imaginings of the heart, justifying the wildest vagaries of passion." More there concludes that without acceptance of the dogma of the Incarnation mankind is in peril of sinking back into barbarism. Such a statement seems a long way from the early essays; but, in reality, it is More's last effort to fortify his "isolated life with the virtue and dignity of experience." He does not attempt to justify revelation; he is willing to dispense with all other dogmas; and even his proof of the incarnation is "whether it corresponds with the lessons and surest intuitions of spiritual experience." His Anglicanism, far from representing a new development, is already fully stated in the sixth volume of the *Shelburne Essays*: "The strong distaste of the English mind for logical conclusions enabled, and still enables, the church of that country at its best, to open a door through the walls of superstition and rationalism into the garden of liberty planted and watered by the spiritual imagination." In fact the thesis and theory of the Greek tradition is expounded in 1905 in the same manner and with the same cogency as it is expounded to-day. "But if, intellectually the vision of the Divine Light was vouchsafed to Plato more than to any other man, historically it has been presented to the gross, unpurged eyes of the world in the life and death of Jesus. The precision of dogma, even the

295

Bible, meant relatively little to Mr. Shorthouse. 'I do not advocate belief in the Bible,' he wrote, 'I advocate belief in Christ.' Somehow, in some way beyond the scope of logic, the ideal which Plato had beheld, the divine idea which all men know and doubt, became a personality that one time, and henceforth the sacraments that recall the drama of that holy life were the surest means of obtaining the silence of the world through which the inner voice speaks and is heard."

More's ideas have not changed, but only his emotional reactions. Some attitudes that he once maintained now seem cold and harsh, and need the support of authority; some superstitions that he once condemned now seem desirable; but always he has held to "the inviolable individuality in which lie the pain and glory of our human estate," and he has never demeaned it by an explanation or a defense. At times he seems to confuse the salvation of his soul with the salvation of mankind, but that is only incidental, for he is scarcely interested in mankind. At times he seems concerned with literature, but if we recall his dictum that "the hardest test of the critic, in the exercise of his special function, is his tact and sureness in valuing the productions of his own day," and recall his neglect of contemporary literature and his occasional wrathful utterances about it, we realize that he has not attempted to be a critic. The best of his essays are on men like Crabbe, Pope, Lamb, Hazlitt

296

and the wits, when More forgets his moralizing and chats in the intimacy of his library.

The pity of his life is that though he has set out to be a moral teacher one can learn no lesson from him. He has said too much and conveyed too little; he has fortified his garden and failed to cultivate it. He has not been an eclectic; the principles of assimilation, either a personal moving center, or an accepted tradition, he lacks. He has not explored the possibilities of the American scene, like Hawthorne, or retired from it, like Emily Dickinson, or remained aloof while within it, like Santayana, or left it, like Henry James. His purpose from the beginning was vague; he has followed no line to the end; and one lays down his work with the feeling that his great erudition was wasted because it was not directed, because it was not disciplined to any definite problems or dignified by any consuming interests.

POETRY, MORALITY, AND
CRITICISM — Winters

POETRY, MORALITY, AND CRITICISM

BEFORE attempting to analyze a poetry so difficult and so elusive as that of the best moderns,
it would appear wise to summarize as clearly as
possible those qualities for which one looks in a poem.
We may say that a poem in the first place should offer
us new perceptions, not only of the exterior universe,
but of human experience as well; it should add, in
other words, to what we have already seen.   This is
the elementary function for the reader.   The corresponding function for the poet is that the practice of
his art should sharpen and train his sensibilities and
render them more acute, and that the very exigencies
of the medium as he employs it in the act of perception should force him to the discovery of values
which he never would have found without the con-
vening of all of the conditions of that particular act,
conditions one or more of which will be the necessity
of solving some particular difficulty such as the loca-
tion of a rime or the perfection of a cadence without disturbance to the remainder of the poem.   The
poet who suffers from such difficulties instead of
profiting by them is only in a rather rough sense a
poet at all.

   If, however, the difficulties of versification are
merely a stimulant to the *poet,* the reader may argue
that he finds them a hindrance to himself and that

301

he prefers some writer of prose who appears to offer him as much with less trouble to all concerned. The answer to such a reader is that the appearance of equal richness in the writer of prose is necessarily deceptive. Language is a kind of abstraction, even at its most "concrete"; such a word as "cat," for instance, is statistical and not specific. Such a word becomes specific only in so far as one gets it into some kind of experiential complex, which qualifies it and limits it, which gives it, in short, a local habitation as well as a name. Such a complex is the poetic line or other unit, which, in turn, should be a definite part of the larger complex, or poem. That is, I imagine, what Mallarmé had in mind when he demanded that the poetic line be a new word, not found in any dictionary, and partaking of the nature of incantation (that is, having the power to materialize a previously non-existent experience). The poem, to be perfect, should likewise be a new word in the same sense, a word of which the line as we have defined it is merely a syllable. Such a "word" is, of course, composed of much more than the sum of its words as one normally uses the term and its syntax. It is composed of an almost fluid complex, if the words are not too nearly contradictory, of relationships between words (in the dictionary sense), relationships involving meaning-content, cadences, rimes, juxtapositions, literary and other connotations, inversions, and

302

so on almost indefinitely. These relationships, it should be obvious, extend the poet's vocabulary almost incalculably. They partake of the fluidity and unpredictability of experience and so provide a means of treating experience with some degree of accuracy as well as of freedom. If the poet does not wish, as he seldom does, to reproduce a given experience with approximate exactitude, he can employ the experience as a basis for or an ingredient in a new experience that will be just as real, in the sense of being non-statistical, and perhaps more valuable. Now verse is more valuable than prose in this process for the simple reasons that its rhythms are faster and more highly organized than are those of prose, and so lend themselves to a greater complexity and condensation of relationship, and that the intensity of this convention renders possible a greater intensity of other desirable conventions, such as poetic language and devices of rhetoric in the best sense. The writer of prose must substitute bulk for this kind of intensity; he must define his experience by giving all of its past history, the narrative logic leading up to it, whereas the experiential conclusions given in a good lyric poem, though specific in themselves, are applicable without alteration to a good many past histories. In this sense the lyric is general as well as specific; in fact, this quality of transferable, or generalized, emotion might be regarded as the defining quality of lyric

303

poetry. What I have just said should make plain the difficulty of comprehending a poem exactly and fully; the sum of its intentions may be very different from its paraphrasable or purely logical content. If one take, for instance, Mr. Allen Tate's sonnet, "The Subway," and translate it into good scholarly prose, using nothing but the individual dictionary meanings of the words and the syntactic logic as a reference, one will find the author saying that, as a result of his metaphysics and of his metropolitan environment, he is going mad. Now as a matter of actual fact, the sonnet says nothing of the sort; let the reader consider it carefully:

Dark accurate plunger down the successive knell
Of arch on arch, where ogives burst a red
Reverberance of hail upon the dead
Thunder, like an exploding crucible!
Harshly articulate, musical steel shell
Of angry worship, hurled religiously
Upon your business of humility
Into the iron forestries of hell:

Till broken in the shift of quieter
Dense altitudes tangential of your steel,
I am become geometries—and glut
Expansions like a blind astronomer
Dazed, while the worldless heavens bulge and reel
In the cold revery of an idiot.

The sonnet indicates that the author has faced and defined the possibility of the madness that I have mentioned (a possibility from the consideration of which he has doubtless found it impossible to escape and from the consideration of which others may therefore have found it impossible to escape) and has arrived at a moral attitude toward it, an attitude which is at once defined and communicated by the poem. This attitude is defined only by the entire poem, not by its isolated logical content; it is a matter not only of logical content but of feeling as well. The feeling is quite specific and unparaphrasable, but one may indicate the nature of it in a rough way by saying that it is a feeling of dignity and of self-control in the face of a situation that is of major difficulty, a difficulty which the poet fully apprehends. This feeling is inseparable from what we call poetic form or unity, the creation of the "word" in the Mallarméan sense, for this act of creation is nothing more nor less than an act of evaluating and shaping (or controlling) a given experience. It hardly seems to me too much to say that Mr. Tate's sonnet is as brilliant a stylistic triumph as Keats' sonnet, "On the Sea," and that the initial emotion may have been more difficult to manipulate; the values of tone and cadence alone are of indescribable perfection, and they represent only the beginning of the poem's beauty. To reënforce my point, I shall take the liberty of quoting another sonnet on another subject, but in which something comparable occurs. The poem is by Mr. Howard Baker:

So he was first to love you, first to hold
Wild girlish eyes in that translucent charm,
That gold-tipped net like fireflies on the mold,
The trembling limbs gone weak to trembling harm.
You say a mockingbird increased your pain
While his oration bruised the mint and cress—
And each word echoing the former vain . . .
Ah, you in your great hat and party dress!

And now I have no stumbling vows to call,
No laws to fix the magic of your hand.
But yet I think there comes a time when all
Is oratory, all dead moments stand
Like figures on a frieze, each icy gesture
The residue to prop an empty vesture.

The spiritual control in a poem, then, is simply a manifestation of the spiritual control within the poet, and, as I have already indicated, it may have been an important means of arriving at a complete realization of that control. The laxity of the one ordinarily involves the laxity of the other; the rather limp versification of Mr. Eliot and of Mr. MacLeish is inseparable from the spiritual limpness that one feels behind the poems, as the fragmentary, ejaculatory, and over-excited quality of a great many of the poems of

Mr. Hart Crane is inseparable from the intellectual confusion upon which these particular poems appear to rest (see, for examples, "The Dance," "Cape Hatteras," and "Atlantis"). Mr. Crane possesses energy in a high degree, but his faculties function clearly only in a limited experiential range (see "Repose of Rivers," "Voyages II," "Southern Cross," and "Cutty Sark"); outside that range he is either numb (see "My Grandmothers' Loveletters" and "Harbor Dawn") or unsure of himself and hence unintegrated (see "The River," a very powerful poem the lack of sureness and hence of integration in which may be due to the Whitmanian fallacy of trying to get at humanity "en masse" instead of in particular and hence clearly and definitely) or both (see "Indiana, probably one of the worst poems in modern literature). Many of the poems of Mr. Eliot and of Mr. MacLeish could be paraphrased down to about the same thing as Mr. Tate's sonnet; the difference between them and Mr. Tate in this respect is that, as their form is much looser to start with, the process of paraphrasing would constitute a much smaller degree of betrayal. And we must not forget that this "form" is not something outside of the poet, something "esthetic" and superimposed upon his moral content; it is essentially a part, in fact it is the greater part, of whatever he may have to say about himself in any poem, even though he may be arriving at the final perfection of the condition he is describing while he describes it and in part as a result of the act and technique of description.

I should pause here to remark that many writers have sought to seize the fluidity of experience by breaking down the limits of form, but in so doing they defeat their own ends. For, as I have shown, writing, as it approaches the looseness of prose and departs from the strictness of verse, tends to lose the capacity for fluid and highly complex relationships between words; language, in short, reapproaches its original statistical stiffness and generality, and one is forced to recognize the truth of the apparent paradox that the greatest fluidity of statement is possible where the greatest clarity of form prevails. It is hard to see how the existence of such a work as Mr. Joyce's most recent creation can be anything but precarious, despite its multitudes of incidental felicities; for it departs from the primary condition of prose—coherent and cumulative logic—without, since it is, finally, prose, achieving the formal precision of verse. These remarks should not be construed, however, as an argument against "free" verse. The free verse that is really verse is not in the least free; and the meters of Dr. Williams and of Miss Moore are among the firmest and most valuable of our time.

Thus, in getting over the second step in my ex-

308

position, I have nearly got over the third. The poet, in striving toward an ideal of poetic form at which he has arrived through the study of other poets, is actually striving to perfect a moral attitude toward that range of experience of which he is aware. Such moral attitudes are contagious in the history of literature from poet to poet, and, within the history of the poet, from poem to poem. The presence of Hardy and Arnold, let us say, in so far as their successful works offer us models and their failures warnings or unfulfilled suggestions, should make it easier to write good poetry; they should not only aid us, by providing standards of sound style or feeling, to test the soundness of our own poems, but, since their experiential range is very wide, they should aid us, as we are able to enter and share their experience, to extend our own range, to grow into regions that we have not mastered or perhaps even discovered. Too often a minor poet or other reader will recognize in such a master the validity of only that part of the master's experience that corresponds to his own limited range and will rule out the poetry to which he is consequently numb as sentimental or insignificant. Inflexibility of critical opinion in such matters is not particularly conducive to growth. The discipline of imitation is thus valuable if it leads to understanding and assimilation. Random experiment may likewise be valuable: one may hit on a form that induces some new state or states of mind. I regard as fallacious the notion that the attitude necessarily precedes the form: the form *may* precede, and the attitude, in any case, is never definite till the form is achieved. I can offer no authority for this belief save my own experience, as I have been able to observe and analyze it. It does not follow that any attitude resulting from random experiment is intrinsically desirable; it is here that criticism becomes necessary. A failure, however, may offer a valuable hint to some one else. The poet who has succeeded once or twice in mastering difficult and central emotions and in recording his mastery for future reference should find it easier to succeed again. I am not, in saying this, setting up art as a substitute for religion or formal ethics. Religion is highly desirable if it is really available to the individual; the study of philosophy is always available and is of incalculable value as a preliminary and as a check to one's activities as a poet and as a critic (that is, an intelligent reader). I am merely attempting to define a few of the things that poetry does. It would perhaps be wise to add another caution: I suffer from no illusion that any man who can write a good poem has a naturally sweet moral temper or that the man who has written three good poems is a candidate for canonization. Literary history is packed with sickening biographies. But it is worth noting that the poetry of such a man, say, as Rochester (who in this is typical of his age) displays a mastery of an extremely narrow range of experience, and that his moral brutality falls almost wholly in those regions (nearly everything except worldly manners) with which his poetry fails to deal. One does not find such brutality in the author of "Dover Beach" and of "Philomela." Aquinas, I believe, says that a demon is good in so far as he may be said to exist, but that he is a demon in so far as his existence is incomplete. Rochester, we may say, was as dead as a thug in most of the regions of the human heart. Most poets have been and are pathetically blind to the limitations of their being and to the possibilities of their chosen medium for the perfection and extension of their being. All of this, however, does not detract from the quality of Rochester's poetry, which is remarkably fine; Rochester does not extend the standards that he recognizes into fields to which they do not apply, and he so falsifies nothing. In reading him, one is aware that he is a wholly sound and beautiful poet and that there are more complex and greater poets. That is all that one has a right to be aware of.

If a poem, in so far as it is good, constitutes a moral success in the face of a certain experience, it is only fair to add that some experiences offer very slight difficulties and some very great, and that the poem will be the most valuable, which, granted it achieves formal perfection, represents the most complex and

311

difficult victory. In the great tragic poets, such as Shakespeare, Hardy, and Racine, one feels that a victory has been won over life itself, so much is implicated in the themes; that feeling is the source of their power over us, for they completely absorb us, whereas a slighter poet will absorb very little of us and leave the rest untouched. This requisite seems to be ignored in a large measure by a good many contemporary poets of more or less mystical tendencies, who avoid the difficult task of mastering the more complex forms of experience by setting up a theoretic escape from them and by then accepting that escape with a good deal of lyrical enthusiasm. Such a theoretic escape is provided us, I fear, by Mr. Crane, in one of the most extraordinary sections of his volume, *The Bridge,* the piece called "The Dance," and such escapes are often indulged in by Mr. Yeats. In the religious poets of the past one encounters this vice very seldom; the older religions are fully aware that the heart, to borrow the terms of a poem by Janet Lewis, is untranslatable, whatever may be true of the soul, and that one can escape from the claims of the world only by understanding those claims and accustoming oneself to the thought of eventually putting them by. The attitude is humane, and it does not belittle nor evade the magnitude of the task; it is essentially a tragic attitude. The religious fervor of Gerard Hopkins, of John Donne, or of George Her-

312

bert should in no way weaken the force of their verses for the non-believer. Neither should the deterministic doctrines, whatever their nature or extent, that can be found in Hardy, in any way weaken his poetry, and for the same reason. Though a belief in any form of determinism should, if pushed to logical conclusions, eliminate the belief in and consequently the functioning of whatever it is that we call the will, yet there is no trace of any kind of spiritual disintegration in Hardy's work. The tragic necessity of putting by the claims of the world without the abandonment of self-control is just as definitely the theme of Hardy's poetry as of Herbert's; and as self-control, or what is equivalent to it in this case, poetic form, is not abandoned but is maintained and even strengthened and purified up to the end of Hardy's life, the "will" is obviously present, and his experience is no less universal than that of any other tragic poet. There is probably not another master of English verse and of the English language, that is, of human experience materialized in the poetic terms of our tongue, so rich and so profound this side of Shakespeare. To wonder if his deterministic theories can invalidate his poetry, as several recent critics have been disposed to do, is mere pedantic twaddle.[1]   Mr.

[1] Hardy's determinism does damage his novels occasionally, however. Those incidents in which fate meddles with the plot, those ironical coincidences (as in *A Pair of Blue Eyes*, for example), may have their prototypes in experience, but one feels

313

Crane's attitude, however, very often (though not always, and sometimes only in a measure) suggests a kind of theoretic rejection of all human endeavor in favor of some vaguely defined but ecstatically asserted existence on a higher plane. As the exact nature of the higher plane is uncertain, it forms a rather uncertain and infertile source of material for exact poetry; one can write poetry about it only by utilizing in some way more or less metaphorical the experience of the plane from which one is trying to escape; but as one *is* endeavoring to escape from this plane, not to master it and understand it, one's evaluations of it and feelings about it are certain to be incomplete

that Hardy insists on using them merely to justify his theory; they break up the organic unity and independence of the action. It is, one feels, not fate, but Hardy, who is meddling, just as definitely as Dickens occasionally meddles to save the day for some one. Dickens' meddling is likely, because of his prejudices, to involve sentimentality; Hardy's meddling is always melodramatic. The novels have to be accepted, because of their sheer grandeur, even though one cannot overlook the flaws. The same kind of melodrama gets into the lyrics occasionally, when an isolated incident of the unlikely and ironical sort, a satire of circumstance, is described in a short poem. The thing that ruins the poem in such a case is not in the nature of the incident, but the fact that the stress is laid on the nature of the incident rather than on the emotion resulting. The poem is anecdotal rather than lyrical, and the anecdote is obviously selected to prove a point. Such incidents are common in life, and are likely to be in the background of many of Hardy's best pieces—"The Wind's Prophecy," for example, or "I Say I'll Seek Her." The emotion is universal, but the incident really *proves* nothing whatever.

314

and confused, though they may be infused with occasional magnificence. There is then here, if I understand rightly such poems as "The Dance," an attempt
to apply to two fields terms that are in one's initial
hypothesis applicable to neither, that is, to apply to
each of two mutually exclusive fields the terms of
the other. The result is confused evaluations and
poetry that, whatever its occasional grandeur, is incoherent and basically unmotivated. This is a vice of
the mind and of the feelings of which Rochester was
not guilty. If it be replied that Mr. Crane can ap-
prehend the state of absolute felicity that he postu-
lates in terms only of this less felicitous life, since he
is, for the time, of the world, the answer is that of
religion: he should discipline himself in the understanding of the terms of this world as a preliminary
to all other activity. That there are large regions
of experience to which Mr. Crane reacts crudely and
without comprehension is shown by the stiffness of
certain poems that I have already pointed out. Further, even when he faces his experience without
evasion, as in "Repose of Rivers" and "Voyages II,"
one feels that the experience is curiously limited and
uncomplicated; it is between the author, isolated
from all human complications, and Eternity. Objective proof of this limitation cannot be found in the
paraphrasable content of the poems (though there is
little there to disprove it), any more than proof of

315

the opposite quality can be found in the paraphrasable content of Hardy; it is in each case a matter of feeling that invades the poems mainly by way of the non-paraphrasable elements: one *feels* the fragility of Mr. Crane's finest work, just as one feels the richness of Hardy's. Hardy is able to utilize, for example, though this is not the whole of the matter, great ranges of literary, historical, and other connotation in words and cadences; one feels behind each word the history of the word and the generations of men that embodied that history; Hardy gets somehow at the wealth of the race. It should be observed, again, how the moral discipline is inherent in the literary discipline, how it becomes almost, at times, in Hardy, a matter of living philology. From the greater part of this wealth Mr. Crane appears to be isolated and content to remain isolated. Mr. Crane becomes, of course, in his best work, a universal symbol of the human consciousness in a particular situation, a fact which is the source of his power, but of the human consciousness in the simplest form of that situation, a fact which is the source of his limitation. And yet I do not wish to seem to belittle Mr. Crane, whom I regard as one of the four or five most extraordinary poets of our time; a lesser poet would not serve my turn.

I should like to forestall one possible objection to the theory of poetry that I am trying to elucidate. Poetry, as a moral discipline, in the sense in which I am trying to show it to be a moral discipline, should not be regarded as one more doctrine of escape. That is, moral responsibility should not be transferred from action to paper, in the face of any particular situation. Poetry, if pursued either by the poet or the reader, in the manner that I have suggested, should offer a means of enriching one's awareness of human experience and of so rendering greater the possibility of intelligence in the face of future situations involving action; and it should offer likewise a means of inducing certain more or less constant habits of feeling, which should render the possibility of one's acting, in a future situation, in accordance with the findings of one's improved intelligence. It should, in other words, increase the intelligence and strengthen the moral temper; these effects should naturally be carried over into action, if, through constant discipline, they are made permanent acquisitions. I am claiming no more for poetry than Arnold claimed for it; no more, I imagine, than did Homer. I am simply trying to illuminate one or two of the more obscure corners of the theory.

II

Mr. Paul Elmer More, in his essay on Symons, *Shelburne Essays, First Series,* confines himself to a description of the false dilemma in which Symons locates the tragedy of human life, and fails to make any connection between this false dilemma, as such, and Mr. Symons' poetry as poetry. The dilemma of lust versus satiety is, in its way, and under certain circumstances, sound enough—that is, it may be, within its limits, a real dilemma. But when, as in Mr. Symons' poetry, lust is confused with absolute felicity and satiety with disillusionment, or tragedy, the dilemma becomes, as Mr. More claims, false. This was an inherited sentimentality, a false evaluation of sensuous pleasures, that, as it was carried into action (or poetry), corrupted experience. The postulated source of felicity is childish, and consequently the disillusionment appears childish, and the tragedy becomes mere sentimentality and self-indulgence for lack of motivation; the entire scale of values upon which Mr. Symons' poetry rests is an inadequate support for the emotions to which he is laying claim. Consequently, he is forced to depend too much upon other poets, to employ unassimilated emotion from outside sources, and we get the curiously sugared mixture of Swinburne and Verlaine that constitutes Mr. Symons' poetic style. Most of his poetry can be reduced to automatic mannerism, just as can most of the expressions of feeling of the sentimentalist whom one meets in the flesh. But of the viciousness of this *writing*, of the whole diseased state of feeling, there is not a word to be found in Mr. More's essay; Mr. More even praises its "sincerity," whatever that

318

may be. The thing that Mr. More finds reprehensible is purely and simply the actions and false reasoning recorded, and of which, for his purposes, one record would be as good as any other. Mr. More concludes his essay with approbation for a poem containing—if one paraphrase it—sounder doctrine, but—if one *read* it, as poetry—sentiments quite as shallow as those to be found in anything else that Mr. Symons has written.

If Mr. More finds Mr. Symons' sentiments sound, Mr. Symons can answer that Mr. More has no right to object to the doctrine giving rise to them, unless Mr. More can prove that the doctrine is an inadequate formulation of the attitude shown in Mr. Symons' best poems, which, in this event, would transcend the doctrine (as do the best poems of Wordsworth and Blake, and, fortunately, of a great many other poets) and be good poetry. But Mr. More does nothing of the sort; he states arbitrarily that the doctrine is false, without definitely relating it to any body of experience that would prove it false (Mr. Symons' own, as materialized in his style, would be fair evidence in the case), and then adds that the poetry is uniformly reprehensible (though "sincere" and well-written) because the doctrine is "false," until he comes to a poem that seems to him pretty good because the doctrine is pretty good. The process is mechanical and arbitrary.

It is obvious that what I am demanding of Mr. More would lead to a "subjective" evaluation of a body of experience. Unfortunately that is the only kind of evaluation of experience, literary or non-literary, that is ultimately possible, and one has to have the training as well as the courage to make it. In critical, as in ethical, dogma, the abstractions can be pushed just so far (they can be pushed, in criticism, as I have indicated, much farther than Mr. More has pushed them—that is, not only into the terminology of ethics, but from that terminology into the terminology of literature), and then the act of interpretation, or rather of understanding, arises. It may be dangerous, but it is inevitable if one is to get out of mechanical formulæ into disciplined experience. The acceptance of the subjective act [2] is not impressionism, in the criticism of art or of life, if, and only if, the intellectual discipline has been extended first as far as it will go. The act becomes impressionism if indulged in when the intellectual discipline is half completed, as when Mr. More, in the volume I have already mentioned, endeavors to judge the early poetry of Mr. Yeats, as poetry, immediately as a result of his objections to Mr. Yeats' intellectual (if that is the word) preoccupations. And this type

[2] By "subjective act" I mean nothing more than the attempt to understand the non-paraphrasable part of the poetic language, or rather the poem as a whole, after one has done talking about it.

320

of bastard impressionism is perhaps the most dangerous sort, for it offers the illusion of an intellectual
sanction. The essay entitled "Dionysus in Dismay" by
Mr. Stanley P. Chase in the volume entitled *Humanism and America* is a reduction to absurdity of this
sort of impressionism; the essay would appear insolent were it not so ludicrous. Mr. More, in writing
on Tolstoy in the same volume, admits that he is unable to resolve the dilemma that Tolstoy posed, the
dilemma of beauty versus goodness, of art versus philosophy, that is, of getting any kind of workable relationship between ethical and artistic terms, and ends
in a vision of heaven and hell as in a blaze of glory,
which is, however, ambiguous. Mr. More's misapprehension is really as innocent as Tolstoy's—it is only
his ethical dogmas that differ. Both writers are
equally helpless at getting their dogmas into orderly
action since they both accept the Platonic error of
finding the secret of good action ultimately in the
intellect (that is, in the definition of a formula,
which, then, supposedly, can be mechanically applied
to regulate action), not, like Aristotle, in the feelings.
Tolstoy, like Plato, shows some consistency in throw-
ing art, or most of it, overboard. Mr. More is unwilling to do this, but he apparently finds no justification in the intellect; his justification is a feeling
that is sometimes pleasant and sometimes rather unhappy. It is on more or less whimsical sentiment,

321

then, that one expects to find most of his judgments based when he departs from the application of formulæ—he remains either what Mr. Tate has labeled him, a moral mechanist, or a kind of wavering and dubious impressionist. It is only fair to add that Mr. More's method gets farther in dealing with a novelist, as in his essays on Hawthorne, or with a dramatist, as in his essay on Beaumont and Fletcher, than in dealing with a lyric poet; for in fiction and drama moral logic and structural outline are one, and the same terms must be employed to describe both. The language of the novelist, since it is prose, more nearly coincides with that of the moralist; and even in dealing with poetic drama one can get over a large part of the ground before one gets to the poetry.

If the reader happens to be familiar with Mr. More's later essay, "Criticism," *Shelburne Essays, Seventh Series,* he may feel that Mr. More has finally solved the difficulty raised in the earlier volume and that my objections are at best but a set of footnotes. I confess myself skeptical. The terms of Mr. More's essay are pretty general and are not particularly new; and the value of any such theory is likely to reside in the footnotes, if it possesses any value at all. Mr. More's actual critical practice, both before and since, has been usually such that one imagines that, should he supply his own footnotes, they would not greatly alter his initial position. The application of his formulæ to modern literature is both arbitrary and ill-tempered—and, one is forced to add, Mr. More discloses great ignorance of the actual data of the literature that he treats so brusquely. He finds a literary issue in a comparison of James Russell Lowell (the New England Poet) and Amy Lowell (the Modern Poet)! (See *Shelburne Essays*, XI, p. 25.) It is a comparison that the student and admirer of Emily Dickinson and of Allen Tate will find curiously irrelevant. Ordinarily Mr. More's thrusts at modern literature, like Mr. Babbitt's, are thrusts in vacuo, no victim being named. Occasionally Mr. More or one of his colleagues does mention the victim, but it is usually a man whose reputation is journalistic rather than literary, such as Sinclair Lewis, Mencken, or Cabell. The Humanist movement may perform a commendable task in purifying our journalism of such influences—that is a subject which I feel myself incompetent to discuss—but it should not delude itself with the thought that it is dealing with literature. The younger writers—Tate, Cowley, Crane, Louise Bogan, Léonie Adams, Howard Baker, Elizabeth Roberts, Janet Lewis, Caroline Gordon, Katherine Anne Porter, Glenway Wescott, and others related—have never been touched by, indeed they have scarcely been aware of, mid-Americanism and Menckenism. They stem from the great stylists of the middle and earlier generations—Pound, Stevens, Williams, Miss Moore,

H. D., Eliot, Joyce (the early Joyce, largely), Lawrence, Hardy, Cunningham Graham and others. There is a steady line of development that is in Mr. Crane alone tinged with Whitmanism, and in relation to which the Humanists' bugaboos are largely a journalistic sideshow. There has been, in other words, a steady tradition of discipline, which, though it may not have been perfect, is at least organic and living, and with which the Humanists (for, as a literary critic, Mr. More is incomparably the best of them) have shown themselves wholly incapable to deal. It is hardly likely, therefore, that they will exert any profound influence on the future of American letters.

Mr. Chase, in his essay "Dionysus in Dismay," illustrates the dangers lurking in Mr. More's method as well as in Mr. Foerster's theory of the reformed professor (i.e., the Humanist), and it is only fair to all concerned to state that Mr. Chase is very little more fatuous than Mr. More himself when Mr. More mentions modern literature. Mr. Chase writes of Wallace Stevens' "Anecdote of the Jar":

Now the elements of this experience—the jar, its shape, color, and quality, the hill in Tennessee where it is placed, the behavior or appearance of the wilderness, the bird, the bush—stand doubtless in some kind of relation with each other in the poet's mind, have possibly certain symbolic values. Since we have no clews to these relationships and values, our mind is free to do anything it pleases with the bare gray jar, the hill, and the wilderness. This freedom, however, and any pleasure we may take in the separate images, in the rhythms, or the placing of the words, are not sufficient compensation for the state of uncertainty and slight irritation in which we are left. Very likely the little poem [*sic*] is meant to suggest nothing more than the superiority, to an intensely civilized person, of the simplest bit of handicraft over any extent of unregulated "nature," [3] but it has been seriously interpreted to me, by devotees of recent poetry, as, respectively, an *objet d'art,* a sex-symbol, and a burial urn containing the remains of a valued friend. And so it must remain, for me, not only like nothing else in Tennessee but like nothing else in the universe.

For the reader's convenience, I quote the poem:

> I placed a jar in Tennessee,
> And round it was, upon a hill.
> It made the slovenly wilderness
> Surround that hill.
>
> The wilderness rose up to it,
> And sprawled around, no longer wild.
> The jar was round upon the ground
> And tall and of a port in air.

[3] Observe the Humanist's preoccupation and compare it with the curious nostalgia for savagery running through all of Mr. Stevens' more ironic pieces, and then return to this poem.

It took dominion everywhere.
The jar was gray and bare.
It did not give of bird or bush,
Like nothing else in Tennessee.

Mr. Chase's phrase "devotees of recent poetry," of course, is particularly devastating; it is one of those phrases that, like "the typical modern poet" (which Mr. Chase likewise employs), are so general and hence so meaningless as to be wholly unanswerable; it should prove an especially telling stroke with the reading public. Any one at all familiar with the workings of Mr. Stevens' extremely ingenious and sensitive (and occasionally, be it said, profound) mind will suspect him of being too witty by at least a little to indulge in any such arbitrary symbolism, such "childish hieroglyphics," as Mr. Chase is bent on finding in his work. For myself, while admitting that all humans are fallible and that in dealing with Mr. Stevens I may be getting beyond my depth, I have always believed that Mr. Stevens was writing in that poem about a jar on a hilltop. With that simple notion of the poem, I have succeeded in extracting from it a good deal of amusement and enjoyment, off and on, for some ten years; it is, as a matter of fact, one of the half dozen or so of Mr. Stevens' lesser achievements that have pleased me most. There is no more reason for seeking a hieroglyphic significance in this

poem than there is in *Lear;* Mr. Chase admits that
Mr. Stevens has given him no clews to one, yet it does
not occur to him that Mr. Stevens had in all likeli-
hood no idea that the reader would go around looking for any.   Mr. Chase has overlooked the poetry in
an attempt to find the formula.

I quote also the witty and humanistic criticism of
Dr. W. C. Williams, the author of "The Destruction
of Tenochtitlan," "To Mark Anthony in Heaven,"
"The Widow's Lament in Springtime," and other
trifles:

The enigmatic character of Dr. William Carlos
Williams' poems, we are told, is due in part to his
habit of jotting down free verse impressions in the
intervals between his professional visits to patients.
I can only hope that in writing out his prescriptions
he makes a greater allowance for the mental capacity
of the pharmacist than he seems to make for mine.
To speak bluntly, the difficulty of reading much
"modernist" verse is due less to the superior sophisti-
cation or cleverness of these writers than to their
essential lack of art.

It is my opinion that Dr. Williams is a major writer;
I cannot here defend that opinion, nor is the defense
in any way necessary.   What here concerns us is the
Humanist's critical technique.   That Mr. Chase
should find the influence of Whitman in Mr. Rob-

inson is amusing enough, but that he should find
the same influence in the Imagists in the form of
a "certain buoyancy and expectancy of mood,
and most characteristically as an underlying trust
in a life force which is felt to be working here in
America to high unforeseen ends" is a bit overwhelming. He should acquaint himself with the
rough outlines of the careers of Mr. Pound and of
H. D. and with Mr. Pound's occasional writings.
Just where these qualities are to be found in Mr.
Pound's *Cantos* or in the earlier "Fish and the
Shadow," it might be embarrassing to say; they are
not to be found in Mr. Aldington's "Choricos"; nor
are they to be found in H. D.'s "At Ithaca," a poem
which, incidentally, though by an imagist, deals, and
really in a remarkably fine fashion, with the very important Humanistic virtues of constancy and love of
home.

Perhaps the finest passage that one could quote
from Mr. Chase is the following:

Considerable damage was done to this shallow
affectation of knowingness of the last few years by
Max Eastman's witty article in the April (1929)
Harper's. A young intellectual from one of our well-
known private schools told me that members of his
group were observed to discontinue their perusal of
transition upon the appearance of Mr. Eastman's
"The Cult of Unintelligibility."

The seriousness with which Mr. Chase takes the reading habits of the "young intellectuals" of "one of our well-known private schools" would be in a different context so charming as quite to disarm one. Mr. More writes of Arnold: "There is no surer way to detect the weak side of a leader than by studying the career of his disciples, or even of his successors." Absurd as Mr. Chase may appear, his method illustrates unmistakably the weak side of Mr. More's and nearly the whole of Mr. Babbitt's in so far as Mr. Babbitt deals with literature.

III

It is an unpleasant task to profess skepticism about the value of a group of writers who are aiming at the betterment of conduct. The philosophical difficulties that may inhere in Mr. Babbitt's particular defense of sane conduct, I do not feel myself competent to discuss; I have a feeling that they may be rather easily and unjustifiably exaggerated. I am particularly grateful for Mr. Babbitt's brilliant exposition of our educational chaos, which appeared in *The Forum* for January, 1929, and I have profited by other things that he has written. I have profited from Mr. More's admirable background studies and even from some of his critical statements. The kind of conduct that is being advocated by the New Humanists, however, is not markedly different from that being advocated from our better Presbyterian pulpits, and it is unlikely that the Humanists reach as large an audience; it is possible that they reach an audience that stands in greater need of predication. The important question is, Do the Humanists transcend our Presbyterian practitioners and their on the whole fairly sound formulæ for behavior as Matthew Arnold's ideal Hellenists transcend his Hebraists, or are the New Humanists, as Mr. William Knickerbocker has already suggested in a recent issue of the *Sewanee Review,* merely a new group of Hebraists who have decided to take the stoa by storm?

If one applies to them the test that Mr. Babbitt has applied to the romantics, "By their fruits ye shall know them," one is bound to encounter anomalies. There is, first and foremost, the helplessness of the two leaders of the movement in the face of the very humanities they proclaim; Mr. Babbitt's aversion to Blake and Mr. More's reiterated and almost plaintive inability to understand the "character" (that is the principle of consistency, the clear relation to the Humanist's dogma) of Swift, of Machiavelli, of Leonardo, and of others, come at once to mind, as does their united dislike for Baudelaire, who is, beyond much doubt, one of the two or three chief sources of a truly humane discipline to be found in the last two centuries. There is Mr. Norman Foerster, who reproves the American scholar for his lack of interest

330

in pure (as Mr. Foerster understands the term) literature in a prose style that will not reassure the majority of the good gentlemen addressed concerning the qualifications of their would-be preceptor. There is Mr. Robert Shafer, who, in defending the doctrine of decorum, has recently been so carried away by his eloquence as to accuse of deliberate dishonesty and complete incompetence Mr. Allen Tate, who, regardless of the merits of the essay which Mr. Shafer was discussing and which it is at least theoretically possible that Mr. Shafer failed in some measure to understand, has given indisputable proof over a period of some eight or ten years of his honesty and profundity both as a critic and as a poet. Such behavior on the part of Mr. Shafer is exemplary not of the Aristotelian ideal of mediation, which he so vociferously professes to uphold, but of very common pedantic ill-breeding. There would seem to be some danger, then, that the famous Horatian phrase, which, Mr. Babbitt tells us, is the cornerstone of the New Humanism, may be translated by a good many of Mr. Babbitt's disciples as "brazen mediocrity."

The ethical code of the Humanists, as a code, is probably sound enough, but, however sound these abstractions may be, they are of no use to the Humanists or to us so long as they retain the status of pure abstractions; the abstractions remain what Mr. Tate has called wisdom in a vacuum. The arbitrary

331

and mechanical application of these principles to organic experience, whether the experience be literary or non-literary, does not constitute a discipline but rather a pedantic habit. If one is to arrive at any valuable conclusions concerning literature one will have to begin with the study of literature, to discover its nature and master its means. To approach it from the outside with the latest set of handy rules, suggests too nearly the five-foot shelf approach to culture or the latest mystical approach to salvation. The literary critic, to have any value, must be in the most profound sense of the expression a man of letters, not a man of theories; it seems to me hardly likely that the terminology of literary criticism, loose as it may be, will be permanently replaced in the second quarter of the twentieth century by a handy summary of Mr. Babbitt's ethical terminology.

How original Mr. Babbitt's and Mr. More's contribution to contemporary thought may be, it would be hard to say. There is probably little in their philosophy that could not be extracted, and in a richer form, from Matthew Arnold. Nor is it certain that Arnold may not have his direct share in the fringe of Mr. Babbitt's apparent influence or that, in fact, a good many others may not. Mr. Babbitt's reiteration of certain ethical values has probably had its effect, however, and, where it has influenced such younger men as R. P. Blackmur, Francis Fergusson,

Robert Penn Warren, T. S. Eliot, Allen Tate, and others, men who can incorporate these values into a richer experience, the influence, in so far as it may have been at work, is doubtless good. It is hard, however, to respect most of the followers of Mr. More and Mr. Babbitt—that is, their professed and immediate followers—who appear to share their deficiencies and to add nothing to their accomplishments. A few years ago the doctor was looking at literature; to-day it is the Humanist. Literature is either way lost in a welter of journalistic careers. One's objection to the Humanists is not to their humanism but to their lack of it; one cannot read many of their volumes without being overwhelmed with a sense of their spiritual bankruptcy.

TOWARDS AN ORGANIC
HUMANISM — Mumford

LEWIS MUMFORD

Towards an Organic Humanism

> Man, as the savage first conceived him,
> man, as the mind of science still affirms,
> is not the center of the world he lives in,
> but merely one of her myriad products,
> more conscious than the rest and more
> perplexed . . . He may cower before it
> like the savage, study it impartially for
> what it is, like the man of science; it
> remains in the end, as in the beginning,
> something alien and inhuman, often de-
> structive of his hopes. But a third way is
> open. He may construct, within the
> world as it is, a pattern of the world as
> he would have it. This is the way of
> humanism, in philosophy, in life and in
> the arts.
>
> GEOFFREY SCOTT.

DURING the last twenty years, two definite philosophies of life have been emerging in America. One of them seeks to carry further the
processes of life and thought that have given us the
Industrial Revolution, and all its issues and by-prod-
ucts in politics, social custom, literature, and the arts.
This philosophy has assumed many guises during the
last few hundred years, but in the form that it has
finally made itself manifest here, one may call it the
New Mechanism. The other philosophy, in its point
of departure and its ethical formulæ, has much in
common with the traditional religious conventions of
the past; but it differs from earlier doctrines in that

337

it acknowledges the ethical insight of the Hindus and the Chinese, as well as the nearer virtues of Christianity; and in that it makes no pretense to revealed knowledge. This second philosophy calls itself the New Humanism; and it stands in opposition to many of the things that the New Mechanism seeks to further.

One uses the terms "New Mechanism" and "New Humanism" as convenient party labels, not by way of accurate description, still less of either praise or disparagement. Neither seems to me a sufficient philosophy of life; but since their rival programs of action are embodied in movements as diverse as communism, fascism, the new capitalism, neo-Catholicism, and educational formalism, one may reasonably search out their weaknesses now, before their defects become plain through the more tedious processes of disintegration and decay.

In America, the leaders of both camps are able and distinguished men: Mr. Irving Babbitt, Mr. Paul Elmer More, Mr. John Dewey and Mr. Charles Beard have all made important contributions to scholarship, philosophy, history and criticism; and however insufficient their broad formulations may be, a certain part of their work nevertheless has great positive value: their several superstructures are, at many points, far more solid than their foundations. Rejecting their total views, one will still prize many of their specific contributions; in fact, to do otherwise would be to ally ourselves with those trivial minds that place an opprobrious label on a whole body of diversified work in order to relieve themselves of the embarrassing task of separating the bad from the good—as if there were not a modicum of honesty in a thief, or a remnant of charity in a Charity Organization!

Both philosophies, however, are partial; and the mistake of every partial philosophy is that it seeks to make a single element in experience dominate, or interpret, the whole. The New Mechanists give this priority to external events, and to physical science, as an instrument for interpreting and controlling these events. The rôle of the personality is looked upon in this philosophy as a passive and subsidiary one, and the notion that the balance and equipoise of the personality might impose adjustments upon the "external" environment has seemed to the New Mechanists absurd. That arts and disciplines could be instrumental to the personality, without affecting any major changes in the physical scene, without producing more goods or minimizing the expenditure of energy, is a notion that is equally remote from the New Mechanists' outlook: hence their disparagement of the fine arts, as opposed to technology, and their belief, either openly expressed or poorly concealed, that physical science will one day serve as a key to every aspect of experience.[1]

It is the merit of the New Humanists that they reject much of what is false and shallow in the creed of the New Mechanists; it is our misfortune that they also neglect many elements that are valuable, and dismiss, in a sweeping condemnation of all that has happened in art and science since Rousseau, a diversity of sound purposes and excellent achievements. Like most doctrines that recoil from a dominant error, the New Humanism carries a part of the error into its own reactions; and for good measure it adds one or two fallacies of its own making. Let us first, however, see what is valid in the creed of the pseudo-Humanists.

Perhaps the most important fact about the New Humanism is its very reaction, its assertion of the dignity of the human spirit. The New Humanists oppose, to the blind drift of technology and art and science and literature during the last two centuries, the force of their own convictions. They refuse to bow down to a fact, just because it happens to be an accomplished one, and they insist that the goodness or badness of a piece of literature, a political doctrine, a habit of mind, cannot be determined by whether it

[1] In the paper here presented Mr. Mumford gives his chief attention to the New Humanists. His critique of the New Mechanists may be found in *The Saturday Review of Literature,* April 12, 1930.—Editor.

is "modern" or "practical" but by whether it supports and fosters fine human ends, or whether it undermines and cripples them. Whereas most of our criticisms of the current order are, like Marx's criticism of Ricardo's economics, formulated in terms provided by that order, the New Humanists take as their standard the independent tradition of thought that comes to us in the sacred writings of the Hindus, in the philosophy of Confucius and Aristotle and Plato, in the poetry of Horace and Virgil and Dante. The New Humanist confronts the New Mechanist with these rational ends, and asks how far they are subserved by our present political and technological scheme, and how far a fine type of personality has been fostered. While the New Humanism has been allied, more or less overtly, with a defense of the privileged classes—I would cite, for example, Professor Babbitt's shrill vituperations against those who would endanger the sanctity of private property by a social interpretation of the Constitution—the connection is a social accident, rather than a logical necessity, and it is conceivable that a New Humanist might hold most of Mr. Babbitt's doctrines without being any more impressed by the sacredness of private property than Plato was.

Because of its literary leanings, the New Humanism has been most specifically formulated, not against the New Mechanists in philosophy and social life, but against more purely literary expressions that arose about the same time, some like "Realism" under the direct influence of the industrial revolution, and some, like the Romantic movement, more or less consciously in revolt against it. Their attack on the New Mechanism is vitiated by their failure to recognize the virtues of their enemy: they speak, for example, as if they themselves had a monopoly on humility—a claim which they make, it is true, in a tone of extreme arrogance—whereas the fact is that the sciences, apart from any practical effects they have achieved, have a positive value in that they have created a working-habit of humility, and have produced a long roster of saintly personalities who have learnt to displace their own wishes and prejudices and biases when they confronted actuality. The coöperative research, the collective testing of ideas, the elimination of idiosyncrasy, the reliance upon determinable measures of weight and number, in short, the whole morale of science has a value which is slowly taking possession of other departments of thought and action: the pervasive impersonality of science has done not a little perhaps to temper the asperities of social intercourse; and as this technique becomes more ingrained, the ethical contribution of science will become more obvious. It is unfortunate that the New Humanist recognizes as ethical only an earlier canon of conduct.

The New Humanist's attack on Romanticism, on the other hand, has been a little belated. What was unreal in Romanticism was already dead when Mr. Babbitt bravely stabbed the surviving phantom: and the chief force that killed Romanticism was our growing positive knowledge about the nature of society and the place of the individual personality. Romanticism grotesquely misconceived these relations: it exaggerated the function of the individual ego: it failed to reckon with the pervasive effect of the social heritage in forming the personality: and it divorced the private life of the individual from his public functions in the community, although the good life is impossible in either department without the establishment of a close reciprocal relation. All these weaknesses were examined and criticized long before the New Humanism had come into existence. De Bonald had pointed out the rôle of social tradition, through language itself, in the formation of the individual mind, and, following him, August Comte established the importance of the social heritage as the mark of differentiation between man and animal societies; in our own time, Messrs. Charles Cooley and John Dewey have demonstrated the actual social nature of individuality, while the new psychologists have made plain that the typical romantic myths of Individual Greatness, Isolation, and Irresponsibility were the manifestations of inferiority and maladjustment in an ego that had lost the social connections which were capable of sustaining it and guiding it towards more coherent ends.

Why should the New Humanists ignore these important contributions of science, and take to themselves the sole credit for upholding these truths? The reason, I think, is that they seek to make a "case" out against the modern world, and particularly against the disintegrating effects of science; and they are conscientiously ignorant of science—Mr. Babbitt has quoted approvingly Socrates' half truth: The trees and the fields can teach me nothing, but men in the city can —out of fear that either their case or their personal vanity might be hurt by acknowledging the genuine achievements in the scientific tradition. Mr. Walter Lippmann has pointed out that modern psychiatry often merely reënforces with additional evidence the ancient empirical precepts of religion and ethics; but the New Humanist is a little chary of being caught in such an alliance. Suspecting, quite rightly, that the scientific principle of continuity may be inimical to his traditional dualism between man and things, which is a fundamental though gratuitous dogma in the New Humanist philosophy, Mr. Babbitt prefers to insulate his beliefs against truths that might upset or modify them.

In his unfriendliness towards contemporary fact, the New Humanist cuts himself off deliberately from the vital forces of our day, preferring the mummy to the embryo and dead lions to live dogs. Like Mechanism, this pseudo-Humanism has no faith in the principle of growth and no understanding of its processes: hence its dogmas malign both our actual life and the possibilities that arise out of it. The New Humanist, impatient to achieve the final stage of growth, its fruition in a mature and competent personality, scorns all the preparatory phases: in his distrust for the erratic experiments of childhood, he puts a premium upon the fixations of senility. In the name of Dante, the New Humanist rejects the long anterior social experiments and efforts that made Dante possible, just as he chooses to forget the actual turmoil and division in the poet's personal life, out of which the magnificent composure of the Divine Comedy was achieved. So, too, in his regard for the decorum of Confucius, he forgets the slow accretion of habits in a stable agricultural society that made it possible for the great master to crystallize by brief example and briefer sentence, the spirit of a whole culture. To assure the final results of growth, namely an ordered pattern of life, the pseudo-Humanist would halt the process itself.

For what, indeed, is the New Humanist's preoccupation with the "inner check," the "moral veto," the "will to refrain," if it be not an effort to protect the personality from the risks and mischances that all creatures must run in the course of their development—experiences which, though they may divide and wreck the personality if there is no integrating center, capable of absorbing these elements and transforming them, are nevertheless the source of much that is precious, and unobtainable by any other process. The search for strict rules, narrow injunctions, a definite program is in part an effort to evade continuous vigilance and responsibility. This no doubt explains the great hold Mr. Babbitt often has, for a while, over the young, overwhelmed as they frequently are by the crisis of adolescence and incapable of directing their energies towards any durable ends. For the finer spirits who are not content to swallow the superficial values of industrial society, Mr. Babbitt provides a series of patent substitutes. If his disciples do not believe in comfort and mechanical improvement, they can believe in the viciousness of Rousseau and the wickedness of "expansion," and espouse, in contrast, a life of studious and edifying negations. Glib generalizations about romanticism will bolster up their deficiencies of experience and judgment, and a concentration upon a purely individual scheme of salvation will satisfy the narcissism of a still immature personality. The result is not a coherent philosophy of life; but at least it is a stopgap. As a purely temporary protest, paving the way for a more central and capacious philosophy of life,

346

the New Humanism has perhaps its chief justification.

II

The truth is that the New Humanists believe, like the New Mechanists, in adjustment to an external environment; but in their case it is to the Past, a select part of the past which verbally has embodied certain moral dicta and has projected a stable, decorous society. The New Humanists make a fetich of morality precisely as the New Mechanists make a fetich of the machine; that is to say, they read art, literature, philosophy, social custom in terms almost solely of their ethical significance and their effect upon practical conduct. Actually, a good part of our activities is conducted on neutral ground, and even over the remainder, habit and the usages of one's group often take the part of deliberate moral choice—only kleptomaniacs are tempted to run off with their neighbor's spoons. This fact does not dispense with the need, which Mr. Bernard Bandler II points out in *Humanism and America,* of deliberately formulating relevant goals and purposes in society, or of integrating one's own conduct into that of the finest endeavors of one's group, nor yet does it overlook the need for critical opposition to prevalent custom, when that falls below the standard of the best life possible.

All this is necessary; but while conduct may be

three-fourths of life, ethical standards are only one aspect of conduct. Conduct has also a physiological aspect, an esthetic aspect, a psychological aspect, an economic aspect; and to isolate ethical judgments from these organic relationships to the whole of life, and reduce good conduct, as Mr. Babbitt does, to the application of the moral veto or the inner check is to lose the significance of ethics itself: since if living well were only a matter of restraint and a limitation of "expansiveness" a chronic invalid would be the supreme type of an ethical personality. All the great religions of the past have admitted the close relation between ethical standards and every other aspect of life; not merely have they surrounded the act of worship with the most intoxicating kind of esthetic ritual, but in their emphasis upon physical acts such as washing the body, anointing the head, feasting and fasting, breathing, exercise and the dance, they have recognized the inefficacy of a purely verbal and didactic approach to a higher life. The one instrument that the Sacred Books have been wise enough not to rely upon exclusively is the Sacred Book.

Samuel Butler's sardonic thrust at the Church, that "as an instrument of warfare against vice, or as a tool for making virtue, Christianity is a mere flint implement," holds even more true of the narrow literary tradition that the New Humanism affiliates itself with. This failure necessarily lies in wait for

348

every creed that formulates its ideal without survey-
ing the groundwork in actuality, and that seeks to
achieve certain humane ends without attaching these
ends to their proper organic sources. Just as the tor-
mented abstentions of an Alexandrian hermit may be
further away from true chastity than the physical
union of a happy marriage, so every ideal end which
ignores the nature of the universe and of man's constitution tends, as Mr. John Dewey has wisely pointed
out, to be both meretricious and ineffectual, since it is
divorced from the means of realization. The good
life is not only good for one's conscience; it is good
for art, good for knowledge, good for health, good
for fellowship. Almost a generation ago the necessary
relations between ethical standards and their underlying conditions of fulfillment were set forth, with
great justice and insight, in Mr. George Santayana's
masterpiece, *The Life of Reason*. It is a little ironic
to realize that, merely by his damnable iterativeness,
the pseudo-Humanism of Mr. Irving Babbitt should
have temporarily displaced the robust and genuine
humanism of Mr. Santayana, and that a plaster
Laokoon should divert attention from a Fifth Century marble!

What a truly humane mind seeks, contrary to Mr.
Babbitt, are not checks and bridles; for there is no
more virtue in negation than in affirmation, in con-
traction than in expansion, apart from the rational

349

ends that are achieved. Obviously, there is a time to laugh and a time to weep; a time to expand and a time to contract; a time to invoke reason and a time to permit passion its ascendancy; and the essence of morality is to recognize the time and the place and the attitudes that are appropriate to them, not bringing irresponsible hilarity into a busy committee meeting, or the prudence of a good businessman into the situation of a drowning child, calling for help. Nor is what we seek a mere elaboration of instrumentalities, as the Mechanist so naïvely believes: what a truly human life demands are positive channels of effort, useful and dignified tasks, fine and significant actions, and quiet states of beatitude, which by their very pursuit or enjoyment provide, incidentally, such checks and restrictions as may be necessary to their success. It is the pride of getting his train into the station on time that saves the engineer from drunkenness quite as much as company regulations; and every good society begets a multitude of such prides and enthusiasms and hopes.

In making concrete suggestions towards these tasks, the New Humanists are quite as sterile as the New Mechanists. Whereas the belittled Romantics influenced happily a score of activities from the planting of gardens to the writing of histories, restoring his sense of dignity to the degraded machine worker and reawakening cultures which had lain dormant under political tyranny, the New Humanists have merely opposed to the weaknesses and infirmities of our present society a series of anxious negatives—negatives just as impotent to produce new values as the optimistic assent of their Mechanist rivals. In short: the New Humanists are empty. No wonder they are so strong in polemics; for they derive their chief significance from the presence of their enemies.

III

In laying down the terms for a more sufficient philosophy of life than either the New Humanism or the New Mechanism, two conditions must be observed: one must not, like the latter, ignore vast tracts of existence merely because they cannot be appraised by the quantitative methods devised by the physical sciences; nor must one adopt the curious error of the New Humanists, and seek to abolish every expression of life except that which conforms to our particular dogma. Let us recall Emerson's words: the new philosophy will comprise the skepticisms as well as the faiths of society. The synthesis we seek must be an open one: that is, it must not merely hold the knowledge and belief that is at present available, but it must be capable of keeping a place open for new areas of expression and interest; thus it differs from the synthesis which satisfied St. Thomas Aquinas and Dante, for that was unable to absorb the discov-

351

eries as to the nature of the physical world which followed so soon after its formulation.

What, then, is our point of departure? We know the world we live in only as the environment of life. That there is an external universe, independent of life and indifferent to it, is an assumption of Newtonian physics which is of great practical convenience: but it is an inference, and not an immediate datum, since every such datum demands the existence of an observer: that is, life. The universe as we know it implies not merely the interlinkages of organic life and all the sustaining conditions in the physical world, such as those which Professor Lawrence Henderson has brilliantly demonstrated in *The Fitness of the Environment:* it also implies the developments of human history. Our thought itself, our concepts, our grammatic structure, are the products of the multitude of human beings that came before us; and the existence of human society is a much surer fact of experience than the existence of Betelgeuse, or, for that matter, the whole physical universe—all of which is derivative and inferential, since it assumes the existence of human instruments like language, mathematics, measurements.

Instead of beginning with a portentous sterile physical universe, and finally discovering man, with all his aims and values, as a pathetic, ludicrous by-product at the end of it, we begin with the human personality itself. The abstraction of an "independent world" from the ego itself is the result of a long difficult process which begins in the cradle; and while this abstraction is a genuine aid to growth, the present convention of regarding the human personality as merely an insignificant fragment of that world is quite as false as the infant's original hallucination of creating milk or warmth out of the void merely by crying for it. We find ourselves, at the very beginning of our adventure, in a state of complicated interdependences which unite us not merely economically and spiritually with other men and societies, but to remote parts of the world and to physical conditions which were established long before human forms appeared upon the earth. Value and significance are the marks of human society: hence our task is not merely that of maintaining or reproducing the species, but of enlarging the domain of value and significance. Art and science, social custom and ritual, reflection and communication, set the seal of significance upon all the immediate data of consciousness or animal existence. Man is never found in a state of nature, because, even in the most primitive parts of the earth, nature is always, so to say, in a state of man. Man's ability to repeat and modify and pattern valuable experiences is achieved, chiefly, through the aid of symbols; and this is what releases him from the blind habit or even blinder chaos.

Personality—human society—the organic world—the physical universe: as one passes from the first category to the last, the degree of certitude in our knowledge increases because the content itself is more limited and derivative and the number of incalculable factors can be reduced; but at the same time, values are lost, and qualitative standards give place to quantitative ones: we feel our kinship with the animals in the universal acts of eating or mating, but we are a little cold, despite Erasmus Darwin, to the loves of the plants, and cannot speak with any conviction of the affinities of atoms, so attenuated do our feelings and emotions become as we reach the sub-basement of life. Reading upward, from the physical world, and applying the statistical methods and techniques to the behavior of more complex organisms, we are determinists: provisionally we can learn much about our own nature as personalities and members of society by regarding ourselves as the products of inexorable causes, closely linked together. Beginning at the top, however, and reading down, we introduce the elements of feeling, choice, personality, into our most abstract accounts of the universe, observe how much our thought owes to such accidents as the fact that we have two hands instead of three and ten fingers instead of twelve, and in general, discover how many qualities we have bestowed upon "reality" by the original and the socially created facts of man's nature.

When the external environment has the upper hand, man functions deterministically: there is not much room for free will when one is being swallowed up in an earthquake. When the tissue of social relations is knit firmly together and man is in the ascendant, he functions voluntarily: every aspect of life shows the force of his imagination and his purpose: the pattern of his streets, the plants in his garden, the contour of the landscape, the paintings on his wall, the food on his table, all have an orderly reference to that creative will which brings value and significance into even his most barren or automatic activities.

That we are entirely creatures of the external world, or as the solipsists would have it, entirely the creators of that world is, as Messrs. Geddes and Branford have pointed out, contrary to human experience: the inner and the outer, the subjective and the objective, the world known to personal intuition and that described by science are, rather, aspects of a single experience. In terms of the dead past, all relationships, including human ones, are fixed: the series is completed. Unfortunately, the scientific method has been based upon the use of mechanical movements, like clocks, rather than upon the reaction of living organisms. The first can apparently be satisfactorily described without introducing the notion of "future," potentiality, choice of possibilities, direction; whereas it is in the nature of all organisms to carry, in any given reaction, anticipatory responses and movements which merge with the previous en-registrations of memory, and in turn to alter both the past and the future by the direction taken from moment to moment. A philosophy which takes account only of a "dead" past and a statistical future is incapable of grasping the essential nature of life: in leaving out the ideal element in man's calculations, it leaves out that which distinguishes his behavior from the actions of a planet or a falling stone. The doctrine of emergent evolution, formulated by Mr. Lloyd Morgan, does away with the necessity for positing a dualism here which separates the law of man from the law of thing: one may preserve the continuity necessary for scientific coherence without denying the existence of a new emergent element; which in man is his social heritage.

In our conceptions of Nature and Man and Society and Personality we have now arrived, I think, at a somewhat deeper and richer understanding of the relationships than either the New Mechanism or the New Humanism have any notion of. We do not necessarily renounce the stopwatch, the micrometer scale, the balance, the spectroscope, the thermometer; but we no longer ask them to answer questions they are unfitted to solve, and we know, too, that both answer and question will tell us as much about the nature of our own impulses as they do about the world: for we have provided the conceptual framework, the ideology, in which such answers must be given. While we agree, on the other hand, to provide a wider scope for our ideologies, we shall beware of projecting hallucinations or neurotic fantasies back upon the unsatisfactory milieu which produced them: we realize that a superstitious theology, for example, can work as much havoc to the human spirit as the most servile mechanical routine. But the way to safeguard against the perversions of personality is not to depersonalize man or banish his ideologies, advising him to conform to a pattern outside of himself: the proper way is to enrich his personality itself so that man will react creatively upon his materials, and be able to carve fine molds of conduct as well as an apparatus for the regulation of his utilities. The most complete personalities are precisely those that have assimilated the most diverse elements in their cultures and have lived least to themselves. Personality provides not merely our original nucleus of experience: it is also the summit of our social achievement: and the apex of every culture is accordingly neither its technology nor its positive science nor its works of art, but all of these together, and many other parts of the universe besides, as they are concentrated and fulfilled in the highest personality: a Confucius, a Plato, a Dante, a Goethe, an Emerson. In such individuals, a society finally lives; and in such societies fine individualities become widespread and frequent.

IV

Once the organic nature of human life and experience is granted, a number of false problems are demolished and a number of more significant ones appear. The belief that there is any single end, towards which society should move, such as the abolition of pain or the achievement of universal comfort or the increase of pleasure, becomes untenable: for life involves a multitude of functions, some pleasant, like eating, some burdensome, like childbirth, some dangerous, like climbing mountains or digging in mines, some relaxing, like playing on a sunny beach, and some demanding stern effort, like prolonged research or gathering in the crops before a turn of the weather: again, some matters require social tact, like the entertainment of superficial acquaintances, and others require defiant isolation, like the enunciation of unwelcome truths. Out of all these habits, discoveries, risks, pleasures, pains, the human personality develops: action and knowledge and emotion, ideal purposes and animal impulses, are all equally necessary to it: and a program which erects a single function or end, like pleasure or efficiency or decorum as the real goal of life, is nothing but an impudent denial of the nature of life itself. The real problem of life, both for men and societies, is to keep the organism and the environment, the inner world and the outer, the personality and its creative sources, in the state of tension wherein growth and renewal may continually take place. That balance is always a precarious one; and it was badly upset for the western world by the industrial revolution. It is for us to restore it. An organic attitude towards life can truly be called humanism; for it will reconcile by its superior comprehension the one-sided philosophies which men have formulated out of a raw and imperfect experience. In our new bed, Romanticist and Classicist, "Humanist" and Mechanist, naturalist and idealist will lie down happily together; but they must cast off, before they do so, the soiled and tattered philosophical clothes in which they now parade.

BERNARD BANDLER II
Born, 1904. Educated at Harvard University
(1926). Editor of *The Hound and Horn*. Contributor to *Humanism and America*.

R. P. BLACKMUR
Born, 1904. Formerly an editor of *The Hound
and Horn*. Contributor to *The New Republic*.

KENNETH BURKE
Born, 1897. Author of *The White Oxen*. A
former editor of *The Dial*. Contributor to
Broom, *The Bookman*, *The Hound and Horn*
and New York Herald-Tribune *Books*. Translator from the German and the French of many
books and stories.

JOHN CHAMBERLAIN
Born, 1903. Educated at Yale (1925). Assist-
ant editor of New York Times *Book Review*.
Contributor to *The Bookman*, *The New Republic*, *The Commonweal*, and *The Forum*.

MALCOLM COWLEY
Born, 1898. Educated at Harvard (1919).
Author of *Blue Juniata* (poetry). Translator of
Variety by Paul Valery, *The Sacred Hill* by
Maurice Barres, *The Count's Ball* by Raymond
Radiguet, *On Board the Morning Star* by Pierre
MacOrlan, *Joan of Arc* by Joseph Delteil, etc.
An editor of *The New Republic*. American
Field Service Fellow to Paris.

C. HARTLEY GRATTAN
Born, 1902. Educated at Clark College (1923).
Author of *Bitter Bierce*, a critical study, *Aus-*

tralian Literature, Why We Fought, a political and economic study, and the last nine chapters of *The Peerless Leader: William Jennings Bryan,* started by the late Paxton Hibben. Edited, with a preface, *A Bookman's Daybook* by Burton Rascoe. Contributor to *The Second American Caravan, The Bookman, The American Mercury, Scribner's, Foreign Affairs, The Nation, The New Republic* and the literary sections of the principal New York newspapers, etc.

HENRY HAZLITT

Born, 1894. Literary editor of the New York *Sun* (1925-1929); now literary editor of *The Nation.* Editorial contributor to *The Century.* Contributor, as a writer of finance, to the New York *Herald, Revue Economique* (Belgium), New York *Mail,* etc.

HENRY-RUSSELL HITCHCOCK

Born, 1903. Educated at Harvard (A.B., 1924, A.M., 1926) Carnegie Fellow. He has taught at Harvard and Vassar and is now at Wesleyan. Author of *Modern Architecture.* Contributor to *The Arts, Architectural Record, Architecture, The American Architect* and *The Hound and Horn.*

LEWIS MUMFORD

Born, 1895. Author of *The Story of Utopias, Sticks and Stones, The Golden Day, American Taste, Herman Melville.* Contributing editor, *The New Republic.* Contributor to *The Freeman, The American Mercury, Harper's Maga-*

362

zine, Die Form and various other American and European magazines.

BURTON RASCOE

Born, 1892. Educated at University of Chicago. Formerly literary editor of *The Chicago Tribune, McCall's Magazine,* the New York *Herald-Tribune.* Formerly editor of *The Bookman.* Now associate editor, *Plain Talk.* Member of the Board of Judges of The Literary Guild. Author of *Theodore Dreiser* and *A Bookman's Daybook.* Regular contributor, dealing with books, to *Arts and Decorations.*

ALLEN TATE

Born, 1899. Educated at Vanderbilt University (1922). Author of *Mr. Pope and Other Poems, Stonewall Jackson, Jefferson Davis.* Guggenheim Fellow. Contributor to *The New Republic, The Nation, The Bookman, The Hound and Horn, This Quarter* (Paris), *The Criterion* (England), etc.

EDMUND WILSON

Born, 1895. Educated at Princeton (1916). Author of (with John Peale Bishop) *The Undertaker's Garland, Discordant Encounters, I Thought of Daisy,* and *Poets, Farewell!* Formerly managing editor of *Vanity Fair.* Now an editor of *The New Republic.*

YVOR WINTERS

Born, 1900. He has taught French and Spanish at the University of Idaho and is now instructor in English at Leland Stanford University. He is author of *The Immobile Wind, The Magpie's Shadow* and *The Bare Hills,* all verse. Contributor to *The Dial, transition, Poetry, The Hound and Horn,* etc.